BERKSHIRE OUTDOORS

Natural Places

A Guide to
Natural
Places

IN THE BERKSHIRE HILLS

Revised Edition

BY RENÉ LAUBACH

Maps and Illustrations by Alison Kolesar

BERKSHIRE HOUSE, PUBLISHERS
Stockbridge, Massachusetts

The text of this book was designed by Jane McWhorter and composed by Philip Ruderman. Typefaces are Palatino and Helvetica. Cover photography of Monument Mountain Reservation (view from Squaw Peak looking south) is by A. Blake Gardner. Maps are based on U.S. Geological Survey quadrants.

Editor: Glenn Novak

Library of Congress Cataloging-in-Publication Data

Laubach, René.
   A guide to natural places in the Berkshire Hills / by René Laubach : maps and illustrations by Alison Kolesar. — Rev. ed.
   p. cm. — (Berkshire outdoors)
   ISBN 0-936399-85-6
   Includes bibliographical references (p.) and index.
   1. Natural history—Massachusetts—Berkshire Hills—Guidebooks.
   2. Berkshire Hills (Mass.)—Guidebooks. I. Title. II. Series.
QH105.M4L381997
917.44′1′0443—dc20   96-44737
                                                       CIP

ISBN: 0-936399-85-6

Berkshire House Publishers
480 Pleasant St., Suite 5
Lee, MA 01238
800-321-8526

Printed in the United States of America

10 9 8 7 6 5 4 3 2 1

*To my parents who encouraged me and to my wife
who shared these adventures with me*

CONTENTS

Key to Location of Sites viii
Introduction ix
Acknowledgments x
How to Use this Book xi
Health and Safety in the Outdoors xvi
Outdoor Ethics...................................... xvii
Wildlife Observation Tips xviii
Berkshire Geology, Vegetation,
   and Cultural History............................. xix
Relief Map of Berkshire County.................... xx

NATURAL PLACES

SOUTH COUNTY

 1 • Campbell Falls State Park 1
 2 • Bartholomew's Cobble 7
 3 • Sage's Ravine 17
 4 • Mount Everett State Reservation 23
 5 • Bash Bish Falls State Park 33
 6 • Mill Pond 41
 7 • Beartown State Forest......................... 47
 8 • Monument Mountain Reservation 57
 9 • Tyringham Cobble............................. 65
10 • Ice Glen and Laura's Tower 71
11 • Goose Pond................................... 79
12 • Stockbridge Bowl............................. 87

CENTRAL COUNTY

13 • Pleasant Valley Wildlife Sanctuary.............. 93
14 • Housatonic Valley Wildlife Management Area .. 101
15 • October Mountain State Forest 111
16 • Canoe Meadows Wildlife Sanctuary 125
17 • Central Berkshire Lakes 135
18 • Pittsfield State Forest & Balance Rock State Park 147
19 • Wahconah Falls State Park 157
20 • Eugene D. Moran Wildlife Management Area ... 163
21 • Notchview Reservation 169
22 • Windsor State Forest and
       Windsor Jambs Scenic Area 177

NORTH COUNTY

23 • Hoosac Lake 183
24 • Savoy Mountain State Forest 189
25 • Mount Greylock State Reservation 199
26 • Field Farm 211
27 • Natural Bridge State Park..................... 219
28 • Eph's Pond and Hoosic River 225
29 • Pine Cobble and East Mountain 233

A map of each location is at or near the beginning of each chapter.

Common and Scientific Names
   of Species Mentioned in Text 242
Natural Places Categorized by
   Amount of Walking Required.................... 253
Selected References............................... 254
A Note on the Author 257
County Road Map................................. 258

MAP LEGEND

paved road

unpaved road

trail described in text
(except where it
coincides with
Appalachian Trail)

Appalachian Trail

900 — contour lines

river or stream

wetlands

seasonally present
stream

rail line

MASS
CONN — state line

7 — U.S. highway

8 — State highway

90 — Interstate highway

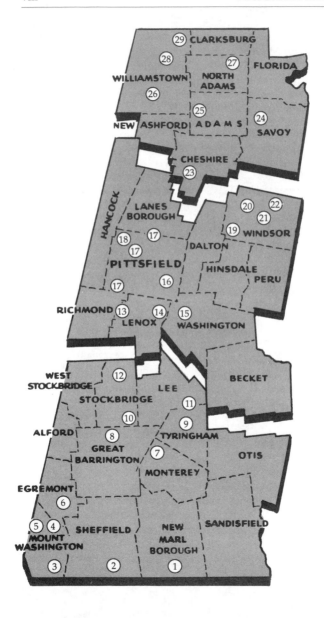

INTRODUCTION

The Berkshire region has long been famous as a center for the arts. Since early in the nineteenth century, writers, poets, musicians, composers, sculptors, painters, actors, and other creative people have been coming to the Berkshire Hills for inspiration and recreation. The largely unspoiled natural beauty of the area has stimulated and abetted this creative output. Henry David Thoreau, an apt example of a writer who was deeply affected by the natural world, was one of the first prominent writer-naturalists to visit the area and partake of its natural delights. Since the 1840s many other nature lovers and naturalists have made pilgrimages to Berkshire, where tourism is now a major industry. It is an industry and a livelihood inextricably linked with the health of our natural environment — and our own health.

Berkshire is blessed with year-round and seasonal residents who deeply cherish the ecological integrity and natural beauty of the area. A significant proportion of land has been safeguarded for posterity through a wide variety of land protection arrangements. The state owns and manages over 116,000 acres of public forests, reservations, parks, and wildlife management areas. Numerous non-profit groups own additional lands that are open to the public, and many towns now have private land trusts whose mission is to preserve the scenic and rural qualities that make life in Berkshire so attractive. The fertile cultural environment, and the healthy natural environment that in large measure gave genesis to it, combine to produce a high quality of life here.

This guide is an attempt to give the visitor to the area, as well as the resident, information about where to find the fascinating flora and fauna, interesting geology, and inspiring vistas that abound in our area. I hope that it will lead you to discover for yourself the many wonderful natural areas that the Berkshire Hills have to offer. I am sure that you, too, will appreciate and want to protect the wild things that make these places so special.

Here's wishing you countless hours of enjoyment and enlightenment as you explore the natural places of Berkshire!

ACKNOWLEDGMENTS

The time and talents of many people went into the production of the first edition of this book. Two individuals in particular contributed major portions to this guide. Pamela Weatherbee of Williamstown provided substantial botanical information to each chapter, as well as other material about Berkshire fauna and flora. I am also indebted to James Ervin of Miss Hall's School in Pittsfield for providing nearly all the geologic material contained in this guide. In short, I could not have written this book without the avid participation of these two people.

Many other persons willingly provided technical information, computer assistance, and aided the author during the production of the first edition in other ways. They include Timothy Flanagan; Thomas Tyning of the Massachusetts Audubon Society; Marilyn Flor, formerly of the Massachusetts Audubon Society; Leo Daly and Tony Gola of the Massachusetts Division of Fisheries and Wildlife; Carl Curtin of the Massachusetts Department of Environmental Management; Richard Miska of the Connecticut Department of Environmental Protection; Stanley Piatczyc and Delphine Phelps of the Trustees of Reservations; Ned Swanberg, formerly of the Trustees of Reservations; Paul Boudreau of the Berkshire Regional Planning Commission; Dennis Regan of Appalachian Mountain Club; Gene Chague and the late Al Les of Trout Unlimited; and George Wislocki of the Berkshire Natural Resources Council.

In addition, many area naturalists provided information about specific sites while introducing me to the many treasures that Berkshire has to offer. Among them are Richard Daub, Edna Dunbar, Robert Goodrich, Bartlett Hendricks, Edwin Neumuth, Ronald Roncatti, David St. James, and Alvah Sanborn.

Individuals who reviewed earlier drafts of the second edition for accuracy are: Paul Adams, Patrick Gammeli, Robert Hatton, B. H. Ingerson, Conrad Ohman, Mike Tirrel, Mark Todd, Dave Wood, and Tim Zelazo of the Massachusetts Department of Environmental Management; David St.

James of the Massachusetts Division of Fisheries and Wildlife; and Andy Bernardy, Jim Caffrey, Stan Piatzek, and Don Reid of the Trustees of Reservations. Bartlett Hendricks also made many helpful suggestions, and Pamela Weatherbee reread the entire text, revising and updating the botanical information in the species list at the back of the book.

General introductory material about the Berkshires was taken from *The Berkshire Book: A Complete Guide* by Jonathan Sternfield, and from *Hikes & Walks in the Berkshire Hills* by Lauren Stevens, both published by Berkshire House. Lauren, also the co-author of *Skiing in the Berkshire Hills,* another Berkshire House title in the Berkshire Outdoors series, gave helpful advice during the preparation of the first edition.

I wish to thank former publisher David Emblidge and the fine staff at Berkshire House for giving me the opportunity to write about a subject dear to my heart. Former managing editor Sarah Novak also made many useful suggestions throughout the process. Glenn Novak served as copy editor for both editions and made many improvements to the manuscript.

I also enjoyed working with artist Alison Kolesar, whose meticulous maps and line drawings added greatly to the usefulness and attractiveness of the first edition.

Lastly, but by no means least, I wish to thank my wife, Christyna, who was my constant and enthusiastic companion in the field for both editions. Together we have shared many wonderful hours.

For this new edition, I wish to thank Berkshire House publisher Jean Rousseau, and especially editor Philip Rich for enabling me to produce an even better book.

HOW TO USE THIS BOOK

This book attempts to be accurate and helpful. Neither the author nor the publisher can be responsible beyond that effort. Many things, both natural and manmade, are subject to change and out of the author's control. And, with the best intentions, errors are possible.

This guide contains information about 33 sites within Berkshire County, Massachusetts. One of these, Campbell Falls State Park, is partially in the state of Connecticut. Several chapters include more than one site when these are located within the same property or close to each other. Some can be reached by motor vehicle and so are handicapped-accessible, although most involve a brief walk. A few involve walks exceeding one mile in each direction; none requires one-way walks longer than 1.5 miles.

Each chapter contains the essential information needed to get you to the site as well as basic information about outstanding features, views, geology, flora, fauna, and seasonal highlights. It is hoped that this material will enable the reader to get the most from each visit. Information provided is current as of the publication date. Readers are advised to contact the managing agency of the property before their visit to ascertain current hours, admission fees, etc.

For more extensive walks and hikes and for specific information about skiing and bicycling in the area, the reader should consult three other guides in this series: *Hikes & Walks in the Berkshire Hills, Skiing in the Berkshire Hills,* and *Bike Rides in the Berkshire Hills.*

Key Terms, Important Names, and Abbreviations

As to what constitutes a *natural area,* I have applied no hard and fast rule. Although largely wooded now, Berkshire was extensively cut over for agriculture, charcoal, and timber in the eighteenth and nineteenth centuries. You will find no true wilderness here (almost every spot is within a few miles of a gravel road), but there are places that do impart that special feeling of wilderness. Most places described in this book remain largely in a natural (if somewhat altered from the original) state, although some, such as many of the larger lakes, have been "created," as it were. In this book, a natural area, then, is defined as a site that is of outstanding interest with regard to scenery, geology, flora, or fauna.

Each chapter contains a treatment of the site's wildlife. Wildlife here is defined as animals that fall into the groups (classes) of vertebrates (animals with backbones). *Fishes* are characterized by jaws, paired fins, and a single gill slit and gill cover. *Amphibians* (frogs and salamanders) are recognized by limbs instead of fins, no claws on their toes, and moist skin instead of scales, feathers, or hair. *Reptiles* (turtles and snakes) are defined by the fact that they lay eggs on land or that they bear living young on land or in the sea. They are not dependent, as are amphibians, upon a return to water to breed. Fertilization is internal, there is no larval (tadpole) stage, and the young as well as the adults have a dry skin bearing scales or horny plates. *Birds* are unique in that they possess feathers. There is no animal with feathers that is not a bird. *Mammals* are air-breathing, endothermic ("warm-blooded," except for two Australian exceptions), milk-producing vertebrates with hair.

Major public and private agencies that manage land in Berkshire have been identified by their abbreviations in the introductory information for each chapter. The full name of the agency or organization and brief information about each follow. Readers are encouraged to contact these organizations regarding membership and their full range of activities.

DEM (Massachusetts Department of Environmental Management) This is the primary land management agency of state government. Its Division of Forests and Parks manages the system of state forests, parks, and reservations. In Berkshire alone, the DEM manages more than 100,000 acres of lands open to the public. The department's regional headquarters is at 740 South St., Pittsfield, 01201.

MDF&W (Massachusetts Division of Fisheries and Wildlife) This state agency has statutory control over wildlife. It also manages more than 12,000 acres in Berkshire. These lands are open to hunting in season. The division's western regional office is at 400 Hubbard Ave., Pittsfield, 01201. The division also includes the Massachusetts Natural Heritage Program, the branch concerned with non-game wildlife and plant conservation. This agency maintains a list of Endangered, Threatened, and Species of Special Concern for flora and fauna. One of its major functions is statewide inventory and mapping of non-game species.

WMA (Wildlife Management Area) is a designation for some lands administered by the MDF&W. These areas are managed primarily for the hunting of specific game species.

AT (Appalachian National Scenic Trail) The Appalachian Trail, along with the corridor of lands it passes through, is owned and administered by the National Park Service, a federal agency. Actual management of the trail has been delegated by the Park Service to the Appalachian Trail Conference. This private, non-profit group's office is at P.O. Box 807, Harpers Ferry, WV, 25425.

AMC (Appalachian Mountain Club) A private, non-profit conservation organization in New England that maintains an extensive trail network. In Massachusetts, the group's volunteers help to maintain the Appalachian National Scenic Trail in cooperation with the National Park Service and maintain a cabin staffed by a summer volunteer at Upper Goose Pond. The AMC also manages Bascom Lodge and the Visitor Center on Mount Greylock for the DEM. Its Berkshire office is at Rockwell Road, Lanesborough, 01237.

MAS (Massachusetts Audubon Society) The major private non-profit land-holding organization in the state. The MAS owns and manages three wildlife sanctuaries in Berkshire totaling more than 2,000 acres. Two properties in the county are currently open to the public, and a wide variety of educational programs are conducted on- and off-site. The MAS Berkshire Sanctuaries office is at 472 West Mountain Road, Lenox, 01240.

TTOR (The Trustees of Reservations) A major private, non-profit conservation organization in Massachusetts. In Berkshire, the TTOR owns and manages both conservation lands and historic sites. The conservation lands encompass more than 6,100 acres in Berkshire County. These lands are open to the public, and educational programming is conducted at some. TTOR's regional office is at P.O. Box 792, Stockbridge, 01262.

CT DEP (Connecticut Department of Environmental Protection) The agency responsible for the management of state lands in Connecticut. Land managed by this agency and included in this guide is Campbell Falls State Park on the Connecticut-Massachusetts border in New Marlborough, Massachusetts.

HEALTH AND SAFETY
IN THE OUTDOORS

There are several basic rules that should be followed by anyone on an outing. A little planning can go a long way toward insuring that your excursion is a safe and enjoyable one.

1. Carry enough water if you are going to be walking. Even clear mountain brooks may not provide drinkable water.

2. Wear sturdy, comfortable shoes and take along a jacket, hat, and rainwear as weather conditions can change rapidly. Dress in layers. Take along an extra pair of socks. If you venture into the woods during the hunting seasons, wear signal orange.

3. Always tell someone where you are going, especially if you will be doing some hiking.

4. Take along a map (this book), a watch, and, if you are going very far afield, a compass. Learn how to use the map and compass in conjunction.

5. Learn to recognize poison ivy. All parts of this plant are poisonous.

6. Although there may be some debate about this matter, I am not aware of the existence of the Lyme disease-carrying tick (deer tick) in Berkshire County at this time. That may change in the future, however, and bears close monitoring.

7. Always wear a life preserver when in a boat, no matter how accomplished a swimmer you may be.

8. An aluminum cross-country ski pole is a helpful walking aid, especially when conditions are icy.

OUTDOOR ETHICS

To do your part to protect and conserve our natural resources, observe the following simple guidelines:

1. Stay on marked trails. Creation of new trails results in erosion and the loss of plants and animals.

2. Carry all your trash out with you.

3. In wetland areas especially, tread lightly so as not to destroy fragile plants and animals.

4. Wildflowers should not be picked, since the removal of their seed-producing organs (flowers) may result in the loss of the species from this place in the future.

5. Animals should be left in their natural communities. Amphibians and reptiles may be handled and observed briefly with care, but should immediately be returned to the exact place where they were found. Always return stones and logs to their original positions.

6. Leave suspected "orphaned" baby birds and animals where they are. Such animals are seldom truly orphaned, since many animals leave their young untended for varying lengths of time. Their chances for survival are greatly reduced if you take them out of their natural element.

7. Observe wildlife unobtrusively, without harassment. The use of play-back tape recordings of bird songs should be used sparingly, if at all. This technique should not be used during the breeding season.

8. Respect posted property; don't trespass. Many land-owners will grant permission if you ask first.

WILDLIFE OBSERVATION TIPS

1. Dress in subdued earth tones except during hunting seasons, when signal-orange attire is strongly advised (only birds can see color, so the orange is to make you visible to other humans).

2. The best times for wildlife observation tend to be during early morning and late afternoon. Many mammals are active at dawn and dusk.

3. Binoculars (7x35 to 10x40) are an extremely useful tool whether one is watching birds, beavers, butterflies, or stars. Learn how to use them properly. A spotting scope and tripod are helpful for waterfowl observation.

4. Your motor vehicle often makes a good blind from which to observe waterfowl and other wildlife. Animals seem less intimidated by a car than by the sight of a human.

5. Photography can add another dimension to your adventures and can make you a better observer.

6. A 10x hand lens comes in handy when you want to take a closer look at insects, plants, etc. If you turn your binoculars upside-down, they will serve as a magnifying glass.

7. Try remaining still for ten or more minutes at a time when in the woods. This may result in wildlife not noticing your presence or at least allowing wildlife to become accustomed to it. In either case, you will usually be afforded closer views of many birds and mammals if you remain still and quiet.

8. Learning the songs and calls of resident (and later, migrant) birds will give you a great advantage toward your successful identification of them and add a large measure of enjoyment. You'll be surprised by how much

better a birder you will be once you have mastered the vocalizations of common species.

9. Take a small notebook and pencil with you to record your observations. You can also use them to sketch plants and animals for later identification. Keeping records of your observations can add greatly to your pleasure and even serve as important documentation for new discoveries.

10. Learn to recognize the tracks and other signs produced by mammals and birds. Even though you might not see the animals, you'll learn a good deal about what lives in the area based upon these clues.

11. You may want to consult field guides, checklists, and other written materials (including those listed in the selected references section of this guide) *before* you go into the field so that you will have some idea of what to expect.

12. For wildlife observation after dark, a head lamp (similar to the type worn by miners) is a handy way to illuminate the trail while freeing your hands.

BERKSHIRE GEOLOGY, VEGETATION, AND CULTURAL HISTORY

The area's considerable topographic relief (the greatest in the state) and its situation in a zone of overlap between the oak-dominated forests to the south and the spruce and fir forests to the north make Berkshire rich in natural diversity. Two major river systems, the Housatonic in Central and South County and the Hoosic in North County, are underlain by a thick layer of limestone rock, buffering the effects of acid precipitation and producing soils colonized by a variety of unusual lime-loving plant species. The uplands of the Berkshire Plateau are pock-marked with nu-

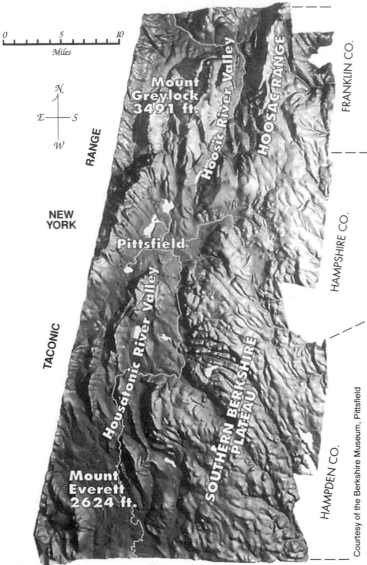

VERMONT

0   5   10

Miles

N

E   S

W

RANGE

NEW YORK

TACONIC

Mount Greylock 3491 ft.

Hoosic River Valley

HOOSAC RANGE

FRANKLIN CO.

Pittsfield

HAMPSHIRE CO.

Housatonic River Valley

SOUTHERN BERKSHIRE PLATEAU

Mount Everett 2624 ft.

HAMPDEN CO.

Courtesy of the Berkshire Museum, Pittsfield

CONNECTICUT

merous wetlands and that most fascinating of all wetlands, the bog. These glacial remnants, harboring so many interesting plants and animals, are fairly numerous in the cool, moist uplands. The majority of the region's larger trees are 85 or 95 years old. Within the next century, Berkshire forests may once again resemble the primeval forests that the colonists discovered.

Geology

In the final analysis, an area's plant and animal life as well as its land-use patterns all depend in large measure upon its geology. It is the geology of an area coupled with its climate that makes it what it is.

Today, Berkshire is composed primarily of valleys with limestone and marble bedrock and upland areas primarily of schists and gneisses (pronounced "nices"). The valleys are indeed valleys because the limestone rocks are softer and more easily eroded than the harder rocks of the uplands. The valleys are bordered on the east by the north-south-trending Hoosac Range and on the southeast by the Southern Berkshire Plateau. Towering over North Berkshire is Mount Greylock. At 3,491 feet above sea level it is the highest point in Massachusetts. Overlooking the county from the south, near its border with Connecticut, is Mount Everett at 2,602 feet above sea level.

The present-day Berkshire Hills are the roots of once great mountains that probably rivaled today's Rockies in stature. They are in fact one of the most ancient mountain systems of the continent. Created when two great continental plates collided with each other, those lofty peaks were ground down by the forces of erosion during the intervening hundreds of millions of years to the rounded hills that you see today.

Six hundred million years ago Berkshire County granites were covered by a shallow sea, into which washed sands, silts, and clays that would eventually harden into sandstone and shale deposits. On top of those sandstones and shales in that ancient sea bed, thick layers of what would become limestone were deposited and formed through the compaction of limy sea-floor ooze and mud, along with fragments of shells in the shallow sea environment.

About 430 million years ago, those sedimentary layers of sandstone, shale, and limestone were subjected to heat, pressure, buckling, and folding as the first of three mountain-building events (called orogenies by geologists) took place. Imagine entire continents as rafts floating on the crust of the earth, much as huge ice sheets float on the ocean. Throughout geologic time, large sections of continents have broken away and floated or drifted off to collide, eventually, with other continents. The process is extremely slow, measured in inches per century, but the effects over millions of years can and do create large mountain ranges (the Himalayas were created when India collided with Asia).

The heat and pressure of this type of collision altered the rocks into their present-day forms: sandstone became quartzite, shale became schist, and limestone was changed into marble. The older granites did not escape alteration either, as they were transformed into granitic gneiss. The roots of that first-formed mountain system are the present day Taconic Range along the Massachusetts-New York border. Most geologists agree that the Taconics comprise all the hills that lie west of Route 7 and Mount Greylock.

After approximately 100 million more years had passed, the area was subjected to another deformation called the Acadian Orogeny. All the rocks were once again transformed by this process of mountain building. Throughout what is now New England, extensive volcanic activity formed rocks by the solidification of molten material. These volcanic lavas were later eroded, exposing the underlying rocks. The younger rocks of the eastern hills in Berkshire County were formed by this later mountain-building process.

The last great earth forces affecting Berkshire took place approximately 225 million years ago during the Appalachian Orogeny. The entire eastern seaboard of what is now North America underwent westward compression. The Appalachian Mountain system was created in this way, and the event tended to further disrupt and change the rock formations of Berkshire.

During the most recent one million years, extensive continental ice sheets covered the area during four major advances of the glaciers and contributed to shaping of Berkshire by weathering and erosion. The effect of the mile-thick glacial ice was to soften and round off, through grinding action, the overall topography of the area. Here and there you will find scattered deposits of exotic rock types that were transported to this area from more northerly locales by the glaciers and dumped out of the ice as the temperature warmed and the ice receded; the last time this happened was somewhere from twelve thousand to fourteen thousand years ago. Glacial lakes were left behind that have long since vanished, but evidence of their former presence remains.

Erosion is still going on today as the two major river systems of Berkshire continue to down-cut, namely the Housatonic, which drains to the south and eventually empties into Long Island Sound, and the Hoosic River, which drains to the northwest and flows into the Hudson River.

According to archaeological evidence, humans made their first appearance on the Berkshire scene in only the last minute of the 24-hour geologic timetable, or some twelve thousand to ten thousand years ago. After the last glacial retreat, small bands of nomadic Paleo-Indian hunters wandered into the area. Fluted projectile points found in neighboring areas attest to the fact that they hunted in Berkshire as well. Their game probably included Ice Age mammals such as wooly mammoth, mastodon, giant beaver, and caribou.

Vegetation

The Berkshire Hills have a greater variety of plant life than any other comparable area in Massachusetts. This is because they have nearly 3,000 feet of elevational relief, from the state's highest peak to the low, broad valleys of the Housatonic and Hoosic rivers. Berkshire is also rich in bedrock types and soils derived from them. Many rare plants that require alkaline conditions are limited to Berkshire's limestone-lined valleys.

Berkshire vegetation has a long history, including many migrations and extinctions. Before the "big chill" that culminated in mile-thick glaciers advancing over the area from the arctic, lush subtropical vegetation extended far to the north. As the cold increased, this vegetation retreated gradually, and by the height of the last glaciation, some twenty thousand years ago, many species had become extinct and others survived only in "refuges" to the south. The bare and desolate landscape left by the retreating ice about twelve thousand years ago soon greened with tundra grasses and sedges, then firs and spruces, which had probably survived close to the glacial edge. A fascinating glimpse into postglacial life was provided by the discovery of mastodon bones and white fir cones in a South County bog (on private land in Egremont), dated at eleven thousand years ago. Soon, pines arrived and other deciduous species straggled back, with American chestnut (now nearly extinct after the chestnut blight of the 1930s) arriving late on the Berkshire scene, only two thousand years ago. As the deciduous species spread into the valleys and lower slopes, where they thrived, the spruce and fir retreated to the cold mountaintops.

Because of these catastrophic climatic events, the Berkshire region now has fewer species, but the ones that remain, especially the trees, are tough and hardy.

Our idea of human community is usually one of interdependent beings, but plant communities are often collections of species that happen to have similar, sometimes competing, growth requirements. Dominant plants, like trees, do create new habitats, either favorable or not, for other plants. Animals are dependent upon vegetation but also produce changes in it.

In general, Berkshire can be divided into four major forest types. Northern hardwoods — the birches, American beech, and sugar maple, with patches of eastern hemlock — form the major forest type of the northern portion. In the southern portion, the forest tends more toward oak, white pine, beech, red maple. On the Berkshire Plateau in the east, red spruce and balsam fir mix with hardwoods. On Mount Greylock, a true boreal (northern) forest of fir and red spruce is found. In reality it is very difficult to generalize. Bedrock, moisture, and exposure (south or north facing) all play major roles in determining what plants grow where. Often the types of vegetation vary all over the map. For instance, you will find sugar maple woods quickly changing to oak or hemlock woods at some locations.

Interspersed throughout all these forest types are many wonderfully varied vegetative communities: bogs, marshes, fens (wet meadows on limestone soils), floodplain forests, beaver meadows, ravines, mountaintops, rock outcrops, and south-facing slopes — each with its own kinds of special plants.

Humans have brought about many changes on the land, such as clearing for farms, introducing new and exotic plants, and cutting the forests for timber. Cleared areas return to deep forest in about one hundred years here, as remaining trees quickly seed in and stumps re-sprout. This results in a patchwork of brushy fields and forests of various ages.

As you explore our varied natural places, be aware that nature is always changing. Plants that once flourished in a certain spot may be gone the next year. Orchids, for instance, are notoriously quirky, coming up one year, but not the next. But after all, variety is the spice of life!

Cultural History

Getting in and out and around the Berkshire area used to be a problem. The native Americans generally thought of the area as removed from their Hudson River homes, a hunting ground to visit in the summer. The Mahicans entered from the south or north, along the river valleys. Although the Massachusetts Bay Colony claimed the land early on, Bay Colony residents found it tough to surmount the Berkshire barrier to the west. Early settlers found it easier to enter along the valleys, a few Dutch infiltrating through the Taconics from New York, but especially residents from the area now known as Connecticut, migrating up the Housatonic. Thus the county was settled from the south to the north, the earliest towns in the south dating to the first quarter of the eighteenth century. The main roads, railroads, and even sewer lines now follow the valleys.

The European settlers were primarily farmers, typically working the bottom lands and, as they filled up, moving up the sides of the hills. Remains of walls, cellar holes, and orchards such as you come across in your ambles remind you that even what seem now lofty ridges were at one time home, especially for those who made their living grazing cattle or merino sheep. In Stockbridge, the English Society for the Propagation of the Gospel in Foreign Parts set up an Indian mission, which gradually acceded to the land hunger of the Europeans. By the time of the Revolution, virtually all native Americans had departed.

As a farmer installed a mill to grind his corn or saw his wood, and his neighbors came to have him do their milling, so industry followed the plough. What began as groupings to protect against French or Indian raids became trading centers. Specialty manufactures, depending on natural resources, developed, such as glass, paper, charcoal, and textiles. Even education can be seen as an industry depending on natural resources. After all, Thoreau said of Williams College's position at the foot of Greylock: "It would be no small advantage if every college were thus located at the base of a mountain, as good at least as one well-endowed professorship. . . . Some will remember, no doubt, not only that they went to college, but that they went to the mountain." In Berkshire County, three of the four colleges and many of the secondary schools are at the base of the mountains.

The opening of the Erie Canal in 1825, providing a practical means for younger residents to head west where the thick topsoil had a lot fewer glacial stones than that of Berkshire, drained the county of human resources. One by one lights winked out on the sidehill farms. Whereas by the middle of the century three-quarters of the trees had been stripped for pasture land, charcoal production, or to feed the insatiable maws of the railroad, for the 150 years since then the county has been revegetating. In Berkshire that ratio is inverted today. The county is three-quarters wooded, which is why coyotes, bear, beaver, turkeys, ravens, and even moose are returning to join the populous deer and smaller animals.

The most important industrial event in the county's history happened in 1886, when William Stanley linked 25 shops along the main street of Great Barrington in the world's first commercial electric system. That, in turn, drew the General Electric Co. to Stanley's shop in Pittsfield. GE has been here ever since, only recently supplanted, through corporate spinoffs and buy-outs, as the county's largest employer. The second most important industrial event was the opening of the Hoosac Tunnel, at 4.75 miles the longest bore in the world in 1875, breaking through the Berkshire barrier for direct train service in the North County from Boston to Albany.

Yet even in the heady days when industry was king — the population of Pittsfield growing from 25,000 to 58,000 in the first 60 years of the 20th century — second homes, tourism, and culture were already crown princes. In the Gilded Age that ended the 19th century, the wealthy collected great estates and built luxury palaces, known as "cottages," some 75 in Lenox and Stockbridge.

As the county now, somewhat painfully, recognizes that industries will never again be what they were through World War II, it is coming to rely on a service economy to which, at least, it is no stranger. Filled with fine educational institutions, public and private, with museums and musicians, with art and artifacts to grace the green walls installed infinitely earlier by nature, Berkshire now boasts streams that are cleaner and woods that are thicker than since farms and industry first came to these garrison hills. And the hills retain a plentiful supply of ground water likely to become increasingly important to the future of this area.

Berkshire has now, as it has had since the ice left, an indigenous population that cares deeply for the land; witness the many towns in the county that have long had zoning, have now established land trusts, and are considering land use countywide. Berkshire residents listen attentively at town meetings to discussions of protecting ridges and aquifers, saving farmland, and cleaning up hazardous waste.

Little litter mars the many paths. Whether driving its roads or walking its trails, you will soon get the message that this land is cared for.

Natural Places

CAMPBELL FALLS STATE PARK

≈§ 1 §≈

Campbell Falls State Park
New Marlborough, Mass., and Norfolk, Conn.

Managed by Conn. DEP.

Acreage: 102 (Conn.), 4.6 (Mass.).

Elevation: 950—1,260 ft.

Trails: Less than 1 mi.

Hours: Open year-round. Closes at sunset.

Admission: None posted.

Facilities/Other: Pit toilet. No camping. Phone: 413-258-4774 (Mass.).

Directions: From Rte. 57 in New Marlborough Center, turn S. onto New Marlborough/Southfield Rd. Stay left toward Southfield, where Southfield Rd. splits off to the right at 1.4 mi. (no sign). Continue S. on Norfolk Rd. through Southfield for 4.6 mi. to Campbell Falls Rd. at state border (Norfolk Rd. becomes Conn. 272). Turn right onto dirt Campbell Falls Rd. and proceed W. for 0.4 mi. to parking area on left. Follow white-blazed (may be difficult to see) trail downhill to the falls. To reach picnic area in Conn. portion: Continue S. on Norfolk Rd. past Campbell Falls Rd. for 0.13 mi. to paved Spaulding Rd. on right. Turn onto Spaulding Rd. and follow for 0.2 mi. to picnic area on right (table in disrepair).

This relatively small park astride the Massachusetts-Connecticut border contains Campbell Falls, one of the outstandingly beautiful waterfalls of Berkshire. The falls are easily accessible at the end of a short, somewhat steep trail that takes you through huge and impressive white pines to a vantage point below the falls. The Whiting River plunges 80 feet through a crevice in the bedrock, producing a tumultuous roar, especially during wet seasons.

Behind you, as you face the falls, Ginger Creek gurgles along to join the Whiting River just downstream of Campbell Falls. Ginger Creek has cut through tilted layers of pinkish quartzite, one of the oldest rocks found in Berkshire and the same age as the rocks of Monument Mountain (see Ch. 8), to form a lovely hemlock gorge. The steep rock walls bear testimony to the hardness of the quartzite.

A short distance downhill from the parking lot, Campbell Falls Road crosses the Whiting River just above the falls. An attractive keystone arched bridge over the river is constructed of native stone. From here you can look upstream, watching and listening to the river as it flows between hemlock-lined banks.

Views and Vistas

Since the best view of the falls is from below, in the gorge, you will find no panoramic views of the countryside; but the beauty of the falls more than makes up for this. If you stand on the bedrock alongside the river just below the arched bridge, you'll find a very photogenic view of the river flowing with great speed through the stone archway of the bridge. *Watch your footing here, as you are quite near the lip of the falls.* This spot does not provide a view of the river dropping over the edge of the falls itself, however.

Plant Communities

The steep slopes are covered with a dense growth of white pine, many quite massive. The result is a shady, cool environment with limited undergrowth and a cushiony, needle-covered forest floor. The rocky gorge and cliffs are characteristically covered with eastern hemlock, a tree with attractive, dark-green foliage and tiny cones at the branch tips. In addition to these evergreens, deciduous members of the northern hardwood forest community that you'll find here include northern red oak, yellow birch, big-tooth aspen, white ash, and a few sugar maples (near the streams), American beech, and red maple. A few pin oaks, a tree that reaches its northern limits in this area, are present as well. These have slender, deeply lobed, and bristle-tipped leaves.

Away from the falls, along the yellow blazed trail to the picnic area, you'll find white oak, black cherry, and shagbark hickory, an easy-to-identify tree that has platy gray bark which peels away from the trunk in ragged strips. Its nuts are much sought after by squirrels. Many trees, especially cherries, contain the webs of tent caterpillars, bristly insects that can defoliate a tree in short order.

Understory trees on the slopes include the attractive green-and-white striped maple, American hornbeam (also known as musclewood because of the sinewy appearance of its trunk), and eastern hophornbeam (thin scaly brown bark).

The shrub layer is rather meager, but one of the most interesting and attractive evergreen shrubs you'll see in Berkshire is American yew. It looks a great deal like a shrubby hemlock, but it grows to only a few feet in height. The needles of the yew are longer and darker green than those of eastern hemlock; the undersides of hemlock needles are whitish, which is not the case with yew. The fruit of the yew is a fleshy red berry that has a very visible single dark seed imbedded in its center. Yews of various species and varieties are common ornamental plants. Another shrub, mountain laurel, grows along the roadsides in the park. The gorgeous white-and-pink flower clusters were chosen to be the Connecticut state flower.

The forest floor under the year-round shade of the pines and hemlocks sports the lovely green foliage of Christmas fern and spinulose wood fern in abundance. Cliffs and boulders support two other ferns — common polypody and marginal wood fern. All are evergreen. The rocks also have a vigorous growth of mosses and silvery green lichens. Among the forest floor herbs you'll find such species as wood sorrel, foamflower, and common speedwell. Foamflower produces white clusters of blossoms with protruding stamens that give the flowers a soft, "foamy" appearance.

The forest floor under the hardwoods is where you'll find the majority of early spring wildflowers such as dutchman's breeches, red trillium, and bloodroot, among others. Wintergreen and partridgeberry are both attractive low-growing, red-berry producing plants with dark evergreen leaves. Partridgeberry has small, rounded, paired leaves growing along a creeping stem, while the leaves of wintergreen are larger and shiny above.

Wildlife

Mammals: You can expect to find signs of the common residents of the hardwood forest community, including red and gray squirrels, eastern chipmunk, white-footed mouse, hairy-tailed mole, porcupine, raccoon, gray fox, and white-tailed deer, to name a few. In the wooded swamp live such aquatic creatures as muskrat and mink.

Birds: Year-round residents include wild turkey, ruffed grouse, pileated woodpecker, blue jay, and black-capped chickadee. Among the nesting woodland warblers are the gorgeous orange, black, and white Blackburnian, black-throated green, and magnolia, all three partial to conifer stands. Ovenbirds prefer deciduous woods. Red-eyed vireos sing even during the heat of midday. Flocks of golden-crowned kinglets and red-breasted nuthatches glean the conifer branches of insects, spiders, and their eggs in winter.

Reptiles: Turtles are represented primarily by the state-listed wood turtle, which may be found in meadows and woodlands near streams. Among the snakes, common garter is the one that you'll encounter more than any other, and even this species is not seen all that often. Ringneck, red-bellied, milk, and northern water snakes (in alder swamps) occur here as well.

Amphibians: A goodly selection of salamanders lives in the area. Indeed, all the species commonly found in other similar habitats occur in the park. Two-lined and dusky salamanders live under the rocks and logs along the edges of clear streams. Spotted and Jefferson salamanders breed in temporary vernal pools found in the forest and spend the rest of their somewhat mysterious lives below the leaf litter. Frogs are quite common, especially the tiny spring peeper, green, wood, pickerel, and gray tree frog, which has abrasive disks at the tips of its toes, allowing it to cling securely to vegetation. The absence of larger water bodies prevents bullfrogs from being common.

Fish: Cold-water species that live in the Whiting River and in Ginger Creek include brook trout, bluntnose dace, longnose dace, and slimy sculpin. The lack of large ponds prevents a greater variety of fish from occurring in the park.

Seasonal Highlights

Spring is when the greatest volume of water flows over the falls, making for very exhilarating viewing and listening. An early spring visit combines peak flow with the emergence of delicate and beautiful wildflowers prior to the leafing out of deciduous trees. Bird migration is in full swing by the beginning of May. In late spring, colorful butterflies visit the picnic area's flower-filled meadows.

In summer there may be less water flowing over Campbell Falls, but its beauty is still considerable. Bird nesting reaches its peak in late June and early July, so listen for the songs of thrushes, vireos, warblers, and flycatchers. You will have an easier time of it away from the roar of the falls. This is a popular swimming hole on weekends especially.

Fall is also a season of excellent water volume. The fall colors decorate the scene in early October, and late in autumn the leaf fall enhances the visibility of the gorge's rock walls. Southbound migrants make the birding a bit more interesting.

Winter's freezing temperatures produce fascinating ice shapes in the gorge alongside the cataract. The broad, domed surface of the gray bedrock to the right often becomes covered with ice that may have the shape and color of cauliflower. Below the falls, the tumbling water keeps pools bordered by bright white ice open. *Use caution when maneuvering to find the perfect vantage point for that photograph!*

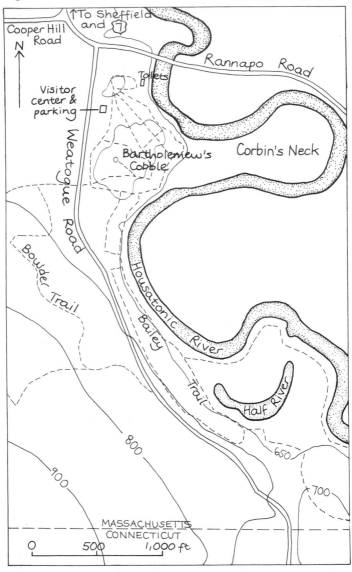

BARTHOLOMEW'S COBBLE

❧ 2 ❧

BARTHOLOMEW'S COBBLE
Sheffield

Owned and managed by TTOR.

Acreage: 277.5.

Elevation: 640—950 ft.

Trails: 5.5 mi.

Hours: Trails open 9-5 daily, year-round. Visitor center open summer daily, 9-5; call for winter hours.

Admission: Adults $3, children $1, TTOR members free. Programs and special events have different fees.

Facilities/Other: Trail maps, self-guided trail leaflets, and bird checklists available at visitor center. Phone: 413-229-8600. Rest rooms available.

Directions: From Sheffield Center take Rte. 7, S. for 1.1 mi. Go right on Rte. 7A for 0.5 mi., turn right onto Rannapo Rd. and continue 1.5 mi., past Cooper Hill Rd. on right, to Weatogue Rd. Turn right onto Weatogue; entrance on left. If parking lot is closed, park along edge of Weatogue Rd.

The Cobble, as it is affectionately known, is one of the most outstanding Berkshire natural areas — indeed, it is a registered National Natural Landmark. This relatively small property encompasses an amazing array of flora and fauna along the Housatonic River. The two 500-million-year-old marble (recrystalized limestone) and quartzite hills (cobbles) provide the proper environment for a host of unusual lime-loving plants. These cobbles owe their existence to the very hard quartzite rock that has resisted weathering far better than the surrounding softer limestone of the valley. The Cobble is justly famous for its great diversity of ferns. The animal life is varied as well, and an extensive and well-maintained trail system makes this fascinating place very accessible. Visitors to South Berkshire should not miss it.

Views and Vistas

Views of the scenic, almost idyllic Housatonic River Valley and bordering hills are wonderful from atop Eaton Trail, which traverses the smaller north cobble. An inspiring view of surrounding uplands and valleys awaits you from the slight promontory of Hurlburt Hill, and a stroll up through the hillside meadows to this point on the Connecticut border will give you a fantastic panorama of the entire area taking in Mount Everett (the highest point in South Berkshire), Mount Race, and Connecticut's highest peak, Bear Mountain, just south of the state line.

Plant Communities

Bartholomew's Cobble is first and foremost a botanist's mecca. It's comforting indeed to know that the many rare and endangered plant species here are protected. More than 800 species have been found. Of these, 50 are ferns or allied species such as clubmosses and horsetails. Without doubt this is the best place in the entire state to find unusual ferns. The limestone bedrock of the Housatonic River Valley is the major reason why plants that thrive in alkaline soils have found this area so appealing. You'll want to get hold of a fern identification guide and search out some of the more unusual forms. Tiny ferns much sought-after by botanists such as maidenhair spleenwort, ebony spleenwort, the delicate purple-stemmed cliffbrake, and walking fern have colonized many rock cavities. There has also been, in the past, an interesting hybrid between ebony spleenwort and walking fern: Scott's spleenwort.

But ferns are by no means the only unusual plants here, albeit the most storied. A small primitive plant, related to ferns and clubmosses, is rock spikemoss, which clings closely to exposed rock. The dry limestone cobbles are covered with a thick growth of red cedar (actually juniper), while eastern hemlock shades the steep slopes. The reservation's trails take you past imposing cliffs covered with lichens, mosses, ferns, and flowering plants like the exquisite red columbine, which blooms in June. The rich deciduous woodland floor is covered with round-lobed hepatica, delicate rue anemone, toothworts (food plants for the mustard, or veined, and West Virginia white butterflies), bloodroot, and many violets in early to mid-April. May apple hides its one white flower under umbrellalike leaves. Another specialty, narrow-leaved spring beauty, more common in the South, is found along Bailey Trail. Seemingly springing from rocks are the bright white flowers of early saxifrage. In summer, delicate blue harebell hangs off ledges. Later, great blue lobelia is the star of the floral show. In summer, meadows and forest edges sport thick growths of purplish wild bergamot and black-eyed susan (an introduced species from the Midwest).

The broad floodplain and banks of the slow-moving Housatonic are lined with silver maple (leaf undersides are silvery green), black willow, American sycamore (with attractive dark and light mottled bark), green ash, American basswood (heart shaped leaves), and cottonwood, all growing in rich, river-deposited soil. You can behold some cottonwoods of truly gargantuan proportions along Bailey Trail and Spero Loop. Hackberry, a southern tree and unusual in Berkshire, characterized by its corky bark, is located midway along Ledges Trail. Many tree species bloom early, before their leaves emerge. An example is silver maple. Its clusters of tiny red flowers add color to an otherwise lifeless scene in early March. Upland woods contain white pine, tulip tree, sugar maple, white ash, and white birch. Tulip tree is uncommon in Berkshire and is found only in South County.

The trail system has been laid out so that you can wander through a mix of interesting natural communities within a relatively short distance. Hayfields and pastures like those on Hurlburt Hill impart a certain peacefulness. They are a nice contrast to the wooded portions of the property and add considerably to the plant diversity.

Wildlife

Mammals: Among the common woodland-edge species to be found here are white-tailed deer, coyote, and red fox. Beaver, muskrat, mink, and river otter frequent the Housatonic and adjacent wetlands. Walking along some of the trails that border the river, you'll be able to find trees recently felled and stripped of bark by beavers. Cottontail rabbits, gray and red squirrels, and eastern chipmunks are common, as is the largest member of the squirrel family, the rotund woodchuck. Raccoon tracks are much in evidence along the muddy shores of the Housatonic, where these masked creatures search at night for frogs and other fare. In the evening or early in the morning, you might see a striped skunk or an opossum, North America's only pouched mammal (marsupial). At dusk, bats sweep the skies over ponds and fields in hot pursuit of aerial insects.

Birds: The Cobble's relatively southern location, its proximity to the Housatonic, and its varied natural communities also combine to make this a wonderfully rewarding place to seek out birds. More than 250 species of birds have been recorded since 1946 — an impressive number for a relatively small site in the Northeast. The milder climate (relative to much of the rest of Berkshire County) enables some species to over-winter here or to return in the spring earlier than elsewhere.

The river provides fine habitat for waterfowl such as Canada goose, wood duck, mallard, black duck, common merganser, and hooded merganser in early spring and late fall. Spotted sandpipers are found along its shores in summer, and during migration solitary sandpiper and other shorebird species frequent the river's mud flats and sand bars. In late summer, big white great egrets hunt for fish and frogs here. Our national bird, the bald eagle, has become a regular visitor — especially in spring and fall.

Hayfields and pastures on Hurlburt Hill are the places to visit if you want to observe open-country species such as eastern bluebird, tree swallow, eastern meadowlark, bobolink, and our smallest falcon, the American kestrel. Hay cutting is delayed until ground nesting bobolinks have fledged their young. Kestrels, bluebirds, and tree swallows are cavity nesters, utilizing abandoned woodpecker holes or other crevices. All three species use the more than 50 nest boxes provided for them here. Large numbers of bluebirds over-winter on the property. On a few occasions in summer, a purple martin has been seen in the Corbin's Neck pasture along the river. This large, dark swallow is not known to nest in the county, and the presence here on June 20 one year of a female caused some excitement. Unfortunately, European starlings, which are numerous here as elsewhere, also nest in cavities and boxes; their presence may preclude nesting here by the martins. Bank swallows also occur along the river. These colony-dwelling birds excavate long tunnels in the gravelly soil of steep river banks for nesting. You'll find them here in summer. A bird currently causing excitement is the black vulture. One or two have been sporadically seen soaring with long-tailed turkey vultures.

Shade trees provide good sites for the pendulous nests of the colorful Baltimore oriole. Shrubby areas harbor the three "mimic thrushes" (birds that mimic other species): gray catbird, brown thrasher (least common of the three), and northern mockingbird. Woodland birds include scarlet tanager, brown creeper, red-eyed vireo, wood thrush, red-breasted and white-breasted nuthatches, several woodpeckers (including red-bellied, which is increasing in South Berkshire), and the state bird, the black-capped chickadee. Both large owls — great horned and barred — nest here and are heard regularly. A band of raucous, mobbing crows is often a telltale clue to the presence of a perched owl.

Reptiles: The late spring, summer, and early fall visitor to the Cobble will occasionally encounter the ubiquitous common garter snake, but you are less likely to find the other species of native snakes. The non-poisonous northern water snake might be chanced upon in wetlands. Both this and the garter seek out frogs. Other locally common species include the red-bellied (characterized by its bright red-or-ange underside), smooth green, ringneck (a small snake with a narrow, light band around its neck) and ribbon snakes, which resemble garter snakes. Wood turtles inhabit the floodplain forests and fields near the Housatonic, but you are far more likely to run across (hopefully not in a literal sense) snapping turtles, or painted turtles sunning themselves on some log. Both these species might be seen in June while they search out sandy, well-drained soils suited for solar incubation of their leathery eggs. You might even find the state-listed spotted turtle, which has an upper shell decorated with small yellow spots, in floodplain pools. This species should be reported to Cobble staff.

Amphibians: In summer you will likely find all the native frogs in suitable habitat. On mild evenings as early as March you may hear the ringing chorus produced by spring peepers in brushy wetlands. Locating one visually is another matter. In the floodplain listen for deep, bellowing calls of huge bullfrogs and higher-pitched croaks of leopard frogs. The latter is an unusual species in Berkshire, far less common than the similar pickerel frog. Leopard frogs have spots, whereas pickerel frogs sport rectangular brown blotches. Another tailless amphibian to listen for is the gray treefrog. This small treefrog has the adhesive disks at the ends of its toes so characteristic of its group. Their calls are reminiscent of the purring of a young raccoon. The sound usually emanates from high in the trees. Listen for them in early summer during daylight hours, sometimes far from water.

All the common native salamanders reside here as well. The bright red-orange land-dwelling phase (known as red eft) of the red-spotted newt is the one you will most often meet on woodland paths, especially during damp weather. These engaging creatures warn potential predators that they have poisonous skins by means of their bright coloration. This species develops from eggs laid in water; the eggs hatch into larvae, which make their way to land, where they will spend from three to five years before developing gills and returning to water to live out the remainder of their lives as red-spotted newts.

Fish: The waters of the Housatonic harbor such species as northern pike, largemouth and smallmouth basses, bluegill, pumpkinseed, yellow perch, brown bullhead, white sucker (very numerous), carp, common golden shiner, spottail shiner, and shortnose dace.

Seasonal Highlights

Spring wildflowers put on quite a show in the Cobble's woodlands. Return on subsequent weekends from early April through mid-May to witness the full range. Also in the spring, the river corridor forms a virtual highway for northbound birds. Even as early as late March, you will be able to find a surprising diversity. The earliest returning residents, such as red-winged blackbirds, will have established their breeding territories in wet fields and marshes by early March. Eastern bluebirds, too, will have returned by March, the brightly colored males preceding the females by a couple of weeks. Many also over-winter. The river itself and flooded fields of Corbin's Neck should be checked for geese, ducks, and shorebirds.

In summer, wildflowers of field and meadow come into their own long after the woodland types have withered and set seed. Watch for colorful hummingbird moths at bergamot, as well as the ruby-throated hummingbirds, with which they are sometimes confused. Flowers are an excellent place to find other insects. Butterflies are among the most appealing, and on a sunny day you may well see 20 or more species, including eastern black swallowtail, tiger swallowtail, common ringlet, question mark, monarch, and its mimic the viceroy, and a variety of small mothlike skippers. During late July, check the short milkweed plants for black-yellow-and-white-striped monarch caterpillars. About one month is required for this creature to complete its miraculous transformation from egg to caterpillar to chrysalis and finally to adult (for a discussion of monarch migration, see Ch. 13). Take walks through various natural communities in order to see the greatest diversity of bird life. A short canoe trip on the river with a stop at the Cobble for a walk is very enjoyable. You can put in at the point where Route 7A crosses the Housatonic in Sheffield. Inquire at the visitor center for a schedule of guided trips.

In fall, the foliage spectacle and sunny, crisp days (sans biting insects) make a perfect time for outdoor excursions. Many ferns are evergreen, and so you can still find them readily (a few examples are Christmas fern, spinulose wood fern, and common polypody, which grows on boulders). Meadow wildflowers, many of which are yellow, such as goldenrods, bloom in profusion. Scan the trees and shrubs for migrant songbirds and, in late fall, the river for waterfowl. After leaf fall, the lay of the land will be visible to its best advantage. If the winds are out of the northwest, a walk up Hurlburt Hill might well reward you with sightings of southbound hawks. It's also a good time to take a closer look at the interesting rock formations and outcrops. If you inspect these rocks, you'll notice that they are oriented from almost horizontal to nearly vertical. This is strong evidence that all rocks of this region have undergone folding by tremendous forces of heat and pressure on several occasions. At various points along Eaton Trail you will also notice small crystals (one to two inches long) of the mineral tremolite. Individual crystals are bluish-white in color and look like little knife blades, often occuring in clusters and radiating from a common center.

Although anything but tropical, winters tend to be less severe in Southern Berkshire. Wetland soils are the last to freeze, so there is often a surprising amount of animal activity in these areas well into the season. Check the roadsides for over-wintering bluebirds, and stretches of the Housatonic free of ice will often be filled with ducks and geese. At first glance the winter landscape may seem without life, but with close observation you will still find a great deal to marvel at. On warm, sunny "thaw" days, a mourning cloak butterfly may flutter by, for instance. Inquire about cross-country and snowshoe programs.

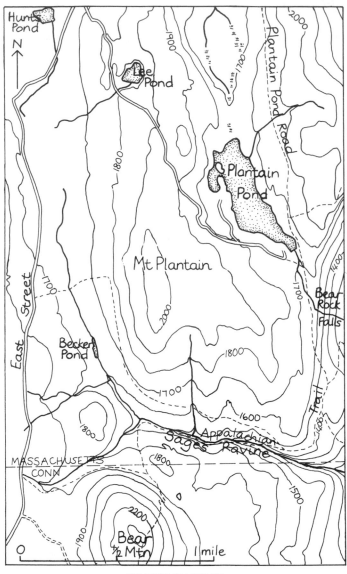

SAGE'S RAVINE

✒ 3 ✑

SAGE'S RAVINE
Mount Washington

Owned and managed by AMC, DEM, National Park Service, and private owner.

Acreage: 1,629.

Elevation: 1,400—1,830 ft.

Trails: Approx. 1.5 mi.

Hours: None posted.

Admission: None posted. Fee for camping at site along AT and for AMC cabin along entry trail.

Facilities/Other: No rest rooms. Phone: 413-443-0011 (AMC field office, Lanesborough). No motorized vehicles or wood fires allowed.

Directions: From jct. of Rtes. 23 and 41 in Egremont, take Mt. Washington Rd. around Mill Pond (see Ch. 6) for 4.6 mi. W. and then S. into town of Mt. Washington, where it becomes East St. Follow East St. to the left when it splits (follow pavement) and continue on East St. past entrance to Mt. Everett State Reservation (see Ch. 4) on left at 7.5 mi. At 7.8 mi. pass road on right to Bash Bish Falls State Park (see Ch. 5). Continue on East St. past Mt. Washington State Forest headquarters (on right) at 9.0 mi. and continue S. on East St. (Mt. Washington Rd. in Conn.), which later turns to gravel, for an additional 2.7 mi. to just across Mass.-Conn. state line (just past granite marker on left). Park in designated area on left (signs indicate AMC parking), being careful not to block gate. Road closed in winter (Nov.-Mar.).

Pick up the trail at the gate and follow it over land owned and maintained by the AMC. In 0.75 mi. this eastbound trail intersects the AT at the base of Bear Mtn. (at 2,316 ft. the highest peak entirely within Conn.). Follow the white-blazed AT N. (left) down the slope for 0.25 mi. to the upper end of the ravine. You can then follow the AT downstream along the brook for nearly another 1.0 mi. to where it crosses

Sage's Ravine Brook over steppingstones on its way out of
the gorge. Continuing N. will take you to Bear Rock Falls
(1.4 mi.), Mt. Race (3.1 mi.), and Mt. Everett (4.9 mi.).

Situated in the extreme southwest corner of Massachusetts, along the Connecticut border, Sage's Ravine is a wild
and picturesque east-west gap cut by Sage's Ravine Brook
through the Berkshire schist of the Taconic Mountains.
Somewhat over a mile in length, the ravine is a damp, rocky
place almost always in shade. Through it the Appalachian
Trail winds along a scenic and loudly flowing brook that
splashes over boulders and logs and creates many clear,
cold pools below each falls as it descends 400 vertical feet
through the gorge. High-speed film or a tripod is a must.

Views and Vistas

As you might expect, there are no panoramic views to
be had from the ravine; for that you'll have to scale some of
the nearby summits. During the seasons when the trees are
leafless, you'll be able to see some of the ridges to the north
as you walk east or west along the access trail from East
Street.

Plant Communities

As you enter the ravine and walk through it downstream along the roaring brook, the contrasting vegetation
of north- and south-facing hillsides will be quite evident.
On your right the rocky slopes are covered with eastern
hemlock, yellow birch, and red maple, all moisture-tolerant
species. Some of the hemlocks are quite large and seemingly perched on boulder pedestals. The shady, rock-stud-
ded slope is blanketed with an evergreen growth of spinulose wood fern, an attractive, lacy fern. This is one of the
most luxuriant growths of the species that I have seen anywhere in Berkshire. There are also Christmas and marginal
wood ferns in small numbers, long beech fern, and, on
some rocks, the small common polypody fern. In a few

clearings you'll see the light-green fronds of hay-scented fern in summer. If you look closely you'll be able to distinguish on the boulders a few American yew bushes, which look somewhat like hemlock, but with longer, darker needles. The moist, shaded hillside has little else in the way of ground cover, other than the green carpet of mosses, ferns, and lichens.

On the opposite side of the brook, the sunnier, south-facing slope is not as rocky. The trees here are mostly American beech, with some white birch and, below them, thickets of mountain laurel, in contrast to the north-facing side of the gorge. In the ravine you'll find some hobblebush in the shrub layer. At the upper, more open, end of the ravine, trees such as northern red oak, black and gray birches, black cherry, and white ash are fairly common. Below them is an understory of striped and mountain maples.

Wildlife

Mammals: The gorge and surrounding slopes are home to gray squirrels, which harvest the abundant acorns and beech nuts. Eastern chipmunks also store this bounty for times of need. The brook entertains mink and sometimes river otter as they search for fish to eat. I've seen white-tailed deer dashing through the forest above the ravine with their warning flags held high. Among the rodents to be found is the ubiquitous white-footed mouse. Bobcat, black bear, and coyote no doubt frequent the area from time to time. Bobcat particularly seem to favor rocky sites.

Birds: Year-round residents include wild turkey, hairy woodpecker, black-capped chickadee, and white-breasted nuthatch. Tiny, golden-crowned kinglets, most often seen in hemlocks, frequent the conifers in spring and fall. Females have yellow crowns, whereas males possess orange crown feathers. Their high-pitched three-part call is especially welcome in late fall, when little else may be stirring. Among the birds that summer and nest in the ravine are the American robin and Louisiana waterthrush, which is actually a warbler. This six-inch bird has a lovely loud ringing song that can even be heard above the roar of the brook. You may see one of these olive-brown birds (white under-side, streaked with brown) along the edge of the brook, constantly bobbing its tail. You may also see and hear her-mit thrush, winter wren, red-eyed and solitary vireos, ov-enbird, Blackburnian, black-throated green, and black-throated blue warblers, and scarlet tanagers, although the sound of the flowing stream makes birding by ear difficult.

Reptiles: The ravine is generally too shady a place to be favored by reptiles, and so snakes are not numerous. Com-mon garter occurs here, as do other species tolerant of cool climes, such as milk and red-bellied snakes. The south-facing side of the gorge is apt to have more of these serpents.

Amphibians: You may encounter wood frogs in the deciduous woodlands above the ravine, as these frogs rely solely upon temporary woodland pools for breeding. Pick-erel frogs find food and shelter along the brook. Obviously the lack of swamps, marshes, and larger ponds restricts the variety of species that can occur at this location. Rocks along the permanently flowing waters of Sage's Ravine Brook create suitable living quarters for dusky and two-line salamanders. The uncommon large orange-brown spring salamander may occur here as well. In the south-facing hillside woodland you may encounter the red eft, wander-ing far from the pond that it will inhabit as an adult red-spotted newt. In the woods the same vernal pools that support wood frogs also provide the necessary breeding sites for spotted (yellow on black) and Jefferson (tiny blue flecks on black) salamanders. These animals spend the vast portion of their lives under the leaf litter and can usually be seen only at night during rainy periods of early spring (unless of course you are fortunate enough to locate a ver-nal pool — see Ch. 18). The most common salamander to be found under rotting logs is the small red-backed species; but some individuals are gray backed and have been dubbed "lead-back" salamander.

Fish: Within the cold, clear, rock-and-gravel-bottomed pools of Sage's Ravine Brook live a few small species that require water with a high oxygen content. Among these are native brook trout, which attain lengths of only two to three inches in some of these smaller streams.

Seasonal Highlights

Early spring rains and melting ice and snow combine to send huge quantities of water churning down the ravine, enabling you to understand how the brook cut this gorge through the hard rock of the Taconics. The large, pleated leaves of false hellebore (Indian poke) emerge early in saturated soils near the stream margin and provide an attractive green border. It is sometimes mistaken for skunk cabbage, which grows in boggy woods. In late spring you'll see several attractive flowering plants in the ravine: starflower, which has seven-petaled white flowers; yellow clintonia (blue bead lily) with nodding greenish-yellow flowers; wild sarsaparilla (which has an aromatic root), distinguished by three round heads of greenish-white flowers; and the low-growing common wood sorrel, a plant that has cloverlike leaves and pretty white flowers with pink veins.

In early summer, mountain laurel shrubs bloom profusely along the entrance trail from mid-June to early July. The ravine is noticeably cooler than adjacent areas. Birds nest in the ravine's trees, shrubs, and on the forest floor. Listen for the loud songs of winter wren and Louisiana waterthrush above the sound of the brook.

The red maples growing on the north-facing slope turn crimson in late September, and the yellow leaves of birches contrast beautifully with the dark-green foliage of hemlocks. Fall rains bring additional water to the ravine, making for a more spectacular flow. This water augments Schenob Brook and its many wetlands in the valley just east of the Taconic Range.

In winter East Road may be closed, so getting here may be a problem. If accessible, the ravine can be a strikingly beautiful place to visit, given the many frozen waterfalls and the numerous icicles suspended from rocky overhangs and boulders. *Icy conditions also make for hazardous footing, and extreme caution should be used in negotiating the trail, especially within the narrower, lower end of the ravine.* You won't see or hear many birds, but you can look for the tracks of aquatic mammals such as mink in the snow and ice along the brook. Mink tracks are paired, show five toes, and are about 1.75 inches long. It may be obvious to you where this luxuriantly furred predator crawled out of the water and onto the snow-covered ice.

⋅ఠ 4 ఠ⋅

MOUNT EVERETT STATE RESERVATION
Mount Washington, Sheffield

Managed by DEM.

Acreage: 1,384.

Elevation: 1,000—2,602 ft.

Trails: 7 mi.

Hours: Memorial Day through Columbus Day. Gate to Mt.
Everett Rd. opens at 8 a.m. and closes at 8 p.m.

Admission: None posted.

Facilities/Other: Rest rooms available at lower parking area.
Alcohol, camping, swimming, and hunting prohibited.
Phone: 413-528-0330.

Directions: From Rtes. 23 and 41 in Egremont, take Rte. 41
and then bear right onto Mt. Washington Rd. (at Mill Pond
— see Ch. 6) and follow it (it becomes East St.) for 7.6 mi.
to Mt. Everett sign on left. Turn left into the reservation. If
gate is closed, park on right or left outside gate. From here
it is 0.9 mi. to Guilder Pond and 1.1 mi. to toilets, trailhead,
and parking. From this lower parking area, it is another 0.6
mi. by steep gravel road to upper parking area, just below
summit.

Mount Everett (2,602 ft.) is the highest peak in South
Berkshire and one of the highest peaks of the Taconic Range.
It is also one of South Berkshire's most visible and picturesque sights. The mountain is made up mostly of bluish-
green Berkshire schist, a heat-and-pressure-altered rock
composed of the minerals chlorite, mica, and quartzite. On
closer inspection you'll be able to see brown garnet crystals
(some up to a quarter-inch) imbedded in the rock. You will
also note the erosion-resistant milky-white quartzite veins.
The rounded summit itself, complete with fire tower, is
accessible by a steep trail. The mountain is traversed by one
of the most scenic sections of the Appalachian Trail in Massachusetts, and it is an excellent vantage point for viewing
migrating hawks as they pass by in fall. The state's second-

highest water body, Guilder Pond (2,042 ft.) is lovely, and circumscribed by a beautiful trail. In late June when the pond's shores burst forth with the gorgeous blossoms of mountain laurel, this is perhaps the most enchanting setting from which to admire this shrub's beauty. The pond trail stands in sharp contrast to the rocky, wind-swept summit.

Views and Vistas

Mount Everett rises almost 2,000 feet above the Housatonic River Valley, and so the views from its summit are nothing short of sublime. As you gaze due south you'll see Mount Race (2,365 ft.) only 1.5 miles away along the ridge and, a few miles farther, Bear Mountain (2,316 ft.), the highest point wholly in nearby Connecticut. Somewhat farther southeast, right where the three states meet, is Mount Ashley (2,390 ft.), and behind it, Mount Frissell (2,453 ft.). Well beyond in the same direction are the Catskills of New York. Less than one mile north is Mount Undine (2,203 ft.), and way beyond is the distinctive double hump of Mount Greylock; between the two is Monument Mountain, which seems out of place in the valley. Its quartzite rock was pushed up through a fault or crack in the younger limestone rocks of the valley. The vast wetlands of the Schenob Brook watershed lie almost 2,000 feet below you in Sheffield to the east. A 14,000-acre "Area of Critical Environmental Concern" was designated by the state in 1990.

Beyond the Housatonic Valley to the east is the undulating surface of the Berkshire Plateau, which posed such a barrier to settlers during the 18th century. This wall extends all the way to the Vermont border and beyond, and is made up largely of tough schists and gneisses. To the southeast in Connecticut, the shining waters of the Twin Lakes (Washinee and Washining) are seemingly close at hand. The view of the upper portion of Mount Everett from the far side of Guilder Pond is very nice, and the entire mountain is readily visible from many localities in South County. Some of the best vantage points are in Sheffield (see Ch. 2).

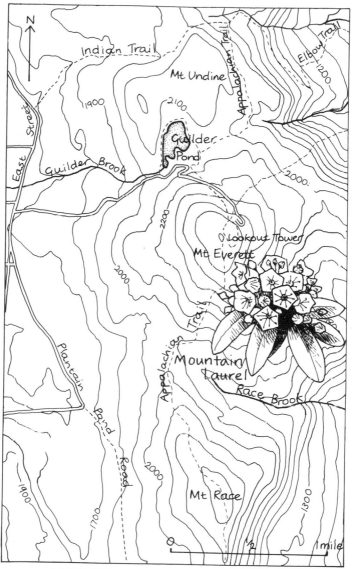

MOUNT EVERETT STATE RESERVATION

Plant Communities

One of the most interesting communities occurs on the ridge line: the pitch pine and scrub (bear) oak "forest" characteristic of the scant rocky soils of the southern Taconic ridges (and also found along the sandplain of the Housatonic River). Although plant diversity may be low on these rocky, windswept ridges, consisting largely of the above trees and low-bush blueberry, huckleberry, mountain ash, and a few other species, the weathered outcrops with their short, gnarled pines present an evocative image fit for the canvas. Little grows in the poor acidic soils below the pines, which are fire adapted. High temperatures are in fact required to open the cones, freeing their seeds. Bearberry, a shiny, ground-hugging evergreen plant, more common in coastal areas, grows atop the escarpment south of Mount Everett.

Upper slopes below the ridge are clad with taller trees: northern red oak, American beech, sugar maple, yellow birch, eastern hemlock, and white pine. Thick growths of mountain laurel form almost impenetrable thickets in some spots. The lovely, large pink-and-white flower clusters contrast wonderfully with the shiny green foliage of this shrub (the Connecticut state flower). When seen in such extravagant displays as are visible here, it represents one of the most beguiling sights of the early summer woods. The shoreline of Guilder Pond is crowded with a virtual thicket of mountain laurel. Here, too, you will find a plant, usually confined to bogs, known as leatherleaf — an apt name. This shrub, which grows along the shoreline, has attractive, small white flowers in May. There are even carnivorous sundew and horned bladderwort (see also Ch. 11), and large cranberry can be found in the peaty soil. In the shallow water, look for common pipewort, with white, buttonlike flowers and "grassy" leaves.

Wildlife

Mammals: White-tailed deer are abundant, and you may see one or more of the graceful animals at any time of year. As elsewhere, the wide variety of mammals rarely present themselves overtly, and so tracks and signs must serve as clues to their presence. Mink live in and around Guilder Pond. Beaver were once in residence, too (as old cuttings attest), but seem to have left the pond's vicinity, at least for now. Black bear, bobcat, coyote, and gray fox will likely not be seen, but after all, that is precisely why an encounter with one of these creatures leaves such an indelible mark on our memories. The gray squirrel, its smaller and engaging relative the red squirrel, as well as the abundant little eastern chipmunk, are the mammals that you will most likely see during a daylight visit.

Birds: The rich woods of the reservation are a fine place to observe the bird life of the southern Taconic Range. Walking through the woods may result in the flushing of a ruffed grouse, in a loud explosion of wing beats. Males of this species annually display for females on favorite drumming logs, upon which they fan out their tails and simultaneously beat their short wings against their bodies so fast as to simulate the low-pitched drone of a lawn mower revving up and sputtering out. Grouse are common in Berkshire woodlands, but witnessing the male's drumming is a spectacle you won't soon forget.

The tall oaks, beeches, maples, and birches provide fine nest sites for such woodland species as rose-breasted grosbeak, scarlet tanager, American robin, red-eyed vireo, least flycatcher, blue jay (one of the many species of wildlife that eats acorns), brown creeper, many species of wood warblers, including black-throated green and black-throated blue (the latter is partial to laurel thickets), and cavity nesters such as downy, hairy, and pileated woodpeckers, yellow-bellied sapsucker, northern flicker, tufted titmouse, black-capped chickadee, and red-breasted and white-breasted nuthatches. Besides the ruffed grouse, birds that build their nests on the ground here include the dark-eyed junco, veery, wood and hermit thrushes, white-throated sparrow, and ovenbird.

In thickets and shrubby field margins as well as on the open summit of Mount Everett you will likely hear the distinctive and clearly whistled *drink your tea* song or *chewink* call of the eastern (formerly rufous-sided) towhee, a large and attractive member of the sizable sparrow clan.

The summit is a well-known hawk-watching site in fall. After the passage of a cold front, and with northwest winds, you may see literally hundreds of hawks pass by, many of which will actually be below your lofty perch. This point, Berry Hill in Hancock, and Spruce Hill in Adams are the premier sites for hawk watching in Berkshire. The same species are seen at all sites, on about the same schedule, and in about the same ratios (see chapters 18 and 24). But even if very little happens by in the way of hawks while you are thus positioned, the views alone are more than adequate compensation. And during fall migration you'll find other birds in the pitch pines of the ridge. In late October, mixed flocks of golden-crowned and ruby-crowned kinglets, black-capped chickadees, yellow-rumped warblers, tufted titmice, and other species scour the tree trunks and stiff needle bunches searching for tiny insects and spiders. This can keep you and your binoculars very busy!

Reptiles: In addition to the common garter snake, you might, if fortunate, encounter the large and glossy black racer sunning itself on an exposed rock outcrop in summer. At the northern end of the ridge is a place known as Jug End, one of the few sites where the endangered eastern timber rattlesnake can still be found.

You'll find painted turtles in the waters of Guilder Pond. This reptile takes its common name from the bright, red-patterned bottom shell. Snapping turtles and the stinkpot (musk turtle), a small species with a high-domed shell, may also reside here. When handled, the stinkpot exudes a foul-smelling secretion, thought to be a deterrent to predators (as well as perhaps a love potion).

Jug End Rattlesnakes

Development and persecution have left the rattlesnake in a precarious position. In the fall these misunderstood creatures move to historic communal den sites where they mass; a slowed metabolic rate and their stored fat reserve enables them to survive the long, frigid winter. This concentration of course makes the animals highly vulnerable. Working against them also is a low birth rate, with the females producing young only once every three or four years — and they don't even begin breeding until age 10. The danger that timber rattlesnakes pose to humans is often greatly overstated. True, these large reptiles do deserve your respect, but an unnatural fear need not keep you out of the woods. In the very unlikely event that you should encounter one of these rattle-bearing reptiles, simply give it a wide berth; the last thing that it wants is to come face to face with you. The area is certainly big enough so that we and the snakes can co-exist. The presence of rattlesnakes on the ridge should be cause for celebration rather than alarm, since it demonstrates that this one element of our natural heritage is still with us, albeit endangered.

Amphibians: The high elevation of the reservation and general scarcity of swamps and marshes result in a relatively small number of frog species. Wood frog, green frog, and spring peeper are the most common. Guilder Pond should be checked in late spring and summer for bullfrogs. These animals, however, are far more numerous in the extensive valley wetlands to the east. Among the common tailed amphibians is the red-spotted newt, found in the clear waters of the pond. Red-backed salamanders occur in the woodlands, and the four-toed, a small Species of Special Concern, lives in mixed woods and boggy places such as along the shores of Guilder Pond. The large and strikingly patterned (yellow on black) spotted salamander breeds in early spring in vernal pools (see Chap. 13 for a bit of their biology). The clear, cold brooks here are home to the relatively common dusky and two-lined salamanders.

Fish: Other than a couple of small brooks that flow down the ridge toward the east, Guilder Pond, at 15 acres, is the only sizable body of water within the reservation. Within it are a few species of fish, including chain pickerel, a species native to southeast Massachusetts, but not Berkshire, and yellow perch, one of the three most common fishes in the state.

Seasonal Highlights

In May, the rich moist woods give rise to a bounty of colorful wildflowers. Among the loveliest are painted trillium and bloodroot. Migrant songbirds in the trees and northward winging hawks are just two more reasons to visit this location in spring.

In the third week of June, mountain laurels reach the height of their bloom, and Guilder Pond has the richly deserved reputation of producing the best show in the area. Sheep laurel blossoms are smaller, but a deeper pink. The flowers of both species have an ingenious method of dusting visiting insects with their pollen. Examine a laurel flower and note that the spring-loaded stamens (which produce pollen) are tucked into little pockets. When an unsuspecting bee jostles the flower, it is whacked by a released stamen, thereby getting a good dose of pollen, which it transports to another flower. Try springing one yourself! Come in June and July and you will have the best chance to see and hear the woodland birds that are in the midst of raising their one or two annual broods. Some, like the scarlet tanager and wood thrush, spend the majority of their lives in the tropical rain forests, about which much has been written of late. These birds move northward to take advantage of the abundant insect hatch in our temperate woodlands during summer. Their stay here lasts only five months, or even less.

Fall is the time for hawk observation from the summit of Mount Everett, from September to early November. (Note that the locked gate after Columbus Day necessitates an uphill walk of over two miles to the summit.) Bring a lunch and a lawn chair, sit back, relax, and contemplate the world around you. In September you might see large kettles of broad-winged hawks taking advantage of the lift created by rising thermals produced when solar radiation warms the earth. Slimmer and faster bird-eating accipiters with long tails and shorter wings come in three sizes: sharp-shinned, which is jay-size or somewhat larger; Cooper's, about the size of a crow; and northern goshawk, a large, powerful predator that nests in the surrounding forests. Goshawks can handle prey as large as grouse or rabbits. A friend of mine once nearly lost his hat (not to mention his head) to a characteristically protective goshawk near the summit!

You'll also see many turkey vultures gliding effortlessly on their long black and (from underneath) white wings. Keep an eye out also for songbird migrants, including tiny, wing-flicking ruby-crowned kinglets in the pitch pines.

You may want to walk a bit of the Appalachian Trail or just sit atop the mountain observing the magnificent fall foliage in early October. In late October, after the leaves have fallen from most trees, the bright yellow leaves of big-tooth aspen stand out dramatically. No matter what you decide to do, this is one of the most magnificent settings in which to do it.

In winter, search for winter seed-eaters such as evening grosbeak, pine siskin, and crossbills in the conifers. That sense of wilderness you may be seeking can also be easiest to achieve in winter, when the forests are virtually devoid of people and the sound of the wind through the white pines is a lonely yet reassuring reminder that all has as yet not been tamed. Cross-country skis are a wonderful way in which to find adventure (see *Skiing*).

Comments

A visit to South Berkshire should include an excursion to Mount Everett even if you have time or ambition only to walk around (or up to) Guilder Pond. The extra energy required to reach the summit is more than worth the effort; the experience will lift not only your physical being to a considerable height but your spirits as well.

BASH BISH FALLS STATE PARK
Mount Washington

Managed by DEM as part of Mt. Washington State Forest.

Acreage: 417.

Elevation: 800—1,890 ft.

Trails: 30 mi. of trails within the state forest.

Hours: Year-round, dawn to dusk (8 a.m. to dusk at parking area in New York).

Admission: None. Primitive camping (allowed only at Mt. Washington State Forest headquarters) $5 a night.

Facilities/Other: Pit toilets available. Maps and information available at Mt. Washington State Forest headquarters on East St., Mt. Washington. Phone: 413-528-0330. Camping also available at Taconic State Park in N.Y. No swimming, rock climbing, motorized vehicles, or alcohol allowed; dogs permitted on leashes only.

Directions: From Rtes. 23 and 41 in Egremont, take Rte. 41 and bear right onto Mt. Washington Rd. (later becomes East St.). Follow it for 8 mi. to Bash Bish Falls Rd.; turn right and follow approx. 3.2 mi. to paved parking area on left. I usually prefer to walk to the falls from Taconic State Park just across the N.Y. line. This parking area is 1 mi. below the parking lot in Mass., off N.Y. Rte. 344. From here you can walk approx. 0.7 mi. across the border, along and above Bash Bish Brook, to the graveled area near the base of the falls.

Bash Bish Falls is the most spectacular waterfall in Berkshire. The falls are composed of two portions, with the lower splitting in two around a huge boulder and plunging 60 feet into a clear green pool — easily one of the area's most photogenic sights. Bash Bish Brook has cut a 1,000-foot-deep valley through which it flows into neighboring New York. From vantage points on the rocky promontory above the upper parking area, you will have wonderful views to the west. The falls and gorge are awe-inspiring at any season.

Views and Vistas

To reach the best view points, make the modest climb up the rock outcrop that abuts the upper parking area. The slick bluish-gray rock glistens because of its high mica and chlorite content. It is also interlaced with thin, milky white stringers of quartz intrusions. Locally, this rock is known as Berkshire schist. From the railing of the metal fence that acts as a welcomed, if somewhat unattractive, safety barrier, you'll see and hear, especially after leaf fall, Bash Bish Brook tumbling through the gorge. Westward you can see well beyond the Harlem Valley, all the way to the Catskill Mountains. The falls themselves are not visible from here. From this vantage point, at 1,270 feet elevation, you'll be gazing down upon the brook 500 feet below you. The steepness of the gorge is indicative of both the down-cutting power of the stream and also the lateral erosion-resistance of the schist.

Bash Bish Mountain (1,890 ft.) forms the northeast-facing wall of the chasm to your left, with Cedar Mountain (1,883 ft.) to your right, forming the southwest-facing wall. The effects of orientation are dramatically visible here. The left slope is covered with dense eastern hemlock, a tree that flourishes under moist, shaded conditions. In sharp contrast, the slopes of Cedar Mountain, to your right, are clothed primarily by oaks, which favor dry, sunny sites. The ridge line of Cedar Mountain is covered by eastern white pine, pitch pine, and scrub oak.

From the graveled maintenance drive area, which can be reached by a steep boulder-laden trail to the right from the upper parking area, you will have a splendid ground-level view of the falls as it plunges with an almost deafening roar into the greenish waters of the pool at its feet. As the brook surges downward, it seems to bounce from side to side in its boulder-filled channel, creating a series of waterfalls. Look up just above the falls and you might notice a white horizontal layer of rock that is a quartz intrusion into the schistose rock of the gorge. The falls is reputedly named for a beautiful Indian woman who lived in a

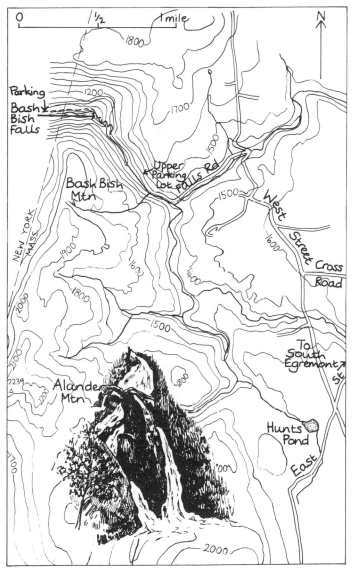

BASH BISH FALLS STATE PARK

nearby village. As legend has it, she was accused of adultery and sent over the falls strapped to a canoe.

Plant Communities

The two sides of the valley support distinctly different types of trees. On the shaded northeast-facing slope and at the bottom of the chasm, large eastern hemlocks and yellow birches predominate, with a dense ground cover of American yew and many ferns; while on the southwest-facing slope, northern red oak is the major species, and hemlock is virtually absent. Other oaks grow here as well. Chestnut oak, the leaves of which have wavy, rounded margins, is numerous, as is white oak. Other species such as sugar and red maples, big-tooth aspen, pignut and shagbark hickories, and tulip tree (the last three being generally southern in distribution) complete the canopy. Understory trees include black birch, eastern hophornbeam, American hornbeam (also known as musclewood because of its very hard, sinewlike trunk), striped maple, and witch hazel, which blooms in late fall. This small tree's flowers are yellow and pleasing, if somewhat scraggly.

Some mountain laurel grows under the oaks near the bottom of the ravine, and on the forest floor you'll find a variety of ferns: Christmas, marginal wood fern, spinulose wood fern, and others. On rock outcroppings, such as at the top of the cliff above the falls and on the exposed bedrock above the parking lot, you'll see another fern, common polypody. All four species are evergreen. In spring the forest floor comes to life with the blossoms of round-lobed hepatica and herb Robert, which has small, fernlike leaves and pretty pink flowers. Later in the year woodland goldenrods and asters give a yellow and bluish hue, respectively, to the forest.

Wildlife

Mammals: Some of the more common species here are white-tailed deer, raccoon, gray squirrel, hairy-tailed mole (which pushes up mounds of earth from its underground burrows), eastern chipmunk, and deer mouse. Although early morning and early evening are best for observation, you may find otherwise nocturnal mammals out and about at midday during cloudy weather.

Birds: The woodlands support a goodly variety of breeding vireos, warblers, thrushes (wood thrush is common), and other birds that winter in the tropics, such as the gaudy scarlet tanager. Vireo nests are fairly easy to distinguish; all four species weave thin strips of birch bark into their nest exteriors, and these small nests are always placed at the end of a forked branch. Another summer resident is the yellow-bellied sapsucker, which drills sap wells (parallel rows of quarter-inch-diameter holes) in a characteristic grid on the trunks of birches, maples, hemlocks, and other trees. It then makes repeated trips to the wells to lick up the sap and to snap up any insects that might have been attracted to it. Hummingbirds also visit the wells in early spring.

Year-round residents include wild turkey, black-capped chickadee, white-breasted nuthatch, downy, hairy, and pileated woodpeckers, brown creeper, blue jay, and tufted titmouse. Many of the birds that reside here, like the wild turkey, blue jay, and white-breasted nuthatch, include acorns as an important part of their diets.

In addition to the resident birds you will likely see in fall, one of the most engaging visitors, in my opinion, is the tiny and active golden-crowned kinglet. While foraging, these smallest of native birds (with the exception of the hummingbird) keep their flocks together with a high-pitched, usually three-note call, which you may hear, even above the roar of the brook and falls.

The red-tailed hawk is a common year-round raptor, and during the summer months watch also for the crow-sized broad-winged and Cooper's hawks, as well as the lordly turkey vulture. Seeing any of these birds soaring over the gorge is a wonderful sight. Cedar Mountain was one of the last places where wild peregrine falcons nested in Massachusetts.

Reptiles: A few species of snakes live here, with the common garter snake being the most numerous. Others include milk, northern brown, red-bellied, and ringneck. The endangered eastern timber rattlesnake may still occur in the area. It seems that the longest individual ever recorded (6 ft., 2 in.) came from this location.

Amphibians: The absence of swamps and marshes within the state park precludes the presence of a larger variety of frogs. The wood frog and the American toad, however, are common. Red-backed, two-lined, and dusky salamanders are the most common tailed amphibians. The latter two live along stream borders and in other wet places. Above the falls, large spring salamanders find conditions to their liking in the clear, cold brook.

Fish: Brook trout are found within the streams of the state forest. There are also other, smaller, cold-water species present in Bash Bish Brook, such as blacknose dace. Brown trout and largemouth bass, fish more commonly found in slightly warmer water, have been introduced into Bash Bish Brook. The only black bullhead (a more western species) ever recorded in the region was found here by state fisheries staff during a survey some years ago — and no one knows how it got here!

Seasonal Highlights

Spring is the season of greatest water flow, when Bash Bish is at its awe-inspiring best. Early spring wildflowers such as round-lobed hepatica bloom in April, and in late May the lovely native wild pink, looking something like a low phlox, blooms near the roadsides. Bird migrants in search of insect food fill the oak trees, which leaf out in May.

In summer the waterfall's flow is reduced, unless the weather has been unusually wet. Nesting birds go about the business of rearing their young; hearing and distinguishing their songs can be challenging, even over the diminished roar of the falls. In July the one-inch-plus magenta blossoms of purple-flowered raspberry adorn the edges of the wide graveled path, while the yellow-flowered false foxglove and pretty pink corymbed spirea bloom along the highway. This is a popular swimming hole despite the prohibition against it.

Fall is second only to spring in the volume of water flow. Bird migration is underway, especially during September, and foliage peaks in early October. After the leaves have fallen, you'll have an easier time obtaining unobstructed views of the gorge and Bash Bish Brook from above.

In early winter, unless deep snow blankets the earth, the site is often still accessible. Nature's ice sculptures, formed by freezing spray, are beautiful. During the coldest weather the falls may freeze completely, resulting in a magnificent icicle of gargantuan proportions!

Comments

Also within Mount Washington State Forest is Alander Mountain (2,239 ft.), from the summit of which you can attain the best views, according to many, in all Berkshire. See *Hikes & Walks* for details about this five-mile excursion.

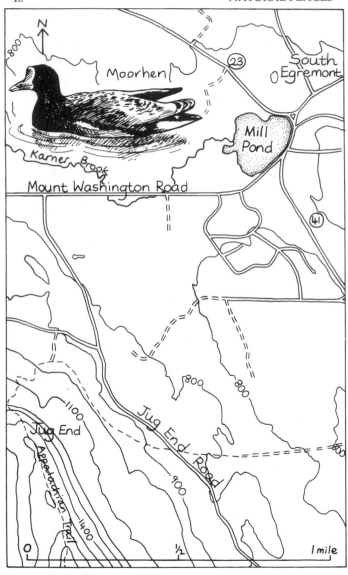

MILL POND

⋙ 6 ⋘

MILL POND
Egremont

Privately owned. Mill Pond is also know as Smiley's Mill Pond and Robinson Pond.

Acreage: 20 (water surface).

Elevation: 728 ft. (water surface).

Facilities: None.

Directions: From downtown Gt. Barrington take Rte. 7, S. to Rte. 23. Turn right onto Rte. 23 and follow it (staying left), past the Rte. 71 split into the village of S. Egremont. Turn left where Rte. 23 meets Rte. 41 (onto 41). Stay right when Mt. Washington Rd. branches off from Rte. 41 in 0.2 mi. Pull off the road and park on the graveled shoulder along S.E. shore of pond. You can get an excellent view of the pond from this location.

Mill Pond is picturesque as well as rich in wildlife resources, notably waterfowl and other aquatic birds. The pond and surrounding marshlands are one of a very few locales in Berkshire where the cootlike common moorhen (formerly common gallinule) has nested.

Views and Vistas

From the edge of the roadway your eyes will fall upon a pleasing scene of open water ringed by cattail marsh. Turn your head to the left to get a very nice view of the rocky promontory known as Jug End (1,520 ft. and traversed by the Appalachian Trail). Beyond Jug End to the right is a rather level ridge, with Mount Whitbeck (1,870 ft.) the high point. Both are part of the Taconic Range, which contains some of the oldest rocks on the continent.

Plant Communities

The dominant vegetation is cattail. Along the western shores, beyond the cattails, is a wooded swamp, with wetland trees such as red maple predominating. There are also numerous white pines. The banks have a shrubby growth of other wetland indicators, including speckled alder and red-osier dogwood. Close to the roadway are several large yellow-twigged willows (noticeable after leaf fall).

Yellow pond-lillies and fragrant water-lilies are the most obvious of the plants that float their leaves on the water's surface. They flower in summer. This pond, like others in the valley, is underlain with marble bedrock, and the resulting alkaline (hard water) conditions encourage the growth of many plants along shore and rooted in the bottom mud (including an invasive aquatic weed, Eurasian milfoil). These plants do provide food and shelter for many organisms.

Yellow iris, an introduced plant, gives the pond an attractive, bright-yellow margin in late spring and early summer. In summer the surface of the pond may be whitened with the tiny flowers of white water-crowfoot, an aquatic buttercup. The flowers spring from submerged, threadlike leaves.

Wildlife

Mammals: A sizable muskrat population thrives in the cattail marsh, and from shore you may view their dome-shaped lodges, constructed of cattails and mud. Perhaps you'll see one of the animals swimming along, carrying succulent vegetation in its mouth. At first you might mistake it for a beaver, which is much larger and usually abroad only from dusk until dawn. Beavers dwell here, too, as recent cuttings on the far shore testify. You're not likely to see other species at the pond itself, but many others inhabit the nearby woodlands and fields.

Birds: The focus here is on water-adapted species. The common breeders — Canada goose, black duck, and the ubiquitous mallard — are here, except in winter. During duck migration, April for instance, other species, such as green-winged and blue-winged teals, our smallest ducks, pay a visit. The latter seem to prefer marshy places such as this. Breeding male green-winged teals have a maroon-and-green-colored head and are certainly one of our most beautiful ducks.

Mill Pond Moorhens

Common moorhens return to the area in middle to late May. These unusual cootlike birds nest in only a few isolated spots in Massachusetts. Unlike coots, moorhens possess bright red bills with yellow tips. They are dark gray on the head, breast, and belly, and brownish on the back. A key feature is a white band running from front to back along their flanks. As you watch these birds swimming you'll notice that they pump their heads as they go. And if you hear odd, chickenlike sounds emanating from the marsh, it may be the moorhens. I have seen up to 13 of these birds on the pond, of which 10 were juveniles. On August 24 one year my wife and I got a chance to watch the ungainly appearing young walking about on top of the lily pads, apparently searching for edible bits — it made for an amusing scene.

In early spring swallows flit over the pond in pursuit of insects. All five species are possible in early May. Other birds that frequent wet places and that you are likely to see and hear are yellow warbler, common yellowthroat, red-winged blackbird, common grackle, and swamp sparrow. Belted kingfisher, another summer resident, hovers and drops like a stone into the water after fish. Wood ducks and the nest boxes that state wildlife staff have erected for them are easily spied; the shallow water and deep muck below currently prevent the boxes' maintenance. In late May you will certainly see adult wood ducks being closely attended to by their young. Fish-eating hooded mergansers use the same nest boxes, and you may see immature birds in mid-summer.

This is also one of the best Berkshire places to find terns. Black terns nest in Lake Champlain's cattail marshes to the north and are uncommon but annual migrants through here. We once watched an even scarcer (this far inland) common tern repeatedly diving for fish one July 15. Even a pied-billed grebe is possible in summer. Great blue herons fish here from August into early November, while cedar waxwings readily consume the red berries of shoreline honeysuckle in summer. In October, migrating rusty blackbirds sometimes perch in bordering trees.

Reptiles: Eastern painted turtles and snapping turtles — perhaps crossing the roadway — are the only reptiles you will likely see from shore. Someone in the know on such matters speculates that the midland painted turtle, a close relative of our eastern variety, may live here also. Northern water and common garter snakes share these water-dominated communities with the other denizens.

Amphibians: Certainly all the frogs reside here or in neighboring woods and fields, but limited access will prevent you from seeing most of them. Better to rely on your sense of hearing. In early spring listen for the high-pitched, ringing chorus of spring peepers and the vibrato whistle of American toads (reminiscent of science-fiction film sound tracks). In summer the resonant *jug-o-rum* of male bullfrogs proclaiming their territorial rights can't be missed. Green frogs can be recognized by their single-note calls (like a plucked banjo string).

Fish: Yellow perch, brown bullhead, and bluegill (introduced) dwell in the pond, providing a repast for such predators as mink, great blue heron, hooded merganser, and belted kingfisher.

Seasonal Highlights

You'll find migrant waterfowl in April. A greater diversity of land birds appears in May, which is also when common moorhens traditionally return to establish breeding territories. In late spring watch for colorful wood ducks and their young.

Summer is the season to watch for young wood ducks and hooded mergansers, while lily blossoms add color to the scene in July. Scan for moorhens and their young too. Great blue herons put in appearances in August after nesting elsewhere. You can sometimes find pied-billed grebes. Even if you don't, the frog choruses in early summer make for pleasurable listening (at least to the trained ear).

In September the shoreline vegetation may be alive with migrant songbirds such as the yellow-rumped warbler. Mallards, American black ducks, and Canada geese are present until the pond freezes over, and you'll find wood ducks nearly that late into the season as well. Great blue herons visit in hopes of securing a frog or fish meal, even in November. The fall colors that brighten up the ridge to your left and the blazing crimson of the wetland's red maples are worth admiring while searching for waterfowl.

In winter it's possible that a river otter or a mink may happen by in search of fish as you arrive, especially if it's just after dawn. This is one of the last Berkshire wetlands to freeze over completely.

Comments

This location is right on the way to Mount Everett (see Ch. 4) and Mount Washington (see Ch. 5) state forests (just continue straight ahead on Mount Washington Road).

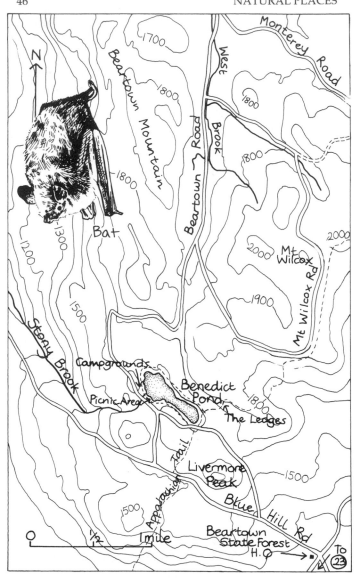

BEARTOWN STATE FOREST

≈ 7 ≈

BEARTOWN STATE FOREST

Great Barrington, Lee, Monterey, Stockbridge, Tyringham

Managed by DEM. Includes Arthur Wharton Swann State Forest.

Acreage: 10,975.

Elevation: 860—2,155 ft.

Trails: 30 mi.

Hours: Year-round.

Admission: None posted. $2 fee per vehicle for swimming and picnicking. $4 per night for camping.

Facilities/Other: Rest rooms, trail maps, pay phone available. Alcoholic beverages prohibited. Phone: 413-528-0904.

Directions: From Rte. 23 in Monterey take Blue Hill Rd. N.W. to year-round state forest entrance and office. Continue straight past office for 1.6 mi. to turnoff on the right for Benedict Pond (Benedict Pond Rd.). Proceed for 0.4 mi. to parking on right. Additional summer entrance is on Rte. 102 between Lee and Stockbridge. From Exit 2 of Mass. Turnpike in Lee, exit left from the turnpike, proceed under the overpass, and make an almost immediate right turn onto Rte. 102. Take Rte. 102 W. for 2.5 mi. to S. Lee. Turn left onto Meadow St., cross Housatonic River, then immediately turn right onto Beartown Mtn. Rd. Follow this road uphill, past forest boundary (at 1.5 mi.) to a fork (at 2.5 mi.). At fork turn right on Beartown Rd. (*not* Beartown Mtn. Rd.) and drive 4 mi. to Benedict Pond (swimming, picnicking). Park on left in gravel lot just past swimming area.

Beartown covers portions of five towns and is the third largest state forest in Massachusetts. Within it are thousands of rugged acres of forested hills, beaver ponds, swamps, and clear flowing brooks. This large tract contains a diverse mix of native flora and fauna. A 6.2-mile portion of the Appalachian Trail crosses the southern portion of the forest, and many other trails make exploration of this relatively high, wet, and wild area possible (see *Hikes & Walks*).

Beautiful views are possible from some vantage points. Benedict Pond, a 37-acre body of water, is circumscribed by a scenic trail lined with mountain laurel shrubs.

Views and Vistas

You'll love the views from a spot along the Appalachian Trail known as the Ledges. This overlook is at the 1,850-foot elevation and is only 0.65 miles from Benedict Pond, which is skirted at its south end by the Appalachian Trail (white blazes). From the Ledges you'll be able to gaze out upon thousands of forested acres, East Mountain State Forest and Warner Mountain in the foreground, the rounded dome of Mount Everett in the Taconic Range to the southwest, and beyond the Taconics, the Catskills. Lake Buel is visible to the south. This rocky cliff-top is also a great place to have lunch.

Plant Communities

Beartown's woodlands are composed mainly of characteristic northern hardwood trees, including northern red oak, sugar and red maples, yellow, black, and white birches, eastern hemlock, and white pine. There are also white oak trees on some south-facing slopes, while sassafras grows under the oaks. Most of the understory below the canopy of large trees is dominated by striped maple and witch hazel. American chestnut sprouts indicate that this tree was dominant here before the blight. The shrub layer is composed largely of evergreen mountain laurel, with lesser amounts of hobblebush and mountain azalea, all three of which produce handsome flower displays.

Along paths, trailing arbutus (mayflower), wintergreen, and goldthread (with orange roots that were once used medicinally), all evergreen, are found. Clintonia, sessile-leaved bellwort, star flower, and wild geranium bloom in late spring in the woodlands. A large and lovely pink orchid commonly known as moccasin flower (pink lady's slipper) grows in acidic conditions below pines, but in general the thin, acidic soil does not favor many spring wildflowers. The delicate princess pine (tree clubmoss) looks like a miniature evergreen in moist woods.

The richer, maple woodlands are home to some interesting and attractive flowering plants, however, including the somewhat comical jack-in-the-pulpit. This odd plant is largely green and brown and consists of a roofed-over "tube" (pulpit) within which stands a fingerlike projection (jack). In fall, a large cluster of bright red berries is produced by tiny flowers hidden from view within the bottom of the pulpit. Other plants in the rich woods include red and painted trilliums (the latter are white with red centers) and bloodroot, an early bloomer with delicate, white-petaled flowers.

In addition to the native conifers, you'll also come across Norway spruce plantations that were planted in the 1930s by the Civilian Conservation Corps. Virtually nothing is able to grow in the dense shade cast by these closely spaced evergreens. Apple trees, a reminder of former human habitation, hang on in some spots, providing fruit now for wildlife. Within forest openings you'll find such herbs as spotted joe-pye weed, hawkweed, heal-all, and, in disturbed areas, raspberries. Bracken fern, one of the largest, prefers dry, sunlit areas. In contrast, cinnamon fern is an indicator of saturated soils.

The state forest's many beaver ponds are ringed by pussy willow, American elm, meadowsweet, and rushes and grasses. Also present are winterberry, a member of the holly family that loses its leaves and sports bright red berries in winter, and the familiar cattail, which produces tens of thousands of fluffy seeds carried by the wind. Marshy beaver meadows that developed over time from silted-in beaver ponds (the eventual fate of all beaver ponds) have a dense growth of speckled alder at the edge, and, in the middle, tussock sedges, the kind you might try to use as steppingstones in crossing a marsh. Brilliant yellow marsh marigold (actually a buttercup) is one of the most attractive species you'll find blooming in boggy spots during spring.

If you closely examine the waters of Benedict Pond, you'll notice a few submergent plants such as pondweeds with their long, stringy stems, sometimes with both floating and underwater leaves. Elodea looks a lot like a plant you might find in an aquarium shop, a use to which it is occasionally put. You'll also find the carnivorous bladderwort, which supports its yellow flower from inflated stems (see also Ch. 11).

Wildlife

Mammals: You'll find the usual northern hardwood forest mammals here and a few others, too. The fisher, a little-known animal and the largest weasel family member in the area, roams the upland forests in search of porcupine and red squirrel, its favorite prey. Other large predators include bobcat, coyote, and black bear (the area's namesake), the latter really more of an omnivore (will eat almost anything). White-tailed deer are the most common large mammal. At the other extreme, there are numerous species of shrews, moles, and mice here.

Beaver and muskrat abound in the wetlands, many of which were created or at least enhanced by the former. Muskrat lodges may be observed at the far end of the Benedict Pond swimming area. An active beaver lodge is located along the north shore of the pond.

Birds: Among year-round residents you might find during a day's search are ruffed grouse, wild turkey, all five species of woodpeckers, both white-breasted and red-breasted nuthatches (the latter mostly in evergreens), brown creeper, blue jay, common raven, northern cardinal, American goldfinch, golden-crowned kinglet (higher elevations especially in spring and fall), tufted titmouse, and black-capped chickadee.

In spring the avian population swells manyfold with the return of such species as turkey vulture, least flycatcher, eastern wood pewee, wood thrush, white-throated, swamp, and song sparrows, solitary and red-eyed vireos and the

Bats in Beartown

One summer my wife and I were called to an old barn in Beartown State Forest to investigate the presence of what turned out to be a sizable brown bat maternity colony (see Ch. 17 for more about bat biology). The bats' small, dark-brown droppings were quite evident as we entered, as was a characteristic musky odor. It seems that the tiny winged creatures had found the barn, used for storing lumber, to their liking. Here several hundred female little browns and their single infants would spend the summer months until the young were full-grown and able to catch their own flying insects. In late summer this colony would begin dispersing, but suitable structures are reused year after year. Although of no real danger to anyone, the bats did unnerve those who had to work in the old building. In this case, increased use of the barn by forest staff discouraged use of the building by bats, and upon a subsequent visit by us a year later, only about 30 to 40 individuals could be seen. Presumably, the majority had found substitute housing elsewhere. Benedict Pond at dusk on warm summer nights should be a good spot for observing these fascinating creatures catch mosquitoes and other insects.

warblers: common yellowthroat, yellow, and chestnut-sided (in or near wet areas), Louisiana waterthrush (along brooks), ovenbird, black and white, Blackburnian, blue-winged (shrubby fields), black-throated blue and American redstart (two of the most common), black-throated green, and magnolia, all in woodlands, and blue-winged in shrubby fields. Almost all are small, brightly colored, and active creatures that consume vast quantities of insect prey, most notably caterpillars. Yellow-rumped warblers nest in the very highest reaches of the state forest, preferring more boreal conditions, but they are abundant migrants here and elsewhere.

Eastern (formerly rufous-sided) towhee and gray catbird prefer thickets, from which they vocalize.

Upon Benedict and other ponds you will see wood ducks, Canada geese, American black and mallard ducks, all of which nest in the state forest. One fall I found a single migrant male black scoter here.

Tree swallows find nesting sites in the standing dead timber of the many beaver swamps, often using an abandoned woodpecker cavity. These lovely birds are iridescent blue-green above and bright white below and chatter almost incessantly as they swoop through the air in pursuit of flying insects. They are certainly a joy to watch. You may also see fork-tailed barn swallows flitting over the ponds. They plaster mud nests against the inside walls and beams of sheds and barns.

The eastern bluebird, nearly everyone's favorite, is also a cavity nester that prefers open country. Near the entrance to the forest along Blue Hill Road you may notice bluebird nest boxes that have been erected on fence posts for their use.

Reptiles: The many ponds, marshes, and brooks sustain a goodly number of painted turtles. You'll see these animals sunning themselves upon logs within the ponds on almost any warm day. In winter these animals venture to the muddy bottoms of ponds, where their reduced biological processes allow them to remain, almost miraculously, until spring. Snapping turtles are common local pond dwellers, too. Wood turtles winter on the bottom of clear brooks within this vast area, wandering about on dry land between June and September.

Nearly all the species of snakes native to the area occur within this large tract. Among the more numerous are the common garter, ribbon, milk, the lovely smooth green, the shy and retiring northern brown, the brightly colored red-bellied, and the tiny ringneck. Less common is northern water snake (sometimes mistaken for the poisonous and very different water moccasin, which does not occur in New England). The one that you're most likely to meet is the garter. This harmless snake preys upon frogs and toads, as well as a wide variety of other fare. On a very few occasions I've found myself transfixed by one of nature's little dramas: Frogs that have been captured by snakes and are in the act of being swallowed emit loud, piercing cries, sounds that will no doubt attract and hold your attention, too!

Amphibians: The abundance of water here sustains a wealth of frog life that includes all the species native to the area, from the largest to the smallest: bull, green, American toad, pickerel, wood, gray tree, and spring peeper. Each has a loud and distinctive call that serves as an advertisement to females for courtship and breeding and as a notice to potential rivals (except for wood frogs, which are not territorial) that "this space is taken." Bullfrogs and green frogs thrive in beaver ponds; pickerel frogs wander long distances from water through wet vegetation; spring peepers form loud choruses on spring nights along the margins of ponds; the purring trill of gray tree frogs can be heard emanating from trees; and the toads are often encountered on woodland paths. The marshy portions of Benedict Pond and the surrounding area are fine places to search for frogs.

As with the frogs, all the native salamanders occur within the expanse of the forest and its many ponds, wetlands, and brooks. The red-spotted newt lives in Benedict Pond, and it is the most aquatic; the familiar land stage of this creature, known charmingly as the red eft, is one that you're likely to meet on woodland paths, especially during warm, wet weather.

Temporary woodland ponds (known as vernal pools), some only a dozen feet in diameter, are the sole breeding habitat of spotted and Jefferson salamanders. (For more detail about their fascinating life histories, see Ch. 18.) The largest salamander in the area is the spring salamander. Up to 8.5 inches long, this orange-brown animal lives in brooks and spring-fed pools at higher elevations. Dusky and two-lined salamanders are smaller and live along the edges of brooks and pools, especially under flat stones.

The state-listed four-toed salamander is quite small
and unassuming in appearance; its back feet, as the name
makes clear, have fewer than the usual five toes. It prefers
boggy pond edges where sphagnum moss grows. This salamander is unusual in that it lays its gelatinous eggs on wet
sphagnum and that the female actually guards the eggs.

The red-backed salamander is the most common in the
entire area. Turning over logs will often reveal these small
creatures — but be sure to return the log and the salamander to their original position. Almost all salamanders
are nocturnal and spend the daylight hours under conceal-
ing rocks, logs, or leaf litter. The attractive (but poisonous
to predators) red eft is the only one you're likely to encounter casually during the day.

Fish: Although Benedict Pond is the only sizable body
of water, the many beaver ponds and clear, cold brooks
support a fairly varied group of fish. Among the species
here are brown and brook trouts, pumpkinseed, brown bullhead, white sucker, blacknose dace (a small fish with a
black line from snout to tail), longnose dace, common golden
shiner, creek chub, and slimy sculpin (a little fish with a
somewhat prehistoric appearance).

Seasonal Highlights

Spring wildflowers abound in the rich woods. Each
week from mid-April on will bring new species to your
attention. Amphibian migrations to vernal pools take place
on rainy evenings in late March and early April. Bird migration begins in earnest at the end of April and peaks in
mid-May.

In summer, the mountain laurel blossoms from mid-
June to early July. Many emergent wetland plants such as
arrowhead and yellow pond-lily bloom at this time. Butterfly activity peaks during warm, sunny days along woodland borders and in fields and meadows. Approximately 70

species of birds are nesting in fields, forests, and wetland communities. Learning their songs is a big advantage.

Fall is perhaps the most pleasant season for walking and hiking, since the biting insects are gone and the heat and humidity of summer are just a memory. The view from the Ledges along the Appalachian Trail south of Benedict Pond is well worth the relatively short climb to reach it. This is also the season of greatest wildlife abundance, when animal populations have been swelled by the addition of so many young.

Winter is the season of hardship for wildlife, not only because of the freezing temperatures but also because of the scarcity of food. For us it can be an enjoyable time to get out and take a closer look at the creatures that have not migrated or hibernated from the season's rigors. The world seems to be on hold, and the summer diversity of flora and fauna is reduced. Since most mammals remain active, following their trails through the snow is an enjoyable and eye-opening activity. Beartown has an extensive trail network for cross-country skiing and snowshoeing, both excellent ways in which to get out and experience nature in winter.

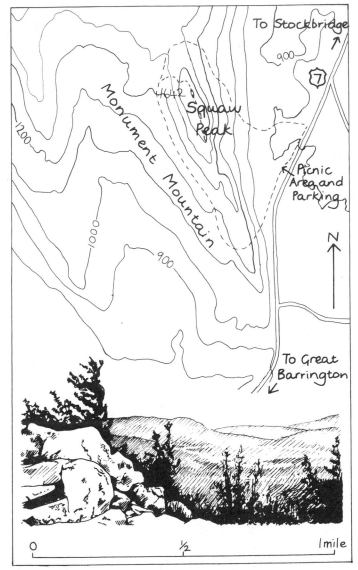

To Stockbridge

900

7

Monument Mountain

1200

4642

Squaw Peak

Picnic Area and Parking

N

1000

900

To Great Barrington

0   ½   1 mile

MONUMENT MOUNTAIN RESERVATION

✍ 8 ☙

MONUMENT MOUNTAIN RESERVATION
Great Barrington

Owned and managed by TTOR.

Acreage: 503.

Elevation: 870—1,642 ft.

Trails: 2.6 mi.

Hours: Sunrise to sunset, year-round.

Admission: Donation requested.

Facilities/Other: Trail maps and information available at TTOR regional office in Stockbridge; phone: 413-298-3239. Picnic tables. No rest rooms or camping. Rock climbing and motorized vehicles prohibited.

Directions: From jct. of Rtes. 7 and 23 in Great Barrington take Rte. 7, N. for 5.9 mi. to entrance and parking on the left. From Red Lion Inn in Stockbridge center take Rte. 7, S. for 3.1 mi. to entrance on right.

Monument Mountain is one of the outstanding scenic and geologic features of South County and, indeed, entire Berkshire. The light-gray quartzite rock has been sculpted over eons by water and ice into a beautiful and august monolith, the upper reaches of which are sparsely covered with pitch and white pines. This peak has exposed crags and, below them, boulder fields (huge rocks that have become detached from the mountain and tumbled down to its base, collecting in a jumbled mass). Freezing and thawing continues to loosen fragments that eventually end up among the mountain's boulder fields.

Monument is composed of some of the oldest rock in Berkshire. It is almost entirely quartzite, a rock that was deposited as sand in a shallow seaway nearly 600 million years ago! This sandstone was changed into what it is today by tremendous heat and pressure and forced up through younger layers of rock along a fault (a crack in the earth's crust). As you stand atop the mountain, notice that the steep east face of the peak lies in a nearly straight north-south line; this is the direction of the fault plane. The white quartzite exposed on the summit is tinged with hues of pink, yellow, gold, and orange. If you attempt to scratch the rock with the blade of a knife you'll quickly appreciate how hard and erosion resistant it is.

The bare quartzite formations give Monument Mountain a look unlike anything else in Berkshire, where smooth, tree-covered contours are the rule. In fact, Monument Mountain reminds me of the Black Hills (where you'll find Mount Rushmore) in South Dakota!

In spring, the mountain can be an excellent place from which to watch the hawk migration, if the weather cooperates.

Views and Vistas

From Squaw Peak (at 1,640 ft., nearly the mountain's highest point) the views are, in a word, inspiring. One such view, looking south, appears in the cover photograph of this book. True, the views are compromised somewhat by the nearness of the highway and a landfill (recently capped), but there is still much beauty to behold from this lofty perch. On a clear day you can see in all directions for many miles, taking in Connecticut's Litchfield Hills to the south, Mount Everett (2,602 ft.) and the Taconic Range to the southwest, New York's Catskills beyond the Taconics to the west-southwest, Mount Greylock (3,491 ft.) to the north, and the Berkshire Plateau to the east. The broad plain of the Housatonic River Valley is readily apparent, running north-south. You'll just be able to make out Stockbridge Bowl to the northwest, behind Rattlesnake Hill.

The twisted, picturesque pitch pines that grow in the thin soils of the summit provide a lovely foreground subject for the photographs you'll feel compelled to take.

Plant Communities

The forests of the mountain's slopes consist of northern red oak, black, white, gray, and yellow birches, white pine (some of tremendous proportions), and eastern hemlock. You may also note black cherry, white oak, chestnut oak, American beech, tulip tree, red maple, and quaking aspen growing here. The smaller, understory trees include the pleasing green-and-white-barked striped maple and witch hazel, whence originates the astringent lotion and which blooms with drooping yellow flowers in late fall. The shrub layer is dominated by shiny green mountain laurel, nannyberry, which has blue-black berries in fall, and hobblebush. Ground cover in the forest includes wintergreen and princess pine, one of the evergreen ground pines.

In the thin soil of the exposed summit, you'll find dwarfed northern red oak, black birch, white birch, red maple, low-bush blueberry, huckleberry, sassafras, mountain laurel, sheep laurel (much smaller than mountain laurel and with smaller, pinker flowers), shadbush, and of course pitch pine. This is the only pine that has needles growing directly from its trunk and branches. To me it is a most picturesque tree of windswept appearance that seems perfectly suited for its lofty position.

Among the ferns that you are sure to see are interrupted, bracken, spinulose wood, marginal wood, Christmas, and common polypody. The latter four are evergreen. The most conspicuous is the common polypody, which grows in a thick mat on top of many boulders.

The quartzite rocks are also covered with various lichens, primitive soil-producing organisms. On the summit of Squaw Peak the light-gray rocks are flecked with a skin-tight growth of roundish, gray-green lichens. Other rocks, especially on shaded slopes, have a growth of foliose (leaf-like) lichens, called rocktripe, which are brown and curly.

The forest floor supports a wide variety of blooming plants, including trailing arbutus (mayflower, the state flower), Indian pipes (virtually all-white because they lack chlorophyll), Canada mayflower (a wild lily similar to the garden-variety lily of the valley), and woodland goldenrods and asters. Indian pipes take their nourishment from decaying organic matter.

The pines with the scaly pink bark, in the vicinity of the parking lot and picnic area, are planted red pines, trees not native to this area.

Wildlife

Mammals: Mammals that frequent woodlands and rocky slopes predominate here. Among them are white-tailed deer, porcupine (which prefer rocky areas for denning), gray fox, striped skunk (an animal that you'll probably smell first), raccoon, masked and short-tailed shrews, white-footed mouse, red-backed vole, and of course eastern chipmunk, red squirrel, and gray squirrel. Wide-ranging animals that visit and pass through the reservation include bobcat, coyote, and black bear.

Birds: The forests contain year-round resident species such as black-capped chickadee, blue jay, hairy and pileated woodpeckers, and brown creeper. Birds that prefer more open habitats include red-tailed hawk and American goldfinch.

Also among the nesting species are common raven (the largest member of the crow family and reputed to be the most intelligent bird in the world), mourning dove, broad-winged hawk, and rock dove, commonly known as pigeon (inhabiting cliff faces, like their wild ancestors). Here these alien birds are a great deal more appealing to me than elsewhere.

Magnificent peregrine falcons, among the fastest of birds, once nested on the quartzite cliff faces of Monument Mountain. The last known nesting in the state (not counting the recent urban reintroductions) in fact took place here during 1957. Ironically, although they have been reintroduced to the skyscrapers of our largest cities, they have yet to reclaim ancestral breeding sites like this one.

Birds that spend the winter in more southerly climes and return to nest each spring include yellow-bellied sapsucker, winter wren, eastern wood pewee (you'll hear its plaintive *pee-a-wee* song in June and July), eastern phoebe, hermit thrush, veery, and wood thrush, scarlet tanager, eastern (formerly rufous-sided) towhee (its whistled refrain is *drink your tea*), red-eyed and yellow-throated vireos (vireo in Latin means "I am green"), and the following warblers: American redstart (a tiny and very active orange, black, and white bird), black-throated green, black-throated blue, black and white, ovenbird, Canada, common yellowthroat, and Blackburnian. Dark-eyed junco and yellow-rumped warbler breed on the coniferous summit. Huge black turkey vultures roost and may nest on the mountain.

Winter visitors to the forests include the pine siskin and evening grosbeak. Ruby-crowned kinglets can be numerous during migrations. You probably won't see the red topknot of the males, so look for the white eye ring and the constant wing-flicking habit of this tiny bird. These sprites nest in the boreal forests of Canada and northern New England.

In spring, Monument Mountain can be an excellent perch from which to watch migrating raptors and other birds. On April 21 one year we were witness to quite a spectacle: 145 hawks were counted within two hours! Among the species passing by, many actually below us, were osprey, northern harrier, sharp-shinned hawk, Cooper's hawk, American kestrel, broad-winged hawk, red-tailed hawk, and turkey vulture. Of these, broad-wingeds were by far the most numerous. We also saw tumbling common ravens, a common loon, and formations of Canada geese. The winds were warm and strong out of the south that day, making for ideal conditions.

Reptiles: The mountain's rocky slopes and outcrops provide numerous sunning and den sites for snakes. Among the residents are common garter, smooth green, northern brown, and red-bellied snakes. Sleek black racers as well could be expected. Rattlesnakes might find the conditions here to their liking, but I am not aware of any records of that magnificent, if misunderstood, creature from this location.

You'll find painted turtles in abundance at Fountain Pond, south of the reservation a short distance; they certainly occur in the marshy Agawam Lake to the north as well.

Amphibians: Frogs that you might see or more likely hear here include wood frog, spring peeper, and gray treefrog, species that don't require permanent ponds for breeding. Wood frogs do require temporary woodland pools; these pools also support inch-long fairy shrimp and certain species of salamanders. Among the salamanders are the red-backed, which has been called the most abundant vertebrate in eastern forests, and possibly two-lined and dusky salamanders. The latter two live along brooks. The larger spotted and Jefferson salamanders may be found, but their existence depends upon the presence of temporary pools, free of fish, for breeding.

Fish: Few if any fish exist on the reservation, with perhaps the exceptions being brook trout and slimy sculpin in the few permanent brooks flowing on the property. Agawam Lake and marsh, on private property north of the reservation, does contain chain pickerel and yellow perch. Fountain Pond to the south contains brown bullhead and sunfish species.

Seasonal Highlights

When spring conditions are auspicious — in particular, strong, southerly breezes — your chances of seeing a significant hawk flight in late April are good. The trees and shrubs hold other migrants as well. Chickadees are excavating nest sites then; look for one chipping away at a dead birch trunk, one of their favorite nesting places.

Wildflowers are in bloom at this time, too. Watch for the lovely white flowers of the low-growing trailing arbutus (mayflower), the state flower, in late April and early May. Many trees are in bloom as well, if less conspicuous in their finery. The tiny but pretty scarlet flowers of red maple attract pollinating bees and other insects during late April. Watch for a picturesque little waterfall that flows over a large rectangular quartzite boulder as you walk along the steeper trail to the summit.

In summer, woodland birds are nesting, and their collective song fills the forest with music. Listen for the high, bubbling song of the tiny, almost mouselike winter wren, especially in the hemlock gorge. Mountain laurel shrubs bloom from mid-June into July; a hike up the mountain at this time is like walking amid pink and white foam. These gorgeous blossom clusters are especially numerous in open, sunlit places.

In fall, a hike to the summit of Squaw Peak will yield a panorama of the foliage from Greylock to Connecticut and from the broad Berkshire Plateau to the Catskills (see *Hikes & Walks*). After leaf fall, you'll get better views from the trail of the rocky crags and boulder fields as you ascend. There may be some movement of hawks past here in September and October if the winds are out of the northwest.

In winter, Squaw Peak can still be accessible, unless the trails are icy, *but caution is urged*. On clear, crisp days, the views can be spectacular — truly some of the best in Berkshire. The little falls may be frozen solid if temperatures have been below zero.

Tracking the myriad creatures in the snow can be fun. Watch for the tiny snow tunnels of masked shrews, roughly the diameter of a pencil, or the larger short-tailed shrews. The tracks of larger white-footed mice trace a six-inch pattern of bounds from one burrow under a protective log to another. Among the most common tracks are those of red squirrels, which usually lead from the trunk of one tree to another nearby. Fox tracks look doglike but are aligned single-file and in a straight line. Nearly everyone will recognize the cloven hoof tracks of deer.

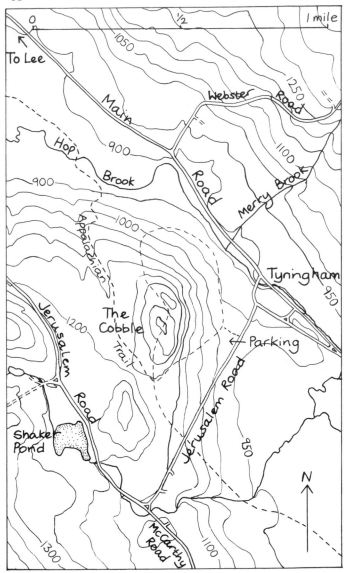

TYRINGHAM COBBLE

❦ 9 ❧

TYRINGHAM COBBLE
Tyringham

Owned and managed by TTOR.

Acreage: 206.

Elevation: 890—1,360 ft.

Trails: Approx. 2.7 mi.

Hours: Sunrise to sunset, year-round.

Admission: Donation requested.

Facilities/Other: Map and information available at TTOR regional office in Stockbridge; phone: 413-298-3239. No rest rooms or camping. Motor vehicles and fires prohibited.

Directions: From Exit 2 of Mass. Turnpike in Lee turn left onto Rte. 20 and proceed under turnpike overpass for very short distance to Rte. 102 on the right. Turn onto Rte. 102 and then turn left (S.) almost immediately onto Tyringham Rd. Follow Tyringham Rd. (called Main Rd. in Tyringham) for 4.2 mi. to village of the same name. In Tyringham center make a right turn onto Jerusalem Rd. Stay right and follow Jerusalem Rd. for 0.2 mi. to parking area on right.

The Appalachian Trail crosses this scenic spot, which is characterized by hayfields, old pastures, and resistant rocky hills and outcrops that afford magnificent views of the lovely Tyringham Valley. The Cobble, actually an isolated promontory that is part of the rather level Berkshire Plateau just to the east, is composed of rock known locally as Tyringham gneiss (sounds like "nice"). It is a rock type that underwent tremendous heat and pressure, being recrystalized in the process. You'll be able to see the characteristic swirls in the rocks, reminiscent of a marble cake. You will also notice milky-white quartz veins in many rocks that stand out within the darker gneiss.

An oddly shaped glacial erratic (to me it resembles a hare), transported from somewhere to the north by the glacial ice sheet and made of weathering marble rather than gneiss, sits near the east slope of the Cobble. Notice the solution cavities eroded into all sides of the boulder. It may remind you of Balance Rock in Lanesborough (see Ch. 18). This erratic rests along the loop trail that winds around the base of Cobble Hill, where you will also see boulders that have tumbled off the hill.

The fields as well as the forests contain a wide variety of interesting plant life, and this is an excellent place to watch birds year-round. Clear and cold Hop Brook, a tributary of the Housatonic, flows along the northern perimeter of the property.

Views and Vistas

The best views are yours from several points atop Cobble Hill. From these somewhat precipitous heights the three-mile-long Tyringham Valley is laid out before you. To the north is Lenox Mountain (2,126 ft.) and to the east and southeast are the uplands of the Berkshire Plateau. The highest point visible along the unnamed ridge is 1,925 feet above sea level; and crouched in front of the ridge is 1,515-foot-high Round Mountain. From your perch, you'll have a bird's-eye view of the village almost 500 feet below, and what an idyllic setting it is!

Plant Communities

You will find an interesting contrast of natural and altered communities on this property. The wooded portions are dominated by hardwoods such as large northern red oak, white ash, black, gray, and yellow birches, sugar and big red maple. You'll also find white pine and eastern hemlock. Understory trees include eastern hophornbeam (one has attained surprising girth — 18 inches), American beech, and in some spots, eastern hemlock. Eastern hophornbeam has thin, very scaly, light-brown bark.

The forest floor has a vigorous growth of Christmas fern in many places, and other ferns include marginal and spinulose wood ferns, lacy maidenhair, sensitive fern, and common polypody, on rock outcrops. Grape and Oriental bittersweet vines (the latter eventually strangles its host) drape trees here, especially along the perimeter of the pastures. Fruits of both are eagerly eaten and spread by birds.

The brushy fields, showing the effects of grazing, contain a dense, shrubby growth of eastern red cedar (cedar waxwings eat the berries), prickly common, Japanese barberry, steeplebush, staghorn sumac, blackberry, and crab apple. The barberry crowds out much of the native vegetation on the pastured hillsides. Its sharp thorns make it an undesirable food plant for cattle. Its numerous bright red berries, however, are eaten by wildlife, which thus effectively spread the species, to the detriment of native plants.

Below the small trees and shrubs grow low-bush blueberry, bristly dewberry (a creeping raspberry relative), and numerous grasses. You will also see goldenrods and thimbleweed (tall anemone), a handsome plant whether in greenish-white flower or thimble-shaped seed head.

Hayfields here contain the usual pasture grasses. Wild thyme, a fragrant plant underfoot with tiny purple flowers, forms a low, thick mat among the short grasses of old pastures. Japanese barberry dominates the upper pastures, forming an almost impenetrable reddish thicket in fall.

Wildlife

Mammals: Among the most common and regularly observed species are eastern chipmunk, gray squirrel (their summer leaf nests being visible in the tree tops in winter), red squirrel, and eastern cottontail rabbit. Other common but less often seen creatures include the red fox, white-tailed deer, porcupine, white-footed mouse, meadow vole, and hairy-tail mole. Larger mammals such as coyotes are also resident.

During the fall, white-footed or deer mice build nests insulated with animal fur and plant down in order to prepare for the onset of sub-freezing temperatures. They will choose almost any suitable cavity, including bird nest boxes. On one outing we discovered a mouse's nest tucked into an eroded crevice of the marble erratic located along the loop trail.

Birds: The mixture of open and wooded communities gives rise to a diverse bird life year-round. Tyringham Cobble is a favorite with local birders, and you will find it productive even during the winter months. Year-round residents include ruffed grouse, red-tailed hawk, American kestrel, pileated woodpecker, northern mockingbird, cedar waxwing, northern cardinal, white-breasted nuthatch, blue jay, black-capped chickadee, tufted titmouse, white-throated sparrow, and brown creeper.

Birds that return in spring to nest here include eastern phoebe, gray catbird, eastern (formerly rufous-sided) towhee (in open, brushy areas where its *drink your tea* song is a pleasing refrain), field sparrow, song sparrow, eastern bluebird (often seen year-round here), wood thrush, hermit thrush, red-eyed vireo, and various warblers, including black-throated blue, magnolia, and blue-winged.

Tree swallows nest in the many boxes near the entrance and barn swallows build their mud nests in the barn. Bobolinks nest in the tall grass of the hayfields. Huge black turkey vultures (so named because of their naked red heads, except in immature birds, which have black heads) ply the skies over the Cobble, searching and indeed "sniffing" out carrion, their only food.

During spring and fall migrations be on the lookout for sharp-shinned and Cooper's hawks, northern harrier, yellow-rumped warbler, and the tail-wagging palm warblers, among others.

Winter visitors include the noisy, flocking evening grosbeaks, which enjoy feasting on maple seeds, and pine siskin, a small, striped goldfinch relative that extracts seeds from the cones of birch and other trees with its needle-sharp beak.

Reptiles: The many rock outcroppings are excellent basking sites for snakes as well as human visitors. Common garter is the most often seen, but I have also found the red-bellied snake here. This small reptile has a bright orange-red underside and feeds primarily upon insects and earthworms. If you are fortunate, you may see other species as well, including the smooth green and the small northern brown snake. Many are more or less nocturnal, and all are harmless.

The lack of standing water means that you won't find turtles here, except perhaps for the wood turtle, which inhabits woods and fields near clear streams like Hop Brook. They spend the winter months in an inactive state on the bottom of a stream.

Amphibians: American toad, pickerel frog, and gray tree frog occur here, and green frogs live along Hop Brook. The abundant red-backed salamander occurs in the woods, remaining hidden under logs during daylight hours. Two-lined and dusky salamanders live along woodland portions of the brook. Spotted and Jefferson salamanders (as well as wood frogs) depend upon the existence of temporary vernal pools for breeding, and I have not found these species on the property, although they may well occur here.

Fishes: Hop Brook, shaded along much of its length by a canopy of trees, contains small cold-water species including brook trout and slimy sculpin. A few species of dace and shiner are also probably present.

Seasonal Highlights

From mid-April to early May, woodland wildflowers are in bloom; a walk along the Appalachian Trail will enable you to see many under the tall oaks. At the same time waves of migrant birds are in the area, some remaining here to nest, others passing through on their way farther north. The heights of Cobble Hill might be a good spot from which to observe hawks moving northward through the Tyringham Valley.

In summer, the fields and pasture edges come alive with wildflowers, providing a source of nectar for many kinds of insects, including butterflies. In late summer, goldenrods and asters are visited by migrating monarch butterflies. The low-bush blueberry bears fruit, which are generally harvested first by the permanent, non-human residents. The woodlands ring with bird song. Wood and hermit thrushes sing their flutelike melodies at dusk.

In fall, an abundance of fruit draws cedar waxwings and migrant species to take advantage of the bounty of grapes, crab apples, bittersweet, cedar berries, and maple seeds. The foliage spectacle from atop Cobble Hill is spectacular. Some views are framed by the bright white trunks of white (paper) birch. In the valley, the corn harvest is underway, making for a bucolic scene. Enjoy it while you can, for farmland is rapidly disappearing in this part of New England.

Winter, when the leaves are gone, affords the most expansive panoramas. The distant hillsides are clothed in contrasting gray-browns and dark greens. The forest floor is covered in spots with the deep green of Christmas fern. Gray squirrels retrieve stored acorns from the ground, leaving telltale round holes beneath the leaf litter that they've scraped away. How do they find the buried bounty? By memory, it seems, although many go unclaimed and grow into new oaks.

Even though few birds are to be found in the forest except for small flocks of golden-crowned kinglets and a few other species, the fields and pasture edges still host a surprising variety of bird life, including the white-throated sparrow, northern mockingbird, and the brilliant eastern bluebird. Try your hand at tracking mammals and birds after a light snowfall.

✍ 10 ❧

ICE GLEN AND LAURA'S TOWER
Stockbridge

Ice Glen owned by town of Stockbridge and managed by Laurel Hill Assn. Laura's Tower (Sedgwick Reservation) owned and managed by Laurel Hill Assn.

Acreage: Ice Glen 58.2; Sedgwick Reservation 256.

Elevation: 830—1,460 ft.

Trails: Approx. 2 mi.

Hours: Closes at sunset.

Admission: None posted.

Facilities/Other: No rest rooms or camping. Vehicles, horses, and fires prohibited. Phone: 413-298-4714 (town hall).

Directions: From the Red Lion Inn at intersection of Rtes. 7 and 102 in Stockbridge take Rte. 7, S. for 0.5 mi. to Ice Glen Rd. on left. Turn onto Ice Glen Rd. and follow for 0.5 mi. Watch for small sign at private drive on left reading "Ice Glen walkers welcome." Pull off the road and park along roadway (not driveway). Parking is very limited. This approach is the most scenic and moderately strenuous. An alternate approach is S. from Red Lion Inn on Rte. 7 and left onto Park St. (before crossing river). Follow Park St. short distance to end and park in lot maintained by Laurel Hill Assn. Trail begins at the footbridge (where map board is situated) crossing the Housatonic River (see *Hikes & Walks*). The tower trail splits off later to the left.

Enormous white pines and eastern hemlocks impart a primeval atmosphere to Ice Glen, a shadowy hemlock gorge strewn with a jumble of huge, angular, fern-covered boulders, which create a myriad of crevices and small caves. These boulders have been pried from the steep slopes of the ravine by frost and root action and tumbled down to their present positions. They are primarily composed of coarse mica schist, typical of the Berkshire Plateau, with some banding of gneiss. This fracture in the earth's crust has been widened by stream action, most likely after the glaciers melted back twelve to fourteen thousand years ago. There is no longer a stream at the surface, but you can hear water trickling through the gorge just below the surface if you listen carefully.

The deep shade and insulating qualities of the rocks create a cool micro-climate and make it possible for ice to remain much longer into spring than in other locales. Ice Glen offers a cool retreat in summer but makes for an enjoyable outing at almost any time of year.

The trail is steep and rocky in places. In addition to the exhilarating walk through the Glen, a trail can take you to Laura's Tower at the top of an unnamed hill for a fine panoramic view of South Berkshire.

Views and Vistas

As you drive or walk down Ice Glen Road near that end of the trail, you will have a wonderful view of Monument Mountain (1,642 ft.) nearby to the southeast. You'll be looking across fields and wetlands at one of the most beautiful peaks in the area — a view that in my opinion begs for painting.

From the top of Laura's Tower, at an elevation of 1,465 feet, you may see the Catskills of New York to the southeast, Mount Everett (2,602 ft.) and Connecticut to the south, and the Housatonic River nearby to the east. You'll also be able to see the hand of humanity on the land in the form of the Massachusetts Turnpike in Stockbridge and Lee to the north and northeast respectively.

Laura's Tower is owned and maintained by the Laurel Hill Association, the nation's first private conservation group. This 25-foot-high metal structure, erected in the 1930s, puts you just above the treetops. The 180-degree view is a fine one any time.

Plant Communities

The orientation of this cleft is north-south, permitting little sunlight to enter the Glen. White pine requires ample

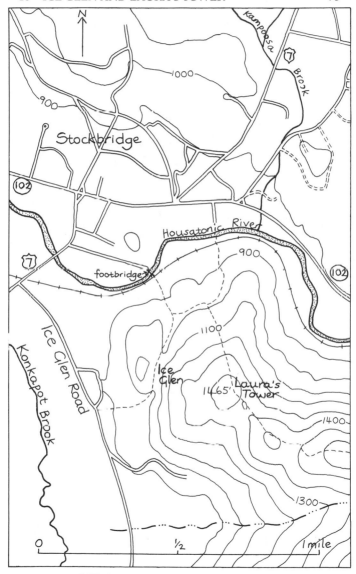

ICE GLEN AND LAURA'S TOWER

sunlight for germination, whereas hemlock is shade tolerant. These mature evergreens have created even more shade.
The result is a cool, wet hemlock gorge. Many of these pines
and hemlocks are of enormous girth and height, giving an
air of primordial wilderness to the place; to me it is reminiscent of an Alfred Bierstadt painting. The rugged terrain
made timber harvesting here impractical, the only reason
why such impressive forest giants were spared. Numerous
large dead trees have fallen across the narrow chasm, adding to the primeval feel.

A particularly huge white pine, four feet in diameter, is
situated at the beginning of the yellow-blazed trail that
goes left into the Glen from the top of the long driveway.
Many hemlocks, some three feet in diameter, are perched,
seemingly precariously, upon boulders. These boulders are
also draped with lichens, mosses, and common polypody
fern (also aptly called rock lover). Marginal wood fern also
grows in the ravine, and both of these species are green all
year long. There are even a few uncommon red pines (pinkish bark) in the gorge.

After the trail levels out atop the gorge, deciduous
species such as yellow birch increase in number. Along the
trail to the tower, northern red oak and big-tooth aspen
become the dominant trees. There are also American beech,
white and gray birch, and sugar maple here. The smooth-
barked striped maple is the main understory tree, and
mountain laurel is a common shrub. You'll also find the
shrub hobblebush, which has large, heart-shaped leaves
and small white flowers in May. The upper portion of the
hill was logged not too many years ago and has revegetated
with small oaks, striped maple, and even a few small American chestnuts. This species, once one of the most common,
was all but wiped out during the 1930s by chestnut blight.
Now only small trees remain, and they are eventually killed
by the disease long before they reach maturity. You can
recognize chestnut trees by their leaves, which resemble
beech leaves but are longer and more sharply tapered, with
larger teeth along their margins.

Herbaceous plants growing in the Glen are those that tolerate shade, fairly high moisture, and acidic soil. Also found in other hemlock gorges in Berkshire, these include spikenard (atop boulders), which has divided leaves and white flower spikes, and white wood aster. In contrast, pretty pink corydalis now blooms in late spring amid the rocks of the summit clearing.

Wildlife

Mammals: This is not a large area, but it is at the north end of the sizable Beartown State Forest upland (see Ch. 7). The coniferous growth within the Glen provides perfect habitat for red squirrel, porcupine, and bobcat. Other species to be found here include white-tailed deer, eastern chipmunk, and a variety of shrews and mice. Larger mammals that surely pass through the site are black bear and coyote. Of all these, the red squirrel is the most noticeable. The chatter of these spritely and often amusing creatures adds a certain charm and atmosphere to the Glen.

Birds: Birds that seek seeds or insects among the evergreen boughs of pine and hemlock are especially abundant. Among the year-round residents you are likely to encounter are black-capped chickadee, brown creeper, red-breasted nuthatch, and perhaps the striking pileated woodpecker. Other nesting species include eastern wood pewee, solitary vireo, and the multi-hued warblers: Blackburnian, Canada, black-throated green, and American redstart. In the deciduous trees above the gorge you are likely to see and hear hairy and downy woodpeckers, white-breasted nuthatch, scarlet tanager, red-eyed vireo, black-throated blue warbler, and ovenbird (which nests on the ground).

In fall, winter, and early spring watch for seed eaters such as the pine siskin (a small, heavily striped finch) and American goldfinch feeding upon the seeds of yellow birch. Nearby, in the thickets and fields along the Housatonic River in winter, are flocks of American tree sparrows, dark-eyed juncos, and cedar waxwings. On the river you may see mallard and American black duck or belted kingfisher.

Reptiles: A variety of snakes live in the area. The eastern timber rattlesnake, an endangered species, has not been found at the once appropriately named Rattlesnake Hill (approximately two miles north of Ice Glen) in more than 50 years. You might see the common garter snake in the open, sunlit spots near the river or atop the hill. Milk, red-bellied, and ringneck snakes also occur here.

The wood turtle is a possibility, since the Housatonic River is so near. If you are lucky enough to see one of these shelled creatures, it would most likely be in the small field areas near the footbridge.

Amphibians: The absence of permanent water bodies precludes a great variety of frogs from calling this spot home. The woodlands do provide the needed habitat for the gray tree frog, the tiny spring peeper, and the wood frog. Wood frogs produce odd, ducklike quacking calls at their vernal pool breeding sites in spring.

Salamanders that require permanent ponds (red-spotted newt) or permanent streams (dusky and two-lined) don't occur here, but you may find spotted and Jefferson salamanders in spring. These two species also require woodland vernal pools for breeding. The red-backed salamander is abundant under logs in the deciduous woods.

Fish: The fish that live in the Housatonic River nearby are discussed in Chapter 14.

Seasonal Highlights

When the snow and ice of winter are all but a memory elsewhere, you may still find stubborn pockets of ice in this gorge. The blooming of spring wildflowers and the arrival of birds from their winter homes in the tropics in late April and early May make this an especially attractive time to visit.

Common wisdom has it that ice may remain in the Glen until July (I've found it as late as June). Whether or not this is true, you'll find this to be a cool retreat even during the hottest days of midsummer. The beautiful haunting songs of hermit and wood thrushes echo through the Glen during the early morning and early evening hours, especially in June and early July. These and other nesting birds add music and color to this charming scene.

In fall, the top of Laura's Tower is a wonderful place from which to survey the colorful scene Look for migrant warblers and the arrival of winter visitors. From the tower you'll no doubt see southbound hawks, especially if the winds are out of the northwest.

During a mild winter, access to the Glen is relatively easy, and the absence of other walkers has its benefits; *but icy conditions can prevail and make the footing hazardous.* The walk to Laura's Tower may still be readily accessible. Watch the hemlocks, yellow birches, and white pines for red-breasted nuthatches, pine siskins, and golden-crowned kinglets.

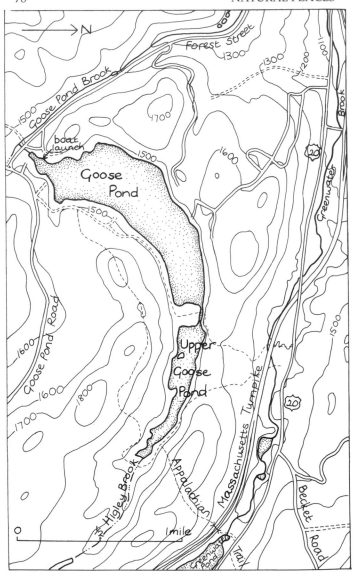

GOOSE PONDS

◄§ 11 §►

GOOSE PONDS
Lee, Tyringham

Owned and managed by National Park Service (along AT corridor), TTOR, and numerous private owners.

Acreage: 284 (water surface).

Elevation: 1,483 ft. (water surface).

Trails: Approx. 4.5 miles of trails in vicinity.

Hours: Public lands open year-round; no overnight parking at boat ramp in Tyringham (managed by County Commissioners).

Admission: None posted.

Facilities/Other: No rest rooms. Camping available along AT. The caretaker's cabin and pit toilets along AT are 2.1 mi. from Rte. 20 (rustic accommodations available, donation requested).

Directions: From Mass. Turnpike Exit 2 in Lee, turn left onto Rte. 20 after exiting from toll booth and travel E. for 0.75 mi. to paved Forest St. on the right. Turn right and follow it uphill for 2.1 mi. to the last left turn before Goose Pond Rd. Turn left onto graveled McDarby Rd. leading to boat ramp (canoes may be launched here). Park on right. By trail from Rte. 20 in Becket: Park along wide paved pull-off near AT sign and walk S. toward Goose Pond.

(Upper) Goose Pond (45 acres) and Lower Goose Pond (239 acres) exist in striking contrast to each other, as much of Upper Goose is an almost pristine environment, while the shores of the larger Lower Goose are lined with cabins. In its natural setting, Upper Goose is a sparkling gem, reminiscent of northern New England, with abundant wildlife and interesting aquatic plants. It can be accessed both by canoe from the boat ramp at Goose Pond and via the Appalachian Trail from either Route 20 in Becket or Goose Pond Road in Tyringham. Whether by foot or afloat, an outing here promises to be equally rewarding.

Views and Vistas

Upper Goose Pond is especially picturesque. The ponds, which are actually one, since they are linked by a narrow channel, are surrounded by hills that rise 300 feet on average above the blue surface of the water. To the northeast the highest points visible are Walling Mountain (2,220 ft.) and Becket Mountain (2,180 ft.), both traversed by the Appalachian Trail. The setting is certainly lovely, and if you arrive early in the day you may indeed get the impression that you are actually in the wilds of Maine.

Plant Communities

The rocky shores of Upper Goose support the trees generally typical of northern hardwood forest, such as yellow birch, sugar maple, American beech, northern red oak, white pine, and eastern hemlock, with an understory of striped maple, mountain maple, small American chestnut (although one larger specimen was seen in flower), and a shrub layer of three viburnum species — hobblebush, wild raisin, and nannyberry — as well as highbush blueberry and mountain laurel. Lower Goose has white birch, red maple, white pine, and willows along its built up-shoreline.

On the moist forest floor grow a wide variety of wildflowers: goldthread, wood sorrel, red trillium (wake robin), painted trillium, clintonia, starflower, and partridgeberry (which has tiny white tubular flowers growing at ground level), to name a few. In summer the lovely yellow-orange flowers of Canada lily bloom in wet spots such as where the Appalachian Trail crosses Higley Brook at the east end of Upper Goose Pond. Dry, open woods is where you might find the large orchid, moccasin flower (pink lady's slipper), or the pipsissewa, with dark-green evergreen leaves.

The ponds themselves support a rich and varied aquatic plant community. At the east end of Upper Goose especially there is a profusion of plant life. An aquatic form of smartweed protrudes its pink flower spikes above the surface from July to early September, and yellow pond-lilies bloom in July. You'll also see arrowhead, tall bulrush, three-way sedge, and the jointed river horsetail protruding from the water. The curious pipewort, with its white, buttonlike head, grows in shallow water. Floating in the water are milfoils (the exotic, invasive Eurasian milfoil is being controlled here through the introduction of a tiny native milfoil-eating aquatic weevil), pondweeds, and the leaves of wild celery, a plant that in late July sends up to the surface its tiny flowers on long, spiraling, corkscrew stems.

Goose Pond Bladderwort

One of the most interesting water plants found at Goose Ponds is the bladderwort, which has an ingenious way of capturing tiny water creatures. Growing from the finely divided leaves underwater are numerous tiny "bladders" that literally suck errant water fleas (Daphnia) into them if the tiny swimming creatures accidentally touch the bladder. The fleas are digested, providing the plant with important minerals it is not able to garner from the nutrient-poor soils of the pond bottom. You might want to temporarily remove a plant from the water to examine the tiny bladders. While you won't be able to see the bladders do their work from your canoe, you will be able to admire the yellow, snapdragonlike flowers that bloom above the surface in summer. At this time the upper end of the pond may be virtually carpeted with a thick growth of bladderwort.

In marshy areas you may be lucky to see the swamp milkweed, a lovely pink to rose-purple cousin of the common milkweed, or perhaps get hooked by the thorny but pretty pink swamp rose.

Wildlife

Mammals: The wetlands and woodlands in the vicinity of the ponds have a rich mammalian life. Beaver, or at least their numerous works, are among the most visible. At the east end of Upper Goose you'll find a short but sturdy beaver dam blocking your boat's progress upstream. Beaver ponds provide excellent habitat for other fur-bearers, such as river otter, mink, and muskrat, as well as many other forms of wildlife. You can observe a muskrat lodge among the bulrushes at the east end of Upper Goose. The forests surrounding the ponds are home to porcupine, bobcat, coyote, black bear, gray fox, raccoon, opossum, red and gray squirrels, eastern chipmunk, red-backed vole, and various shrews, mice, and other small mammals. You may find white-tailed deer in the more open woodlands, but you may feel that seeing a moose would be more in keeping with the wilderness feel of this place.

Birds: This heavily forested area also has a rich bird life. Species such as veery, hermit and wood thrushes, yellow-bellied sapsucker, hairy and downy woodpeckers, solitary, yellow-throated and red-eyed vireos, and the warblers — magnolia, black-throated blue, black and white, chestnut-sided, black-throated green, Canada, Blackburnian, American redstart, and ovenbird — are common nesters. Both ruffed grouse and wild turkey are numerous in the forest, but because turkeys are very wary, you're more likely to see or hear the grouse. The low drumming sound of the male, made to attract a mate, reverberates through the forest in spring and early summer.

You will of course find a variety of water birds at the ponds. Canada geese and mallards breed along the shores or, in the case of geese, on beaver lodges, where they're safer from predators. In late June you might well see adult Canadas with their fuzzy yellowish goslings. Spotted sandpiper, a species in which the larger female mates with several males who care for the young, nests near the pond shores. The belted kingfisher and great blue heron both fish in the waters, and swamp sparrow, common yellowthroat, red-winged blackbird, common grackle, and tree swallows nest in the wetlands just east of Upper Goose.

You're bound to observe turkey vultures flying over-head and perhaps common ravens, whose guttural croaks add another dimension of authenticity to the wilderness atmosphere. Migrating ospreys search the lakes for fish with their keen eyes in the fall.

Reptiles: The painted turtle is the common shelled rep-tilian inhabitant of Upper Goose. Snapping turtles are also fairly common, but less often seen sunning themselves. Common garter and northern water snakes are found in the woods and wetlands, feasting on frogs and, in the case of the water snake, also on fish. Milk snakes are common inhabitants of these cool woodlands as well.

Amphibians: In summer you will see and hear bellow-ing bullfrogs and "hiccuping" green frogs. The latter's song sounds like a plucked banjo string. Wet vegetation is the usual haunt of the brown-blotched pickerel frog, another common inhabitant. Tiny spring peepers climb vegetation bordering the ponds and are difficult to locate. On the for-est floor you might come upon a wood frog, identified by its black "mask." Warty American toads are among the most commonly encountered members of this group of tail-less amphibians.

The clear, cold water of the pond teems with three inch-long red-spotted newts. If you go ashore and take a walk, especially during wet weather, you may find the attractive land phase of this animal, the red eft, crawling slowly over the trail. Red-backed salamanders are common in the surrounding woodlands, and two-lined salamanders live along the brooks feeding the ponds.

Fishes: Fishing is one of the popular recreational activi-ties on these lakes, and the finned vertebrates are numer-ous. Among the introduced game species are chain pick-erel, largemouth bass, and brown, brook, and rainbow trout (the last was recently reclassified as a salmon). Yellow perch, bluegill (introduced), pumpkinseed (a colorful sunfish), white sucker, common and golden shiners, and brown bullhead, a bottom feeder, are common here, too. Even smelt, small relatives of salmon, were introduced some time ago and have adapted to year-round life in fresh water. Normally these silvery, streamlined, eight-inch fish live in salt water, returning to fresh water only to breed. They are a favorite prey of brown trout and largemouth bass in Goose Ponds.

In summer you might notice large masses of a clear, gelatinlike substance adhering to twigs submerged in the water. These are not egg masses — although they do resemble the eggs of mole salamanders and wood frogs — but rather a group of very simple, corallike animals known as a bryozoan colony. These filter-feeding creatures are little changed from their ancestors that have been found as fossils in 350-million-year-old rocks. The shaded channel joining the two ponds is a particularly good place to find these colonies, which sometimes attain volleyball size.

Seasonal Highlights

A combination paddle and hike is an enjoyable way to observe spring wildflowers and migrant birds. Hobblebush shows off its lacy white flower clusters in May. While ashore you may also want to check out some of the rocks, predominately schists and gneisses. Gneiss (say "nice") is commonly a banded rock, with alternating layers of light and dark minerals: quartz (milky white), mica (dark colored), and chlorite (greenish-gray). Schist is usually composed of just one mineral, yet exhibits the tortuous folding caused by intense heat and pressure from long-past episodes of mountain building.

In summer, if you canoe from Lower Goose Pond through the channel to Upper Goose, go ashore and spend some time exploring the rich and fragrant forest. You can stretch your legs, then contemplate the plant and animal life while you're eating lunch. The ponds are among the best places to canoe in Berkshire and offer a beauty markedly different from that of the Housatonic River Valley.

Late June and early July are good times to visit, since aquatic vegetation is in flower and bird nesting is at its peak. Bright yellow Canada lilies bloom in late June along Higley Brook, and mountain laurel blossoms in the woodlands.

The red maples of the wetlands lend a brilliant blaze of color during late September. Migrant birds, searching for caterpillars, feed in the conifers, fattening up for the long flight ahead, and the leaves of hobblebush turn a deep maroon. You should find a few geese and perhaps other waterfowl in October and November. Incredible as it may seem, an Atlantic puffin was observed here in November 1970!

While canoeing may be out of the question in winter, you might try cross-country skiing or snowshoeing on the Appalachian Trail if there is enough snow. Look for the tracks of mink and river otter along beaver ponds and brooks. You might even find the droppings of otter, composed largely of fish scales and bones.

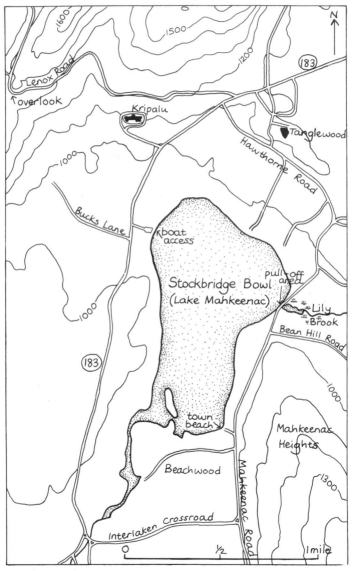

STOCKBRIDGE BOWL

✍ 12 ❧

STOCKBRIDGE BOWL
Stockbridge

Public facilities owned and operated by town of Stockbridge.
 Stockbridge Bowl is also known as Lake Mahkeenac.

Acreage: 372 (water surface).

Elevation: 925 ft. (water surface).

Hours: None posted at boat ramp. Town beach swimming for
 residents only during summer season.

Admission: None posted.

Facilities/Other: Rest rooms available. Phone: 413-298-4714
 (town hall).

Directions: From center of Stockbridge take Rte. 102, W. to
 Route 183. Turn right on Rte. 183 and go N. approx. 3.5 mi.
 to boat access on right; to continue on to the town beach,
 proceed N. (right) on Rte. 183 for 1.5 mi. to Hawthorne Rd.
 on right; keep right and follow it to Mahkeenac Rd.;
 continue to paved pull-off area on left adjacent to marsh
 (1.5 mi. from turnoff onto Hawthorne Rd.); to reach the town
 beach, continue another 0.7 mi. and turn right into graveled
 parking lot.

Stockbridge Bowl may be the most picturesque of all
the large Berkshire lakes. Although much of its shoreline is
no longer natural, the lake still retains much of its beauty.
This is also a reasonably good place, especially during November, to find migrant waterfowl.

Like all the other large Berkshire lakes, the Bowl owes
its existence to the glacial erosion that gouged out a north-
south-trending basin in the softer limestone and marbles
that now underlie the lake. A dam at the south end increased the Bowl's size by impounding more of the original
basin.

Views and Vistas

Several fine drive-up views exist along the perimeter of the lake: from the roadside parking area on the eastern shore there is a nice view of the north end of the lake, with a backdrop consisting of the Lenox-Stockbridge ridge with Stockbridge Mountain (1,828 ft.) as its high point to your left. Nestled on a hill in front of Lenox Mountain, to your right, is Kripalu Center. Bald Head is the promontory at the right end of the ridge. A similar but less dramatic view is yours from farther south along the shore at the town beach.

If you stand at the town boat ramp on the west shore of the lake you will see Rattlesnake Hill to the southeast.

The most breathtaking, albeit somewhat distant, view of the lake and the surrounding hills is from high above the lake off Lenox Road, just across the line in Richmond. To reach it from Tanglewood, take a right at Richmond Mountain Road (which becomes Lenox Road) where it branches off from Route 183 (0.1 mile beyond the Tanglewood gates), for approximately 1.5 miles to a gravel pull-off area on the left called Olivia's Overlook. From this vantage point, almost 500 feet above the lake, the view is spectacular.

Plant Communities

Stockbridge Bowl, like most other area lakes, is virtually ringed with camps and vacation homes. The natural communities near the shore have therefore undergone a radical transformation from the way the shoreline vegetation must have appeared originally. Nevertheless, the scene is a pleasing one, and woodlands still do exist at the north end of the lake and on the slopes behind the cottages. Elsewhere along the shore you will find large shade trees: willows, birches, and white pine.

Lily Brook flows into the lake, creating a marshland near the eastern shore along Mahkeenac Road. The dominant plant here is cattail. The giant plumed reed (*Phragmites*), an invasive alien that colonizes disturbed sites, forms an attractive small stand near the culvert. A dam situated approximately a half mile south of the mouth of Lily Brook allows the lake level to be controlled.

The lake itself contains virtually no emergent or floating plants, although considerable amounts of Eurasian milfoil and other aquatic "weeds" are present (see Ch. 17 for more about aquatic weeds).

Wildlife

Mammals: Aquatic mammals such as muskrat reside in the cattail marsh at the mouth of Lily Brook. The usual highly adaptive mammals (raccoon, opossum, striped skunk, squirrels, etc.) are found about the lake. On two successive early November waterfowl censuses (both warm days) a Hoffmann Bird Club group observed a little brown bat flying above the beach at midday, perhaps the most notable sighting of each outing! Colonies of this species, and probably the big brown bat as well, exist near the lake.

Birds: The birds that matter here are waterfowl. Fall, November in particular, is dramatically better here than spring. During the first half of November you will usually see some water birds, although one or two types may be it. Then again, you may happen upon a flock of 23 red-throated loons, as I did one November day.

Other species I've recorded here are common loon, red-necked grebe, pied-billed grebe, canvasback, oldsquaw, bufflehead, common goldeneye, lesser scaup, ring-necked duck, hooded merganser, common merganser, and of course Canada goose, mallard, and American black ducks. Other species are certainly possible. On two occasions in late October, a double-crested cormorant stopped over. A few ring-billed or herring gulls are usually present. During November you might also witness an osprey patrolling the lake. Other fish-eating birds here from time to time in fall include great blue heron, belted kingfisher, and greater yellowlegs, a large shorebird that sometimes includes small fish in its diet.

In the shoreline vegetation a wide range of perching birds are possible. I've seen rusty blackbird, American goldfinch, golden-crowned kinglet, black-capped chickadee, American robin, cedar waxwing, and house finch (an attractive bird "imported" from the American Southwest and released on Long Island in 1940, eventually becoming something of a pest species all across the eastern half of the country).

Reptiles: Painted turtles live in Lily Brook marsh, and snapping turtles also occur in the vicinity. The garter is probably the only snake you'll see, although the northern water snake is a common wetland inhabitant of this area.

Amphibians: You can expect to find some of the common frogs in the marshy areas, but this is not a particularly good place to observe this group of animals. You can, however, listen to the calling bull, green, and pickerel frogs, as well as gray treefrogs and spring peepers in spring and summer.

The largest species of salamander in the state, the-20-inch-long mudpuppy, has been found in Stockbridge Bowl. It is an almost primeval-appearing animal that is fully aquatic, nocturnal, and feeds upon crayfish and worms. They are active year-round. Since these creatures are not native to the area, it is anyone's guess as to how they got here. As fish bait, perhaps? The lake also contains many red-spotted newts, which are native and common.

Fish: That there are fish in Stockbridge Bowl is attested to by people with the requisite equipment, as well as the presence of fish-eating birds. Species known to exist in the lake include chain pickerel, largemouth bass, brook, brown, and rainbow trout (the last introduced), pumpkinseed, bluegill, rock bass, yellow perch, white sucker, bridle minnow, and killifish.

Seasonal Highlights

In spring, you may want to check the lake for migrating waterfowl, although fall is the most productive season.

In summer, little is here in the way of water birds, but the picturesque views make a stop worthwhile. The town beach, as in other communities, is open for swimming only to residents.

Late October to mid-November is when the vast majority of migrant water birds stop off here, although the number and the variety do not match that of the Central Berkshire lakes. The fall foliage views from Olivia's Overlook along Lenox Road above the lake can be spectacular in early October.

In winter, a river otter out on the ice with a fish is a possibility, but don't count on it.

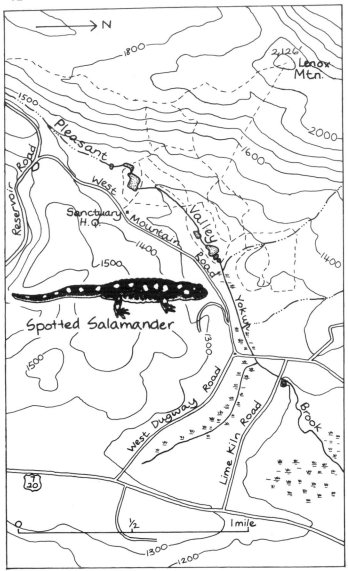

N

2,126′ Lenox Mtn.

1800

1500

Pleasant

West

Valley

Sanctuary H.Q.

Mountain Road

Reservoir Road

1500

1400

1500

2000

1600

1400

Yokun

Spotted Salamander

1300

1500

West Dugway Road

Lime Kiln Road

Brook

7 20

0   ½   1mile

1300

1200

PLEASANT VALLEY WILDLIFE SANCTUARY

◄§ 13 ◊►

PLEASANT VALLEY WILDLIFE SANCTUARY
Lenox

Owned and managed by MAS.

Acreage: 1,585.

Elevation: 1,250—2,126 ft.

Trails: 7 mi.

Hours: Year-round, every day except Mon. and major holidays. Also open Mon. July 1 to Columbus Day and most Mon. holidays. Trails open from dawn to dusk. Office hours: Tue.-Sat., 9-5; Sun. and holidays, 10-4.

Admission: Adults, $3, children 3-15 and persons 65 and over, $2; MAS members and children under 3, free; programs (and there are many all year long) and special events have different fees. Dogs, horses, and bicycles not allowed.

Facilities/Other: Trail maps, checklists, and program listing obtainable at office. Rest rooms available. No camping. Phone: 413-637-0320.

Directions: Pleasant Valley is 6.6 mi. N. of Exit 2 (Lee) of the Mass. Turnpike. From the S. take Rte. 7/20, N. to W. Dugway Rd. on the left, opposite the Quality Inn. Follow this road W. for 0.8 mi. to its intersection with W. Mountain Rd. and continue 0.8 mi. to the sanctuary's graveled parking lot. Register at the office, which is the brown house.

The looming presence of Lenox Mountain (2,126 ft.), an outlier of the Taconic Range, and a necklace of beaver-created ponds along Yokun Brook dominate this sanctuary, established in 1929. Beaver ponds and associated wetlands are easily accessible along the brook, a lovely, clear tributary of the Housatonic River. A feeder stream to Yokun Brook has cut a modest but lovely gorge, shaded by eastern hemlocks, through the marble bedrock near the so-called Bishop's Glen. The sanctuary possesses a beauty and tranquillity that make it a pleasure to visit.

Views and Vistas

The finest view is actually off sanctuary property, on the summit of Lenox Mountain (2,126 ft.), a destination for many visitors. Sanctuary staff maintain the 1.5-mile trail from the office to the summit. Lands surrounding sanctuary property are owned by the town of Lenox, except for the immediate vicinity of the fire tower, which is state-owned. The tower, which was damaged by fire in 1994, is no longer climbable. Nevertheless, on a clear day, your efforts will be rewarded by fine views of the Catskills to the southwest, Mount Greylock and Vermont's Green Mountains to the north, and the Taconics, straddling the New York-Massachusetts border, just five miles to the west. For a nice easterly view of Pleasant Valley itself hike up the steep Trail of the Ledges (*not recommended during wet or icy conditions*) to an overlook known as Farviews (see *Hikes & Walks*). For views of the mountain ridge from the valley, the open fields in front of the sanctuary's Trailside Museum and the northern end of Yokun Trail are best. The scene from the south end of Pike's Pond Trail is also lovely.

Plant Communities

Much of the sanctuary, like most of Berkshire, is second-growth hardwoods. Logging and agricultural clearing during the eighteenth and nineteenth centuries have left us with a relatively young forest. Nevertheless, steep sections of Lenox Mountain contain northern hardwood forest stands with stately old trees such as sugar maple, white birch, and eastern hemlock. Tall, magnificent white pines form a cathedral stand in the vicinity of Beaver Lodge and Waycross trails. Species typical of lower slopes are northern red oak (some quite large), white ash (cross-hatched bark), black cherry, and gray and white birches. You will even find a few, such as shagbark and bitternut hickories, that are more characteristic of southern forests.

Trees characteristic of boreal forests, such as red spruce, are present in small numbers near the summit of the mountain on the southwest face. On the slopes grow painted trillium (white petals with red centers), and in the valley wildflowers included in the spring bloom are hepatica, miterwort, foamflower, jack-in-the pulpit, sweet white violet, long-spurred violet, and red trillium.

Over 25 species of ferns can be found by the careful observer. Some, such as walking fern, grow only on limestone cliffs, while Christmas, evergreen wood fern, and interrupted fern are the most common in rich woods. In wet areas look for sensitive, cinnamon (which has a cinnamon-colored spore-bearing stalk), and royal ferns. You can find all three along Pike's Pond Trail.

The extensive beaver pond system makes it possible for a wide array of plants suited to moist conditions to flourish. Typical marsh plants are cattail, bur-reed (which has spiky green heads), bulrushes, yellow pond-lily, pond-weeds, blue flag iris (very visible in summer along Yokun Trail), and arrowhead. Shrubs that grow in the wetlands and along its edges are speckled alder, arrowwood (a viburnum with very straight branches), silky and redstem (red-osier) dogwoods, and many willows. Red maple, white pine, and gray and white birches grow along the margins.

Notice that beavers have cut a wide swath along the pond borders, which are now full of ferns and resprouting trees and shrubs. Beaver ponds trap silt and organic matter that eventually builds up into rich soil, fostering a wealth of marsh plants that in turn encourage a myriad of animal life. When the pond becomes too shallow, the beavers move elsewhere, the untended dam collapses, and the rich soil eventually grows up to meadow vegetation. These meadows, among the first lands cultivated by European settlers, comprise some of the richest plant communities on the property. More than 650 species of plants were identified on the sanctuary during a 1989 inventory.

Wildlife

Mammals: Without doubt the active beaver population is among the most interesting and easily observed (generally at dusk) of the sanctuary's mammal life. Pike's Pond, an artificial body of water, was one of the very first beaver reintroduction sites in the state. Our native beaver population had been trapped out by 1850, and in 1932 three animals from Bear Mountain Park, New York, were brought in. You can readily observe these fascinating creatures here (at 50 to 70 pounds, beavers qualify as the continent's largest rodents), from Pike's Pond, Yokun, and Beaver Lodge trails. Even if the animals themselves are not visible, you will see their large, dome-shaped lodges and dams, both constructed of mud and sticks. These ponds and attendant wetlands also provide habitat for such aquatic species as muskrat, mink, and river otter.

White-tailed deer are numerous and are sometimes seen in woodlands and fields here. In the fall, look for "buck rubs" — small trees that have had their bark rubbed off by male deer polishing their antlers in preparation for the coming mating season. Predators here include coyote, occasionally heard howling after sunset, bobcat, and red and gray foxes. Sightings of black bears, always bound to cause excitement, are becoming more common, with a few reports each year now.

A wide variety of small mammals are seen annually in the fields and forests of the sanctuary. Among these are the short-tailed weasel (ermine), hairy-tailed mole, red-backed mouse, white-footed mouse, short-tailed shrew, woodchuck (usually seen on lawns), eastern chipmunk, and gray and red squirrels. Except for the last four, all squirrels, the others are seldom seen. Cloudy days improve your chances of seeing the nocturnal types. At dusk on warm summer evenings, you'll find big brown and little brown bats pursuing insects above Pike's Pond.

Birds: Woodland birds characteristic of northern hardwood forest predominate at Pleasant Valley. Conversely, species associated with open country are less common. Woodland birds such as scarlet tanager, rose-breasted grosbeak, least flycatcher, yellow-bellied sapsucker, the magnificent pileated woodpecker, and fifteen or so species of energetic and colorful wood warblers, including the black-throated blue, black-throated green, Blackburnian, black and white (which creeps around branches like a nuthatch), American redstart, chestnut-sided, yellow, and ovenbird, nest on the property. Solitary, yellow-throated, and red-eyed vireos, neotropical migrants all, nest in the woodlands. The thrushes, veery, wood thrush, and hermit, rank among the continent's best avian songsters, and you can hear all three in spring and early summer, especially early and late in the day.

For close-up looks at some of the more common resident species, watch them as they patronize the sanctuary's feeding station, north of the office. Nearby, a hummingbird garden planted largely with red, tubular flowers attracts ruby-throated hummingbirds, especially from May through early August. A few pairs of Canada geese nest on islands or beaver lodges within the pond system, as do a few pairs of mallard ducks. The elegant wood duck has been known to occupy the nest boxes placed for their use in the wetlands, and hooded mergansers also make use of the same big boxes. The male, in display, shows off a spectacular white crest to his best advantage.

Swamp sparrows nest in the cattail and sedge wetlands bordering the ponds, and alder flycatchers can sometimes be heard singing, *fee-bee-o*, quite fittingly, from the alder swamps. At dusk, chunky male American woodcocks perform their courtship flights above meadows bordering the beaver ponds. I'll never forget the first time that I witnessed this spectacle. Dr. George J. Wallace, an early director of this sanctuary, took some of his students to a wetland near Michigan State University, where for years he taught ornithology, and with flashlight in hand proceeded to mesmerize and enlighten us about this bird's nuptial habits!

Sanctuary staff and volunteers conduct bird walks and bird-banding demonstrations for the public year-round. Inquire as to the schedule for these programs. A sanctuary bird checklist is available at the office. So far, 158 species have been recorded, of which 80 have nested here.

Reptiles: The most easily observed reptiles at Pleasant Valley are turtles. Painted turtles are readily visible as they bask on logs during the warmer months. Pike's Pond is a good place to observe them, and you might see the occasional snapping turtle there in summer. The mating activities of two enormous snappers have been observed by some visitors to Pike's Pond the last several summers.

Snakes, although fairly common, are seldom observed, except for the common garter. When they are, it is usually while basking in some open sunlit spot. Don't be alarmed if you happen upon one, as it is harmless. If fortunate, you may find some of the other snakes that dwell at the sanctuary: milk, red-bellied, and ringneck. Milk snakes are light brown with dark, coppery-colored blotches that are wide on the snake's back and narrow along its sides.

Amphibians: Bullfrogs, green frogs, and pickerel frogs are especially visible and audible during the summer months, when males give their characteristic mating calls. Green frogs shriek alarm and leap to safety as you approach them. In early spring, tiny tree frogs called spring peepers can be heard sounding like sleigh bells. You might hear the purring call of an unseen gray treefrog. This one- to-two-inch-long species, which has orange hind parts underneath, is at its northern range limits here. Wood frogs, as the name implies, live in forested areas. These amphibians, whose calls sound remarkably like ducks quacking, and some salamanders perform annual migrations from burrows deep in the leaf litter to small woodland ponds called vernal pools. An artificial vernal pool, once a duck pen, is located just north of the barn.

Fish: Fish are abundant in the sanctuary ponds. You can easily view brown bullhead, pumpkinseed (a sunfish that has a reddish patch on its cheek), and golden shiner from bridges along Pike's Pond Trail and elsewhere.

Salamander Sanctuary

The timing of salamander migrations to vernal pools is triggered by the cool rains of spring in late March or early April, when nighttime temperatures reach 40 degrees or so. On such nights, spotted, Jefferson, and perhaps four-toed salamanders can be seen crossing West Dugway and West Mountain roads. Pleasant Valley in fact was the first place in the nation to have a portion (five acres) of its property officially declared a salamander sanctuary. Marilyn Flor, former staff naturalist, conducted field research into the annual comings and goings of spotted salamanders for more than 10 years. She was able to identify each individual by its uniquely different spot pattern, something no one else had apparently discovered!

Seasonal Highlights

Annual wood frog and salamander migration takes place on rainy nights in late March and early April. This annual ritual of courtship and mating makes for fascinating wildlife observation. Late April to late May is the peak for bird migration. Late April and early May, before the tree leaves have emerged, also is the time of greatest woodland wildflower bloom. Species such as bloodroot, sharp-lobed hepatica, and red trillium are among the most beautiful and common. Wet areas glow with the golden beauty of marsh marigold, which is in reality a buttercup. A good place to observe them is from the boardwalk near the office (Pike's Pond Trail). Late May is the time to appreciate the gorgeous pink blossoms and wonderful aroma of the mountain azalea bushes, also along Pike's Pond Trail.

Mid-June to early July is peak flowering for the mountain laurel shrubs that grace many of the sanctuary's trails (Laurel Trail, naturally enough, has the thickest growth). June and July are also the months of peak bird nesting.

Later in summer, you can see parent birds feeding their insistent fledglings. When the non-native red mulberry trees near the sanctuary buildings bear their ripe, purple-black fruit around the first week of July, they become fairly alive with scarlet tanagers, Baltimore orioles, rose-breasted grosbeaks, veerys, gray catbirds, cedar waxwings, American robins, and other colorful species. If you walk to the shores of Pike's Pond after dusk, you'll see not only beavers but also big and little brown bats, acrobatically going about their nightly business of catching flying insects. Summer also brings a profusion of wildflowers, especially in meadows, with new species coming into the flowering sequence each week.

Fall brings back many of the same bird migrants that passed through on their way north in spring, but in more subdued plumages. The annual migration of monarch butterflies on their way south to central Mexico is a notable phenomenon. Millions of these insects annually make this 2,500-mile, two-month journey, each for the first and only time. You will observe them flying southwest through the valley from late August until early October, with a peak in early September. But certainly the most spectacular show of the season is the autumnal foliage, which tends to be at its best in this area in early to mid October.

Winter is the best season for tracking. After a light snowfall you'll usually find evidence of a wide variety of mammals, including mink and fox. Flocks of evening grosbeaks sometimes visit the sunflower feeders. Crossbills and common redpolls may even be found some years. The intrepid can rent snowshoes at the office for a nominal fee; and a one-mile loop trail has been designated for cross-country skiing (see *Skiing*).

❧ 14 ❧

HOUSATONIC VALLEY
WILDLIFE MANAGEMENT AREA
Lenox, Pittsfield

Managed by MDF&W.

Acreage: 818.

Elevation: 950 ft.

Hours: Year round.

Admission: None.

Facilities/Other: No rest rooms. Camping available at October Mtn. State Forest in Lee. Hunting and fishing allowed in season. Map and information available at MDF&W regional office, 400 Hubbard Ave., Pittsfield. Office hours 8-4, Mon.-Fri., except holidays. Phone: 413-447-9789.

Directions: This area is accessible from several points. To Decker Boat Access, Lenox: From where Rtes. 7/20 and 7A merge in Lenox, travel N. 2.75 mi. to New Lenox Rd. on right. Take New Lenox Rd. for 2 mi. to parking area on right. Do not park along river, but rather in upper lot so as not to interfere with launching activities. To Brielman's Swamp in Pittsfield: From the jct. of Rte. 7/20 and Holmes Rd. in Lenox, take Holmes Rd. N. for 1.1 mi. to Utility Drive on the right and turn right. Proceed under narrow railroad underpass to just short of Pittsfield sewage treatment plant. Park along edge of gravel roadway on left. Walk the graveled road and grassy tracks into area. To Wood Pond, Lenox: From where 7/20 and 7A merge in Lenox, take Rte. 7/20, S. for 1.3 mi. to Housatonic St. Turn left onto Housatonic St. and proceed 1.4 mi. to Wood Pond. Park at end of graveled roadway, being careful not to block private drive on left.

The slow-moving, meandering Housatonic River with its associated floodplain and wetlands is an outstanding area to observe wildlife. Our river corridors, in fact, are among the best places to enjoy nature and witness the interplay of life forms; and a canoe enables you to get right in among the action. The valley is very scenic and was once a long, narrow north-south-trending glacial lake. The natural dam to this lake was near the entrance to the Massachusetts Turnpike in Lee, a few miles to the south. With the final melting and withdrawal of the ice, the dam was breached and the lake ceased to exist. A six-mile flatwater canoe trip between the Decker Boat Access and Wood Pond, both in Lenox, is an ideal way to experience the pleasures of the river. A separate portion of the management area, known locally as Brielman's Swamp, lies to the north in Pittsfield near the sewage treatment plant. It is a great place to seek out aquatic birds, especially such secretive ones as the American bittern, Virginia rail, and sora.

Views and Vistas

Nearly the entire six-mile stretch of winding river will provide you with beautiful views of the Housatonic, the farmland and wetlands along its banks, and the scenic October Mountain plateau nearby to the east. You'll experience a different scene around each bend — and there are many. For a bucolic setting, it's hard to beat the view of the former dairy farm across the river from the Decker launch site. You can get the best views of October Mountain at the beginning as well as near the end of this route. As you approach Wood Pond by canoe, the upland comes to closely parallel the river. For drive-up views, the vistas from Wood Pond and especially the Decker site are very nice.

Plant Communities

The banks of the Housatonic are lined with silver maple, basswood (heart-shaped leaves), green ash, and black willow — all species tolerant of wet soils. At one point on the route you will come to a cool, shaded slope bedecked with eastern hemlocks. The difference in air temperatures on a warm day is noticeable as you canoe through this shaded stretch. In sunnier areas, the globular white flower clusters of buttonbush bloom along the banks in

American Bittern

HOUSATONIC VALLEY W.M.A.

mid-July. In places where the flow of the river has changed, causing a former part of the channel to be partly cut off, you'll find marshes luxuriant with vegetation. In late July the floating leaves and yellow flowers of the yellow pond-lily, as well as the attractive purple flower stalks of the emergent pickerel weed, are much in evidence. In shallower waters at this time it's difficult to miss the arrow-head-shaped leaves and lovely white flowers of arrowhead. Along the banks of some of these backwaters you should look for the brilliant red cardinal flower (a protected species). In late summer many portions of the high river banks are lined with the orange-flowered touch-me-not (jewel weed), from which hummingbirds and bumblebees sip nectar.

One species that belies the problems it causes is purple loosestrife, a Eurasian import. In summer this invasive plant covers entire wetlands with its tall purple-red flower stalks, crowding out our native cattails and other beneficial species. You can't miss seeing this troublesome, albeit attractive, exotic in floodplain wetlands during summer.

At Brielman's Swamp you'll find cattail marshes that harbor much animal life and bordering upland fields with a very different set of animal residents.

Wildlife

Mammals: Beavers have recolonized the Housatonic, perhaps originally by way of Yokun Brook from Pleasant Valley (see Ch. 13). Here they don't build dams, since the river is already wide and deep enough to meet their security needs. A canoe trip will enable you to see several lodges up close. These are constructed on the bank, with the entrance underwater, of course. The beavers themselves are seldom abroad during the day; you are much more likely to see muskrats. These fairly big rodents look something like their much larger cousins, but their tails are long and thin rather than flat and paddlelike. You'll find them active by day at virtually any season. Muskrat lodges, usually built of cattails and mud, are visible from shore at Brielman's Swamp.

A trip on the river, especially at dawn or dusk, will reveal a much greater variety of mammals to you, including perhaps white-tailed deer. The ubiquitous squirrels, both gray and red and eastern chipmunk, will be heard if not seen during almost any trip. While on the river one beautiful June day, a canoeing party I was with chanced upon a young porcupine in a small elm tree along the bank, only ten feet above the water. We were able to maneuver right underneath the animal for excellent views!

Birds: The Housatonic River, its associated wetlands and adjacent uplands, both fields and forests, make this a rich area for bird life. At Brielman's Swamp you'll find species dependent upon thick stands of emergent plants such as cattail. The most sought-after from the birder's point of view are American bittern, Virginia rail, and sora (also a rail). One purported source for the expression "skinny as a rail" may refer to the fact that these birds are somewhat flattened laterally to enable them to move through the thick vegetation with relative ease. They are secretive birds that are much more often heard than seen. For best results you must come early. Dawn is not too early to hear the odd, repetitious clicking call of the Virginia rail, or the bizarre water-pump-like sounds made by the bittern. If you are fortunate, these shy birds may walk momentarily out into the open, affording you a look.

There are usually a few ducks in the open water, and sometimes a great blue heron. In the shrubs and fields around the marsh's periphery you are likely to hear and see, in the breeding season, willow flycatcher, yellow warbler, swamp sparrow, brown thrasher, field sparrow, eastern kingbird, American goldfinch, and perhaps a red-tailed hawk. In the upper hayfields watch for bobolinks from mid-May through July. During migrations, you may find a few shorebirds stopping off to feed on the muddy margins of the wetlands. These include the solitary sandpiper and greater yellowlegs. Common snipe are found in the wet meadows in the spring. The bordering woodlands support many of the same species you'll find in other woodlands of

the area, such as the tufted titmouse and pileated woodpecker.

A canoe trip between the Decker boat launch and Wood
Pond will reveal a sizable number and variety of bird life,
especially in late spring, summer, and early fall. After you
first put in, paddle upstream (left) a few hundred feet until
you're under the highway bridge. This is an excellent vantage point from which to watch cliff and barn swallows (the
latter have long, forked tails) entering and exiting their
nests, both of which are constructed largely of mud. The
cliff swallow nests are the globular ones with small, round
entrance holes. These uncommon birds have returned by
late May, and you will find them carrying out their annual
nesting chores well into July. This is the same species, by
the way, that returns to Capistrano in Southern California
each year. As you travel downstream you will certainly
hear and often see many other species. Most visible perhaps
of these are the belted kingfisher, mallard, American black
duck, and wood duck. Wood ducks nest in the large nesting
boxes provided for them; you'll see these huge birdhouses
with their oval entrance holes at many points along the
river bank. Warbling vireos are difficult to spot, but easy to
hear, as they sing their slow, burry phrases from riverside
trees. Also be on the lookout for ruby-throated hummingbirds zipping by; it's easy to mistake them for large insects.

Other common breeding species in the valley are least
flycatcher, yellow warbler, chestnut-sided warbler, American redstart, indigo bunting (the male appears all blue in
bright sunlight), scarlet tanager, wood thrush, rose-breasted
grosbeak, red-eyed vireo, and ovenbird. You may also
record purple finch, hermit thrush, great crested flycatcher,
yellow-bellied sapsucker, and yellow-throated vireo. Late
summer is the best time to see great blue heron, green
heron, and ducks. You might also see a spotted sandpiper,
bobbing as it walks along the shore; it's one of the few
shorebirds that breed in this area. In mid-July the utility
wires over Wood Pond are sometimes full of swallows,
especially tree swallows.

Beginning in late July and through October, southbound ospreys follow the river valley in search of live fish, their only food. Witnessing one of these majestic birds diving into the river and emerging with a meal (often a large goldfish!) is truly memorable. Sometimes misidentified as eagles, ospreys have a white head with a brown band through the eyes, and they have brownish, not white, tails.

Bald eagles are becoming a more regular sight, especially during spring and fall migrations. From late August through early October, migrant broad-winged, sharpshinned, and Cooper's hawks may be seen gliding southward over the October Mountain ridge. Large black birds may be either common ravens or turkey vultures. Vultures search for carrion on outstretched wings, held above the horizontal, rarely flapping them. Northern harriers patrol low over the fields and wetlands searching (actually listening) for rodents in late summer. Fittingly, their faces are more owllike than those of other hawks.

Reptiles: For many years, the chances of seeing a painted turtle in the river were nil. More recently, however, painted turtles have again been sighted during canoe trips on this portion of the Housatonic. Snakes are not likely to be seen from a canoe. Common garter, milk, red-bellied, and ribbon snakes occur in the meadows but are seldom encountered.

Amphibians: Frogs, as you might expect, are abundant. The most visible in spring and summer are the huge, bug-eyed bullfrogs. Males, with yellow throats, stake out feeding territories along the banks. They can easily be distinguished from the smaller females by their round "eardrums," which are larger than their eyes. Bullfrog-watching can make for great entertainment as you leisurely float downriver taking in all the sights, smells, and sounds. You will also probably encounter green frogs, which are smaller than bullfrogs, have two parallel "pleats" on their backs, and give a call that sounds something like a plucked banjo string. You can find both pickerel frogs and the un-

PCBs in the Housatonic

PCBs (polychlorinated biphenyls) were manufactured and used as insulating agents in electrical transformers built up until the 1970s, when the substances were found to cause cancer in laboratory animals. There is a suspected, although as yet unproved, link to cancer in humans as well. In 1979 the federal Environmental Protection Agency outlawed the use of PCBs. For two decades prior to that, PCBs had leaked from the General Electric transformer operation in Pittsfield, where they were manufactured, into the Housatonic River. PCBs accumulate in the fatty tissues of organisms, such as fish and frogs and birds, that ingest them.

A variety of remedial measures have been suggested over the years to deal with the large quantities of the suspected carcinogen in the river's sediments. Dredging and landfilling were proposed during the mid-1980s but as yet have not been carried out. The introduction of naturally occurring PCB-consuming bacteria into the river was also proposed. Under laboratory conditions, these bacteria actually digest the chlorine portion of the PCB molecule, rendering the remaining substances harmless.

In late 1991 a controlled experiment to test such bacterial stimulation was set up within Wood Pond (a portion of the Housatonic) in Lenox. Here testing and monitoring was conducted for two and one half years with the hope that the bacteria may one day be released into the river, resulting in the complete elimination of the PCB threat in the county's major waterway. Unfortunately, this method has been largely discounted as an effective large-scale solution. You can catch a glimpse of the experimental lab from shore where Housatonic Street dead-ends at the river.

common leopard frog in the damp vegetation of the floodplain. In April and May listen for the high-pitched chorus of spring peepers.

Fish: Most notable, in one sense, of the fish in the Housatonic are the exotic goldfish, which attain surprising size here. As you paddle about in some of the backwaters you'll surely glimpse these foot-long specimens. On several occasions, I have seen an osprey in flight with a bright orange goldfish in its talons. These fish must be a remarkably visible target from above!

Other species in this section of the river include brown trout, rainbow trout (these fish are now considered to be a species of salmon), largemouth bass, bluegill, common shiner, longnose dace, longnose sucker, white sucker, and fall fish. There is even a record of a banded killifish from the river. This area is open to hunting and fishing in season, although consumption of river fish is not recommended because of the presence of PCBs in the sediment as well as in the fish and other aquatic life.

Seasonal Highlights

A springtime river trip is an excellent way in which to behold the wonders of bird migration. On shore, woodland wildflowers dot the forest floor, and you may want to pause to seek them out. One of spring's most enthralling spectacles is the nuptial flight of the male American woodcock. This chunky shorebird with a huge bill puts on an amazing aerial performance that must be seen and heard. Meadows adjacent to wetlands (try the Decker launch site) are where you'll witness his act at dusk in April. Late May is a fine time to make that dawn visit to Brielman's Swamp in search of bittern and rails.

By summer, bird nesting is in full swing, and a canoe trip on an early summer or midsummer morning will reward you with a cacophony of bird music and sights of colorful plumage. June is the perfect month to take a look at the swallow colony under the highway bridge near the Decker launch site. July is best if you want to see the colorful wetland plants of the river's backwaters. Along the river banks, too, there is an endless procession of blooming plants, and bullfrog activity is at its peak. Late summer brings migrating ospreys and views of magnificent great blue herons and perhaps even a great egret (big and white).

Early fall is the season for hawks. Watch the ridge as you float downstream (southward). Fall wildflowers bloom in the meadows, and migrant birds are in the trees. Monarch butterflies, too, are following the river valley southward in September. You may see migrating least, solitary, and spotted sandpipers along the banks and on the river's many sand bars in early fall. In early October the brilliant foliage on the ridge and along the river banks is a sight to see. Red maples and other wetland trees tend to acquire their finery earlier than trees of the uplands. Flocks of ducks and geese stop over in late fall during their migrations to milder climes.

In winter, portions of the Housatonic remain free of ice except during the severest cold. You may find that birding at Brielman's Swamp can still be quite productive.

Comments

You can rent canoes from outfitters in Lenox, Sheffield, and Adams. A few words of caution: The normally tranquil Housatonic can become a dangerous stream in spring after heavy rains and snow-melt cause it to top its banks. The Massachusetts Audubon Society conducts naturalist-guided canoe trips from May to October on the upper Housatonic. Inquire at their office in Lenox for a schedule.

⊷ 15 ⊶

OCTOBER MOUNTAIN STATE FOREST
Washington, Becket, Lee, Lenox

Managed by DEM.

Acreage: 15,979.

Elevation: 960—2,263 ft.

Trails: 35 mi., including 8.5 mi. of AT.

Hours: Daily, sunrise to sunset.

Admission: None. Camping, $6 per site (visitor parking $2).

Facilities/Other: Rest rooms, camping (May to October), trail maps available at office for Lee camping area. Phone: 413-243-1778, 243-9735.

Directions: To office and Lee camping area: Take Exit 2 from the Mass. Turnpike in Lee right onto Rte. 7/20 (N.). Follow Rte. 7/20 through Lee for 1.1 mi. to Center St. on right. Follow Columbia St. left around small pond (watch for herons and egrets here in late summer), past paper mill and along Housatonic River for 1.2 mi. to Mill St. Merge with East St. and follow for 0.3 mi. to Bradley St. (later Woodland Rd.). Turn right and follow for 0.8 mi. to entrance on right. There are a number of other access points in the various towns including: From Rte. 8 in Becket to County Rd. to the "four corners" and Washington Mtn. Marsh (formerly Lake) area in Washington; Rte. 8 to Yokum Pond Rd. in Becket to a signed turnoff to Buckley Dunton Lake in the same town (can also be reached from Rte. 20 in Lee to Becket Rd.); and via two AT crossings — Rte. 20 in Becket, near Greenwater Pond, and where Beach Rd. intersects Pittsfield Rd. in Washington. To reach Felton Lake and Halfway Pond (bog), both in Washington: From Decker boat launch in Lenox (see Ch. 14) take New Lenox Rd. E. for 1.8 mi. Bear right onto Lenox-Whitney Place Rd. (requires high-clearance vehicle) and proceed 1.7 mi. Turn right onto Felton Pond Rd. and drive 1.6 mi. to buried telephone cable crossing. Walk 600 ft. W. along cable right-of-way from Felton Pond Rd., then S. toward Halfway Pond (no trail, wet conditions).

October Mountain is the largest state forest in Massachusetts. Apparently this name was first used by Herman
Melville (who had a good view of it from his house on
Holmes Road in Pittsfield, in addition to his view of
Greylock). Within its vast acreage lie expanses of mixed
and northern hardwood forests, meadows, bogs (such as
Halfway Pond and Washington Mountain Marsh), many
swamps, marshes, fast mountain brooks, ponds (such as
Finerty Pond, accessed by the Appalachian Trail), and reservoirs that supply Pittsfield and Lenox with water. The
land is rolling, much of it around 2,000 feet in elevation and
therefore decidedly cool — ideal for the formation of bogs
and marshes. This wild and rugged park contains a varied
assemblage of flora and fauna representative of the Berkshire Plateau. The Appalachian Trail and numerous other
trails and tracks offer access to its many delights.

The plateau's rocks were once the "basement" of a vast
mountain system that existed over this part of New England
and beyond. The overlying rocks of that system have long
since vanished, owing to the forces of water, ice, and wind
over many millions of years. These rocks exhibit the results
of great heat and pressure; upon close inspection you'll find
that many specimens show swirls, indicating that forces
were great enough to cause this rock to flow in a near-
plastic state. The rocks are both of the schist and gneiss
types, and some are studded with crystals of garnet,
hornblende, mica, actinolite, tremolite, and many other
minerals.

Views and Vistas

Few summits rise sufficiently above the high but rather
level plateau as to afford panoramic views, and those that
do are largely overgrown with trees. There are better views
of the upland (see for instance Ch. 14) than from it, although a few vistas are worthy of mention. A view of Mount
Greylock is possible from Felton Pond Road. You can get a
somewhat limited view of the hills to the west from the
Appalachian Trail atop Becket Mountain (2,180 ft.). Hike

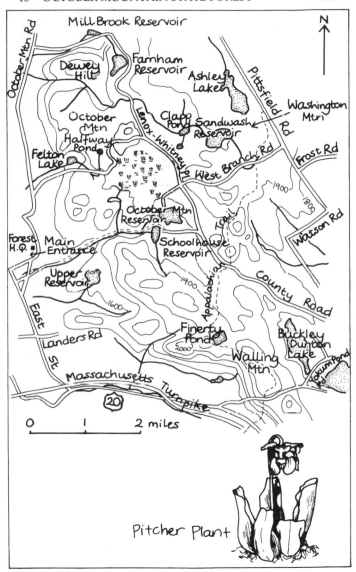

Pitcher Plant

OCTOBER MOUNTAIN STATE FOREST

north from Route 20 or Tyne Road in Becket to reach this vantage point (you can continue to Finerty Pond; see *Hikes & Walks*). For pleasant views of the spruce-studded hills from a paved road, take a drive in Washington along the Pittsfield Road (Washington Mountain Road at its north end in Dalton). A turn onto gravel West Branch Road opposite the old town hall and cemetery (high-clearance vehicle required) will take you into the forest for some exploring on foot or skis. The views of rolling, tree-covered Becket Mountain and Walling Mountain (2,220 ft.) across the lake from the Buckley Dunton Reservoir dam and boat launch are also pleasing.

Plant Communities

What plant communities you encounter during your travels through October Mountain depends largely upon elevation as well as geology and soil type. Orientation toward north or south is also important. The majority of this large area is covered with typical northern hardwood forest. The major trees you'll see are northern red oak (some of which attain considerable size here), American beech, all five common species of birches, eastern hemlock, white ash, sugar and red maples, eastern hemlock, and white pine.

Smaller, understory trees include eastern hophornbeam, American hornbeam, shadbush (which produces lovely white flowers and great quantities of berries), striped maple, and mountain maple.

The major shrubs are two evergreens — mountain laurel and American yew — and the deciduous hobblebush. In spring, red-berried elder flowers along the roadsides, and it produces fruit in summer. Ground-covering plants include wintergreen, partridgeberry, and several species of clubmosses. The ferns that you'll find year-round, owing to their evergreen qualities, are Christmas, spinulose wood, marginal wood, and common polypody. New York fern is also abundant but not evergreen. There are many other fairly common ones, numbering perhaps 30 species in all.

Moist soil and cool climate here favor native evergreens, and in the higher reaches of the forest, from about 1,700 feet elevation and up, you'll find red spruce and balsam fir becoming increasingly common. At 2,000 feet there are thick stands of our most common native spruce. In spring the needle-covered forest floor beneath spruces and firs displays many colorful species of blooming wildflowers, including painted trillium and bunchberry.

Remember, spruce cones hang down, while fir cones stand up. Don't let the planted Norway spruces, with much larger (4-7 inch) cones, confuse you. The forest abounds with Norway spruce, white spruce, and red pine stands, many planted by the Civilian Conservation Corps during the 1930s. Their roots hold the soil and prevent erosion, but little else can flourish in the dense shade of these groves. Other introduced species include Japanese larch, which has larger cones than our tamarack. You'll find many planted larches in the Lee campground.

At the edges of wetlands and moist woodlands you'll be able to see the lovely and fragrant pink-flowered mountain azalea, as well as winterberry shrubs with bright-red berries. Beaver marshes are surrounded by cattails, sedges, blue flag iris, and perhaps royal ferns among the speckled alder shrubs.

In the wet margins of bogs grows black spruce, which resembles its larger relative red spruce. Also found in wet soils is our native tamarack or larch, a conifer that has the distinction of losing all its needles each fall. In fact, they turn a lovely yellow before being shed. Bogs, actually ice-age relics, are very special communities that harbor a distinctive and unusual plant life. Since no more are currently being created, bogs are truly a dwindling resource. True bogs have a floating mat of sphagnum moss around their edges that serves as a platform for other plants. This moss can hold fifty times its own weight in water. October Mountain contains a number of these fragile and biologically fascinating communities.

One such place is Halfway Pond (see directions above). Here black spruce, tamarack, and red maple surround the pond, and Labrador tea and leatherleaf are the common shrubs. Labrador tea has thick, leathery, evergreen leaves with brown fuzz underneath and a cluster of white flowers in mid-June. Wild calla, which looks much like the cultivated variety, is abundant here, and you'll also find large and wren's egg cranberry, round-leaved sundew, pitcherplant (see also Ch. 18), and three-leaved Solomon's seal. The surface of the pond itself is covered in July with yellow pond-lilies. This is a wet place and not for everybody. Other bogs contain the beautiful rose pogonia, an orchid, and other species that tolerate such acidic conditions.

Wildlife

Mammals: Virtually all the mammals native to Berkshire and neighboring areas inhabit October Mountain. In the woodlands and along its edges you'll find white-tailed deer, porcupine, striped skunk, opossum, gray fox, raccoon, long-tailed weasel (which except for its black-tipped tail turns white in winter), red-backed and deer mice, red and gray squirrels, flying squirrels, eastern chipmunk, snowshoe hare, eastern cottontail, hairy-tailed mole, masked, smoky, and short-tailed shrews, and little brown, big brown, long-eared, and red bats. All the wide-ranging and seldom-seen predators occur here, too: bobcat, coyote, black bear, and fisher.

In more open areas the common species include meadow vole and red fox, and in the wetlands (Finerty Pond, for instance) be on the lookout for river otter, mink, beaver, and muskrat. Even two moose were sighted at October Mountain in 1996. I have been fortunate enough to see all but a few of these animals within or near the boundaries of this state forest. The above list is not exhaustive, as other species exist here as well, and you may be fortunate enough with patience and good timing to catch a glimpse of many of them.

Some are seen most often in the blinding beams of car headlights, and quite a few pay the ultimate price for not having evolved along with high-speed motor vehicles. As with mammals elsewhere, you'll likely see most species only after sunset or in the wee hours of the morning. Overcast skies encourage some less nocturnal creatures to venture forth even at midday.

Birds: The list of birds for October Mountain is equally encyclopedic. Among the year-round residents are wild turkey, ruffed grouse, mourning dove, pileated, hairy, and downy woodpeckers, common raven, American crow, blue jay, black-capped chickadee, golden-crowned kinglet, American goldfinch, dark-eyed junco, purple finch, northern cardinal, red-breasted and white-breasted nuthatches, brown creeper, cedar waxwing, red-tailed hawk, and the powerful northern goshawk.

Large but graceful turkey vultures ride the warm air currents seemingly without effort. They may nest in hollow logs or on inaccessible cliffs in the forest. Along with crows and ravens, they serve as a sort of sanitation squad, removing dead animals from roadways and elsewhere. The advent of the automobile actually benefited these birds!

Summer residents in wetlands include Canada goose, great blue and green herons, the spotted sandpiper, red-shouldered hawk, tree swallow, Nashville warbler, northern waterthrush, common yellowthroat, common grackle, red-winged blackbird, and swamp sparrow.

In woodlands and their clearings you'll find sharp-shinned, broad winged, and Cooper's hawks, the ruby-throated hummingbird (the smallest of all eastern birds), yellow-bellied sapsucker, eastern wood pewee, eastern phoebe, winter wren, black-billed cuckoo, wood, hermit, and a few Swainson's thrushes (which usually nest in even higher or more northern habitats), veery, American robin, solitary and red-eyed vireos, and the following species of wood warblers: chestnut-sided (young woodland stages), magnolia (conifers), black-throated blue (mountain laurel and hobblebush thickets), black-throated green (pine woods), yellow-rumped, Blackburnian (quite common in spruce groves), black and white, ovenbird, Canada (wet places), and along woodland brooks, Louisiana waterthrush.

You may also see and hear three of the most colorful woodland breeders: scarlet tanager, Baltimore oriole, and rose-breasted grosbeak.

In the fields, meadows, and brushy edges you can expect to find the American kestrel, American woodcock (close to water), common flicker, eastern kingbird, barn swallow, gray catbird, eastern bluebird (see Ch. 21 for more about this much-loved species), and song and chipping sparrows. Other inhabitants include white-throated sparrow (*old Sam Peabody Peabody Peabody* is its plaintive, whistled song), brown-headed cowbird (the female lays her eggs in the nests of other, usually smaller species), eastern (formerly rufous-sided) towhee, and indigo bunting.

Seldom seen, but more often heard, are the nocturnal raptors — the owls, ranging in size from the diminutive northern saw-whet to the 20-inch-tall and "earless" barred to the 26-inch-tall great horned owl. The great horned sometimes feasts on skunk! By day, most owls roost in thick evergreens, where regurgitated pellets of fur and bones reveal their current or former presence and diets.

In late fall, birds that breed farther north visit October Mountain. Among these are the colorful so-called "winter finches," prized by birders because of their erratic irruptions into our area. They include pine and evening grosbeaks, white-winged and red crossbills, pine siskin, and common redpoll. Of these, evening grosbeaks are of most regular occurrence, and no doubt some nest in the higher parts of the state forest, given that a few, sometimes feeding their fledglings, are seen during the summer months.

American tree sparrows, rusty-capped birds that have a black spot on their clear gray breasts, also migrate down from the southern edge of Canada's tundra to take up winter residence in our brushy fields. These birds arrive here in November and depart in April.

Still other birds pass through the area only during the spring and fall migrations. They include northern harrier, ruby-crowned kinglet, olive-sided flycatcher, blackpoll warbler, northern Parula, and white-crowned sparrow, a handsome creature with a rakish black-and-white-striped head.

On the ponds and reservoirs you may see ring-necked duck (sometimes in large flocks), black scoter, common merganser, red-breasted merganser, and other species of waterfowl.

Reptiles: The many ponds, lakes, reservoirs, streams, swamps, marshes, and vernal pools within October Mountain means that in this vast area you may well find most of Berkshire's native species, given enough searching. Snapping, painted, and wood turtles are common, and one rare species, the spotted turtle, may occur here also. Sightings of the latter should be documented and reported to state wildlife officials. This turtle, which frequents flooded meadows and vernal pools, has a dark shell covered with small yellow spots.

All the snakes native to Berkshire, except the eastern timber rattlesnake, live within the woodlands, fields, and wetlands of the state forest. The most numerous species are the common garter, ringneck, red-bellied, northern brown, smooth green, and milk snakes. The ribbon snake may also occur here.

To find most snakes, you'll have to seek out their preferred haunts: rocky, sunlit spots, grassy fields with places for concealment such as rocks, and logs and wetland edges where they can capture frogs and fish (garter and water snakes). Many snakes are nocturnal, and finding them requires some searching. Be sure to replace overturned rocks and logs (as well as the animals) to their original positions.

Amphibians: All the native frogs dwell within the many natural communities. The most common are bull and green (beaver ponds), pickerel (wet vegetation), spring peeper (vegetation near water), wood (forest floor; vernal pools in early spring), and American toad (ponds and woodlands). Science has recently discovered that wood frogs are able to survive freezing, a remarkable ability they share with spring peepers and painted turtles. It seems that the frogs are able to survive just below the leaf litter because of two remarkable adaptations: their blood contains an antifreeze that lowers its freezing point, and when temperatures fall low enough, the water within the animals' cells is expelled into the body cavity. Were this not so, the cells would freeze and rupture!

All the local salamanders, of which there are nine species, live in the state forest. One of the most attractive and plentiful is the red-spotted newt, which inhabits beaver ponds. It is about three inches long, has a vertically flattened tail, which it uses for propulsion, and has a row of red spots on each side of its yellowish body. This interesting creature also has a land-dwelling stage more apt to come to your attention: the bright red-orange (advertising a poisonous skin to potential predators) salamander is known as red eft. They are a common sight on forest trails during wet weather in summer.

Since the state forest contains many vernal pools, the spotted and Jefferson salamanders (called "mole" salamanders because they spend most of their lives underground) reside here. You may see them on rainy nights in early spring, crossing roads that traverse the forest; many run afoul of vehicles, unfortunately. One biologist I know was involved in the installation of salamander tunnels below a busy roadway in the Western Massachusetts town of Amherst.

Clear brooks and springs are where you might be lucky enough to find spring, dusky, and two-lined salamanders, given that you look under enough flat stones. The last two are fairly numerous, while the first (large and orange-brown) is uncommon in Berkshire.

Another of the uncommon types is the four-toed salamander, classified as a Species of Special Concern by the state. They are usually found in bogs and wet areas where sphagnum moss grows. It is on the moss that the female lays and guards her gelatinous eggs.

The hardwood forest floor, under the leaf litter and rotting logs, is the daytime retreat of the abundant red-backed salamander. It is usually the most readily found species and perhaps the most abundant vertebrate in the entire area.

Fish: Ponds and streams here contain a variety of fishes, including brown and brook trout, pumpkinseed (a colorful sunfish), and blacknose dace. Beaver ponds host populations of brown bullhead and yellow perch, too. The state forest is bordered on the west by the Housatonic River. (For information regarding species found in the Housatonic, see Ch. 14.)

Seasonal Highlights

Spring is a time of renewal after a long season of dormancy for many plants and animals. Check for spotted and Jefferson salamanders making their overland treks on their way to vernal pools on rainy nights in early April. The brief blooming periods of many woodland wildflowers should be an impetus for you to get out often to find what's in bloom. Mid-April is when these "spring ephemerals" usually reach their peak. In April listen and look at dusk for the courtship flights of male American woodcock in open areas near water. Their spiraling, twittering flights are one of my favorite rites of spring. Somewhat later, after the leaves have begun to grow and, in turn, the insects have begun feasting on the tender foliage, the northward flight of birds brings them into the area during a time of plenty.

Mid-June is a perfect time to visit a bog, since that is when many bog plants put forth their blossoms: bog cranberry with its tiny pink flowers, Labrador tea shrubs with clusters of white flowers, and insect-catching pitcher plants all bloom upon the sphagnum mat.

The fields come into their own in July with tall species of flowers (many of which are yellow), and pink blooming meadowsweet shrubs. Over the fields flutter numerous colorful butterflies: Atlantis fritillary (which is especially abundant here), meadow fritillary, red-spotted purple (a species that includes white admiral), and eyed brown, to name just a few of the more than 45 species that occur in the area. The fields at the intersection of West Branch and Whitney Place roads are a good place to observe these delicate creatures.

Meanwhile, birds are nesting, and visits to various natural communities — hardwoods, mixed forest, conifer stands, fields, bogs and wetlands, ponds and reservoirs — will show you warblers, thrushes, flycatchers, vireos, swallows, and lots of others. Take along a field guide. Woodlands near water are particularly productive. Listen for the ethereal, flutelike song of the Swainson's thrush, an uncommon bird that usually nests only in the highest locations of Berkshire. The Nashville warbler is an attractive small bird, bluish-gray above and yellow below, found in cool, boggy sites.

This is also a good time of year for seeking out amphibians, usually by a combination of sound and sight in the case of our frogs.

Beginning in late summer and continuing into mid-fall, many species of goldenrod and aster bloom in fields and along woodland edges. Look for flat-topped aster in cool, moist swamps. Many insects collect nectar and pollen from the bountiful blossoms. Various species of blue gentians bloom in sunny spots during this season.

The beauty of the woodlands in late September and early October is well known to residents and visitors alike. Red maples, especially characteristic of wetland communities, are among the first to turn, with a brilliant crimson display. These same wetlands are where you'll observe beavers busily putting in provisions in preparation for winter. Dawn and dusk are the best times to observe these large vegetarian rodents.

Another cavalcade of migrant birds moves through the area. Check the ponds and reservoirs for ring-necked ducks and other waterfowl in October. Hawks are also on the move, and you may witness dozens or even hundreds of broad-winged hawks "kettling" upward on a thermal and then gliding off toward the south.

In winter the many miles of roads and trails make this a wonderful place to view the landscape from cross-country skis (see *Skiing*). The conifer stands may harbor the elusive "winter finches," and in some years roving bands of red or white-winged crossbills may be common. You may also find a small flock of pine grosbeaks feeding on berries along a woodland track. In the fields, common redpolls make an appearance some years, feeding on weed seeds and birch catkins.

Although black bears are inactive in their dens during this season, other large mammals are out and about. You may chance upon a coyote or perhaps a bobcat or fisher while on a walk or out for a drive. The mountain brooks and ponds are home to fish-eating river otter and mink. Watching otters frolic above the ice is something you won't soon forget. Even if you never see any of these animals, you're almost sure to find signs of them, especially if tracking conditions are favorable (a light coating of soft snow).

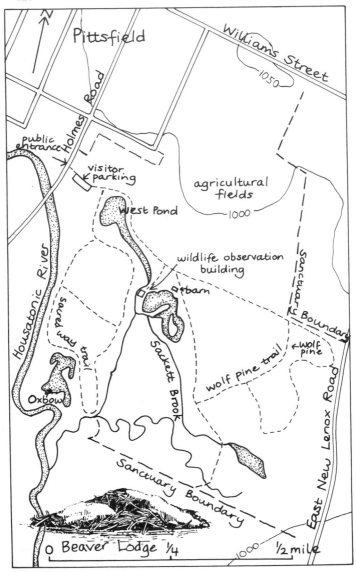

CANOE MEADOWS WILDLIFE SANCTUARY

✺ 16 ✺

CANOE MEADOWS WILDLIFE SANCTUARY
Pittsfield

Owned and managed by MAS.

Acreage: 262.

Elevation: 950—1,050 ft.

Trails: 3 mi.

Hours: Year-round except Mon. and major holidays. Also open most Mon. holidays. Trails open 7 to dusk. Cross-country skiing on weekends only.

Admission: Adults, $2; children 3-15 and persons 65 and over, $1; MAS members and children under 3, free. Programs and special events have different fees. Dogs, horses, vehicles, alcohlic beverages, and camping not allowed.

Facilities/Other: No office or rest rooms. Pit toilets available. For trail maps, bird checklists, or information contact MAS office at Pleasant Valley Wildlife Sanctuary, Lenox. Phone: 413-637-0320.

Directions: From Rte. 7/20 and Holmes Rd. in Lenox, take Holmes Rd. for 2.2 mi. to entrance on right. From Park Square in Pittsfield, take East St. E. to Elm St. Bear right on Elm St., follow to Holmes Rd. on right, and follow Holmes Rd. 1.0 mi. to sanctuary entrance on left. Parking and public entrance at Holmes Rd.

At Canoe Meadows you'll find a varied assemblage of natural communities just a mile and a half from downtown Pittsfield, making this a haven for city dwellers. On some portions of the property it is easy to forget that you are, after all, very near the most populous city in the county. The sanctuary, bordering the Housatonic River, has wetlands teeming with life, as well as natural meadows, agricultural fields, upland forest, and bottomland woods, making it a rewarding and convenient place to observe wildlife. A small wildlife observation building acts as a blind that enables visitors to observe wetland creatures. A huge, spreading white pine, many feet in girth and known as the Wolf Pine, is situated along the trail of the same name. To find it, follow the maintenance road into the sanctuary to the trail-head on the left, opposite the red storage barn. Massachusetts Audubon Society staff conduct programs here year-round; obtain the seasonal program schedule by contacting the MAS office in Lenox.

Views and Vistas

Just beyond the parking lot, an idyllic, pastoral setting greets you. West Pond is in front of you toward your right, with the rounded hills of October Mountain State Forest as a backdrop. If in the summer you visit the Massachusetts Audubon Society's Community Gardens Project — some 150 garden plots located at 350 William Street (turn into the graveled drive and proceed straight ahead slowly and park) — you will be rewarded not only by the sight of colorful and well-maintained vegetable and flower gardens, but by perhaps the most panoramic, non-summit view to be had anywhere in Pittsfield, all laid out before you. Looking southward, the Lenox-Stockbridge Mountain Ridge (2,126 ft.) is to your right, while the October Mountain upland (Berkshire Plateau) is on your left.

Plant Communities

Although there are upland hardwood forests at Canoe Meadows, the visually dominant communities, as its name suggests, are fields, both natural and agricultural. The most attractive of these are to be found bordering the Housatonic, traversed along their periphery by the Sacred Way Trail. To reach it, take the trail to the right from just below the parking lot. It leads along West Pond, then curves to the left, crossing a concrete-slab bridge over the outlet stream of the pond. The low-lying fields are wet meadows vegetated with sedges, reed canary grass, and clumps of speckled alder and pussy willow shrubs. Along the brook grows a thicket of red-twigged red-osier dogwood shrubs, draped with wild cucumber vines that produce prickly fruit. In winter, you can see the fibrous skeleton of the fruit, which held the seeds.

The higher fields beyond are sandy and dry, with an almost solid growth of *Spiraea* (meadowsweet and steeple-bush). Here and there, small white pines, white (paper) birches, and northern red oaks are establishing themselves. Where the trail makes a sharp turn to the left you will see an oxbow pond on the opposite side. This was once the river channel, now isolated from the Housatonic. On its surface in summer are yellow pond-lilies. Here, too, the trail passes very close to an enormous black maple, an unusual species in Berkshire, and then proceeds through a stand of young gray birches and quaking aspen. Beavers have altered the floodplain landscape where Sackett Brook enters the river in the southwestern corner of the sanctuary. Red maples and other trees tolerant of wet soils, including a majestic American sycamore with its strikingly mottled light-and-dark trunk, border the waterway. Other floodplain trees include silver maple, box elder, and American elm. Tall yellow Canada lilies bloom along the trail in early summer.

The trail turns sharply left at this point and continues along the opposite side of the *Spiraea* fields and then down to skirt a large swampy area with many aspens on your right. Water, backed up by beaver activity, has killed many trees, but in the process has also created a rich wildlife habitat. The trail then proceeds through shrubby wet areas of pussy willow (which sport their fuzzy catkins as early as late February), alder shrubs, and tussock sedges, and then follows along West Pond's edge back to the concrete bridge. In summer, the calm waters of the pond often have a green layer of tiny floating plants called duckweed. Each has a pair of "rootlets" that hang down from the underside of the tiny floating pad.

Although the 40 acres or so of hayfields contain few native plants, they make for a pleasant pastoral scene and in summer are filled with such flowers as tall buttercup, bedstraw (used by pioneers to stuff mattresses), and purple cow-vetch, intermingled among the grasses. Along the maintenance road and in the wetter portions of Sacred Way Trail, sizable stands of milkweed, the monarch caterpillar's sole diet, attract a great variety of beautiful butterflies and other interesting insects in June and July.

You should also sample some of the sanctuary's woodlands by proceeding down the maintenance road, with planted red pines to your left and native white pines to your right. Tall, yellow-flowered cup plant blooms along the wet margin of the road near the storage barn in early August. Its paired leaves form "cups" along the plant stem, trapping rainwater.

The Wolf Pine Trail head is indicated by a blue sign on your left, opposite the red storage barn. Proceeding through shady damp hemlock woods that sport abundant wildflower blooms in spring, this trail takes its name from the impressive spreading hulk of a white pine that grew to its enormous proportions, with multiple trunks, when this was an open field. It may have been left to provide shade for livestock. Contrast this wolf tree with the tall, straight trunks of white pines that grew up in competitive environments among other pines.

When the trail exits the forest, turn right to proceed back toward the parking lot. On the way, you'll pass through an eastern hemlock grove with many large trees, followed by a wooded wetland that may remind you of a southern swamp. In spring and summer you'll see the unusual skunk cabbage (so called because the crushed plant has a fetid odor), as well as many other wildflowers, like the beautiful, shiny yellow marsh marigold (a buttercup).

Wildlife

Mammals: As at the Massachusetts Audubon Society's other area property, Pleasant Valley, a large and active beaver population lives here. Felled trees and stumps are visible along various parts of the Sacred Way Trail. For a look at one of their lodges, walk the maintenance road to just past the red barn and look to your right into the large swamp. Beavers here as elsewhere become active at dusk generally, so don't expect to see them during daylight hours. If you do see a beaverlike creature in the water it will most likely be a muskrat. Also, large river otters seek fish in the ponds and are occasionally spotted. White-tailed deer are especially common in the overgrown fields and bottomland woods. You will certainly see their tracks, if nothing more. Deer, raccoons, and even sometimes black bear find ample food in the agricultural fields during late summer. Red foxes are especially common in open country, and you may be fortunate enough to see one patrolling the hayfields in search of rodents such as the abundant meadow vole. It is a real thrill to see one of these handsome animals following in the wake of a haying machine as its rodent food becomes suddenly vulnerable. Gray foxes occur here, too, but it is unusual to see one. These foxes can and do climb trees! Other species include coyote, red and gray squirrels, eastern chipmunk, woodchuck, big brown bat, meadow jumping mouse, short-tailed and masked shrews, star-nosed mole (a creature with a bizarre, 22-tentacled snout), white-footed mouse, opossum, and striped skunk.

Birds: Canoe Meadows is an excellent place to watch birds. To date, 175 species have been recorded. The wide variety of plant communities and the presence of the Housatonic River as a migration corridor make this possible. Any time of year can be productive, and the trail system makes for easy access. Grassland birds such as the bobolink breed in the hayfields near William Street. The bubbling territorial song of the strikingly colored and polygamous (they mate with more than one female) males is given in flight — a fascinating visual and auditory display. The birds return from their wintering grounds in southern South America by late May. Along the wooded edges of the hayfields you'll often see the incredibly blue male indigo bunting. His brilliant color, by the way, is caused by feather structure, refracting sunlight in a certain way, rather than by pigment; in the shade these birds appear blackish.

Wetland species are well represented, too. American

black ducks, mallards, and the regal wood ducks nest in the wooded swamps. Green herons are suspected nesters. Great blue herons, while not breeding at Canoe Meadows, often stalk fish and frogs in West Pond and other sanctuary water bodies. The wildlife observation buildling is a good place from which to scan the pond for all these. Check the swamps in spring and summer for northern waterthrush, which is actually a warbler. Where the maintenance road and the far end of Wolf Pine Trail meet is a good spot to listen for one. In late August and September a great egret may even show up at West Pond. These large, stately, all-white birds are unmistakable. The noisy, somewhat comical belted king-fisher with its ragged blue crest is a virtual fixture at the pond in summer. You might be fortunate enough to see one plunging into the water and emerging with a fish.

The wet fields along the Sacred Way Trail are a good place to see two of the less common species of small fly-catchers: alder and willow. The only reliable way to tell them apart is by their songs. During migration, you might catch a glimpse of the larger olive-sided flycatcher sitting on top of one of the dead trees. Other spring migrants you may see are solitary and spotted sandpipers along the pond shores in mid-May, and tail-wagging palm warblers in the brushy fields. One of the most abundant and beautiful nest-ing birds is the yellow warbler. You can easily observe the attractive blue-green and white tree swallows entering and exiting their nest boxes between the pond and the parking area. Other breeding species you may see here include swamp sparrow, brown thrasher, warbling vireo, and purple finch. A June walk along the short Sacred Way Trail will allow you to see or hear an average of 45 species.

A variety of uncommon to rare species have been spot-ted during recent years at Canoe Meadows, including the Acadian flycatcher, yellow-breasted chat, lark sparrow, clay-colored sparrow, laughing gull, and even yellow-crowned night herons, which were suspected of nesting.

The woodlands, although not extensive, are large enough to accommodate birds like ruffed grouse, veery, tufted titmouse, and a variety of wood warblers, including the pine warbler. This uncommon Berkshire bird has been found in the large white pines near the storage barn in June, indicating possible nesting. Birders are as likely to see the huge pileated woodpecker at Canoe Meadows as anywhere. You will usually hear red-breasted nuthatches giving their nasal calls as you walk through the shady pine groves. Barred owls and great horned owls occur in the deep woods but are much more often heard than seen. Usually it will be the raucous sound of mobbing crows that will attract your attention. Great horned owls begin nesting in January.

The sanctuary's open expanses make this a good place to see hawks — red-tailed and sometimes American kestrel, and Cooper's during the breeding season. Kestrels have nested in cavities on the property several times in recent years. In late summer and early fall, migrating species such as sharp-shinned and broad-winged hawks liven up the mix. Check West Pond, where you may experience the thrill of seeing an osprey plunging into the water after a fish. One mid-November day I was very excited to witness a golden eagle passing high overhead. Other fall migrants include the Savannah sparrow, rusty blackbird (wetlands), and yellow-rumped warbler. The agricultural fields are good places to search for water pipit flocks and killdeer in late fall.

Among the species that move into the area for the winter are American tree sparrows. Northern shrikes sometimes stop off for a time at Canoe Meadows. Robins are even found here in some winters near wetlands where fruit is still plentiful. You should be able to find a flock of cedar waxwings, and a few white-throated sparrows are present all winter long here. Perhaps the most unusual event I've witnessed at Canoe Meadows involving a bird occurred one day in mid-October when a live song sparrow, completely entangled by the hooked seeds of a burdock, was found by our birding group. We released it unharmed.

Reptiles: The painted turtle is the most often seen reptile. Besides seeing these creatures sunning themselves on logs, you might come upon one in late May searching for a place to bury its eggs. They prefer sandy, well-drained soils. Snapping turtles, too, walk about in mid-June along the graveled maintenance road and in recently mowed hayfields, searching for a place to lay their eggs. The state-listed wood turtle also lives at Canoe Meadows. Massachusetts Audubon Society staff, in an attempt to learn more about this animal's life history, fitted several with radio transmitters and tracked their movements. They spend their summers in hayfields and wet meadows and move to stream bottoms for the winter.

The common garter is the only snake you are likely to see. One of the most spellbinding examples of "survival of the fittest" that I've witnessed involved a garter in the process of swallowing a wood frog it had captured. The frog's loud defense screams were startling. Milk snakes are found in the Sacred Way fields but are seldom seen.

Amphibians: Frogs are abundant. From the largest (bullfrog) to the smallest (spring peeper), frogs are one of the most obvious forms of wildlife. Huge male bullfrogs with yellow throats can be seen guarding and actively defending their piece of West Pond from others of their own kind. The ringing chorus of spring peepers represents one of the earliest signs that spring has arrived. Other species found here are green, pickerel, leopard (unusual in Massachusetts), and wood frogs, and the American toad (in river floodplain fields).

Fish: As you might suspect, the sanctuary has abundant fish life, owing to all the watery habitats available to them. Brook and brown trout live and reproduce in the cool, fast-flowing brooks that have their sources in the October Mountain plateau to the east. Species adapted to warmer, less oxygen-rich waters such as white sucker, longnose sucker, common shiner, longnose dace, fall fish, and goldfish live in the Housatonic. The most interesting fish-watching can be had at West Pond in late spring, especially if water levels are low. Take the Sacred Way Trail to the backside of West Pond and look into the shallow waters along shore for the circular depressions that are the nests of pumpkinseeds (a sunfish). In late May you'll be able to observe each female guarding her nest and chasing off other intruding fish that may happen to stray too close for the owner's comfort.

Seasonal Highlights

For early spring wildflowers, walk Wolf Pine Trail. Species such as bloodroot, painted trillium, foamflower, and jack-in-the-pulpit are common here. Spring bird migration makes this an exciting time to be in the fields or woodlands of the sanctuary.

In summer, the meadows and uncut hayfields burst with wildflowers. Watch for the wide variety of butterfly species in the open areas. Birds are nesting, and a tour of both the Sacred Way and Wolf Pine trails will show you a wide variety of species. Of course this is when birds are most vocal and your chances of finding them are best. Bobolinks put on quite a show in the hayfields through mid-July.

Following the fall corn harvest, large flocks of Canada geese can be found daily, gleaning the leftovers from the stubbled fields. Although locally breeding geese have become somewhat of a nuisance here, as elsewhere in the Northeast, the disciplined formations and melancholy calls of migrating Canada geese are still among the most beautiful sights and sounds that can be experienced. If you are very fortunate you might even see a flock of white snow geese in the fields in November with the Canadas; they are on their way to the mid-Atlantic coast from their Arctic breeding grounds. Fall is also the season during which migrant sparrows such as Lincoln's and the white-crowned make a brief appearance. Among the best places to see them are the weedy edges at the Community Gardens. The striking fall foliage in early October is an added bonus.

Even in winter, birds such as the northern cardinal, northern mockingbird, and American tree sparrow are still common along the Sacred Way Trail. A walk through the woodlands will enable you to see golden-crowned kinglets, woodpeckers, and brown creepers, among others. The dead and dried stalks of flowers and "weeds" can be beautiful in their own right; it's fun to test your identification skills. Tracking in the snow is also entertaining, and in addition to the tracks of many species of mammals you may also find evidence of ruffed grouse and wild turkey.

When enough snow has fallen, Canoe Meadows is also an excellent place to cross-country ski (weekends only). The trails are wide and mostly level — good conditions for the beginner, or anyone desiring a slow-paced outing (see *Skiing*). This is also a great way in which to appreciate the stark beauty of the winter landscape.

✺ 17 ✺

CENTRAL BERKSHIRE LAKES
Pittsfield, Lanesborough, Richmond

Public areas on Onota and Pontoosuc lakes operated by Pittsfield Parks Commission. Beach at Richmond Pond owned and operated by town of Richmond.

Acreage: (Water surfaces) Onota, 617; Pontoosuc, 470; Richmond Pond, 217.

Elevation: (Water surfaces) Onota, 1,078 ft.; Pontoosuc 1,098 ft.; Richmond Pond, 1,122 ft.

Hours: Burbank Park (Onota Lake) and Pontoosuc Park, sunrise to 8 p.m. No hours posted at Richmond Pond boat ramp.

Admission: None.

Facilities/Other: Rest rooms at Burbank Park (Onota) summer only, phone. 413-442-6662. No rest rooms at Richmond Pond; phone: 413-698-3355 (town hall).

Directions: For Burbank Park at Onota Lake: From Park Square in Pittsfield, take West St. W. for approx. 1.25 mi. to Valentine Rd.; turn right onto Valentine Rd. and go N. for approx. 0.8 mi. to Lakeway Dr. Turn left onto Lakeway and follow it to Burbank Park. Parking available at boat ramp; for beach area, continue to the right at road split before boat ramp. For Pontoosuc Park, turn onto Hancock Rd. from Rte. 7 just S. of lake; entrance is on right. Two other public access points for Pontoosuc Lake are the beaches at the ends of Sunrise Street (in Lanesborough) and Narragansett Avenue (walk down dirt track on left). Richmond public beach and boat ramp: From Park Square in Pittsfield, travel S. on Rte. 7 for approx. 0.25 mi. to Rte. 20. Turn right (W.) onto Rte. 20 and follow it for approx. 1 mi. to Barker Rd. Turn left onto Barker Rd. and proceed 3 mi. to Boys' Club Rd. (opposite Bartlett's Orchard). Turn right onto Boys' Club Rd., stay left and follow it (it later becomes Richmond Shores Rd. and then Beach Rd.) for 1.2 mi. to boat ramp. Beach area is a 0.25 mi. walk N. past gate on graveled road.

All three lakes, two of which (Pontoosuc and Richmond Pond) are impoundments, host large numbers of
waterfowl, especially during spring and fall. They are in
fact, collectively, the best places in Berkshire to observe
waterfowl — not surprising, after all, since these lakes are
the closest thing that Berkshirites have to a coast. The lakes
are situated in a north-south-trending valley, in the center
of what is called the Berkshire lime belt, because the underlying rocks are primarily limestone and marble. Glaciers
were responsible for gouging out, in the soft limestone bedrock, the deeper parts of the valley, which are now occupied by the lakes.

Views and Vistas

All three lakes serve as scenic foregrounds for unobstructed views, either of summits within Pittsfield State
Forest (see Ch. 18) or, in the case of Richmond Pond, Lenox
Mountain. Pontoosuc Lake lies just east of the rounded
peaks of the Taconic Range. A small park, owned and managed by the city of Pittsfield and known as Pontoosuc Park,
affords very picturesque views through tall pines from a
high point above the south end of the lake. From this vantage point near the dam, you'll see the Taconics to your left:
from south to north, Berry, Honwee (2,313 ft.), and Potter
mountains and the double hump of Mount Greylock (3,491
ft.) straight ahead to the north. The uppermost portion of
Greylock is technically a monadnock, a geologist's name for
a residual mountain mass that stands alone and above the
surrounding terrain.

You will find a somewhat different but still scenic view
of the Taconics from the boat ramp area at Burbank Park.
It's difficult to stand almost anywhere along the shores of
Onota Lake and not encounter a pleasing sight.

For an excellent view of the western flank of Lenox
Mountain (2,126 ft.), the public boat ramp at the southwest
corner of Richmond Pond (in Richmond) is hard to beat.
This view of the ridge is virtually unobstructed.

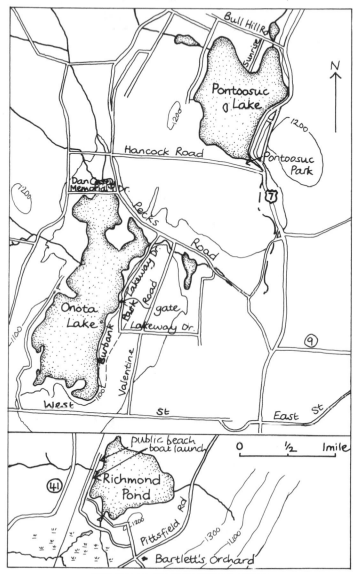

CENTRAL BERKSHIRE LAKES

Plant Communities

All three water bodies have a considerable number of homes, condominiums, cottages, and other structures along their shores. This is particularly true of Pontoosuc Lake, which is virtually ringed with dwellings. Richmond Pond and especially Onota Lake still possess some areas of natural vegetation near their shores. Burbank Park has a few hardwood stands reminiscent of wilder sites. The most obvious trees around the shoreline are tall white pines and gray birches. Richmond Pond has a narrow strip of woodlands along its western shore and extensive wetlands to its south.

For me the wetland plant communities, although most are limited in size and by no means pristine, hold the most interest. Small marsh lands exist at the northern end of Pontoosuc Lake (Bull Hill Rd., west off Rte. 7); at the north end of Onota Lake (Dan Casey Memorial Dr., between Churchill St. and Pecks Rd.); and at the southwest fringes of Richmond Pond near the boat ramp. They contain some of the most easily recognized wetland plants, such as cattail and yellow pond-lily.

There are more extensive marshes along the stream feeding into Richmond Pond, which can be seen from the road leading to the boat launch. The shrubs sweet gale (a member of the wax myrtle family), silky dogwood, and shining willow line the stream, and emergent plants such as bur reed, grass-leaved arrowhead, and marsh cinquefoil (five leaflets) colonize the muddy edges (beavers have flooded this area recently). Along the shorelines in these areas are red maple, white birch, and black ash.

The lake waters themselves contain submerged aquatic plants such as Eurasian milfoil, wild celery, elodea, and coontail. Nutrients entering the lakes from leaking septic systems accelerate the problem of weed growth in many Berkshire lakes. Like many alien plants that have no natural enemies here, milfoil grew quickly out of control, making the water in some lakes almost unusable.

One means that communities have employed in hopes of controlling this situation is the annual draw-down of lake levels, exposing and ultimately freezing the undesirable plants with the onset of winter. In Berkshire this is generally done in late October. Such drastic annual fluctuation of water levels, however, results in a brown zone around many area lakes devoid of most plant life. Other means of control, such as the use of chemical agents, are often more harmful in that they may destroy all aquatic vegetation, not just the undesirable milfoil.

The long-term solutions are to repair existing faulty septic systems and prohibit their placement in the future so close to water bodies.

Wildlife

Mammals: In the aquatic and semiaquatic environments along the shore, muskrats rank as one of the most common and easily observed creatures. They construct their lodges of cattails and mud, both of which are in good supply at Pontoosuc and Onota. Not only do the cattail leaves supply building materials, but the starchy roots serve also as nutritious food for the rodents. You can get a look at these lodges in the marshes at the north end of Onota Lake. Beavers are also widespread in Berkshire, and lakes bordered by woodlots can serve their needs as well. You can view recently constructed beaver lodges at the extreme north end of Onota Lake and along Beach Road at Richmond Pond. At the latter site, the rodents have built a dam up against a large culvert. It's possible you might even see a mink or river otter, if you're lucky. Also white-tailed deer regularly turn up here, as do other common mammals, especially those that have adapted well to human presence — gray squirrels, raccoons, opossums, and striped skunks.

Bats, both little and big brown species (the two common "house bats") establish their nursery colonies within easy reach of water bodies. In summer these colonies are made up solely of females and their young (they bear only one or two babies each year). Bats require ample supplies of water for drinking, and soon after emerging each evening at dusk they satisfy their thirst by skimming the surface of a lake, pond, or river. Our colonies are all located within one mile of water, and usually within a quarter-mile or less. Lakes are usually excellent places to find the flying insect food that bats require and therefore good places to observe flying bats — as most people who have fished from a boat at dusk can tell you. (Not to worry, the bats will not get caught in your hair!)

Birds: Although certainly a wide range of land birds will be found in the trees, shrubs, and fields surrounding these three lakes, it is the water birds (geese, ducks, loons, grebes, and coots) that make them noteworthy from a naturalist's perspective. During many visits to these lakes in the past eleven years, I have had the pleasure of seeing a total of 36 species of water birds. Ducks accounted for 23 of these.

Should you visit the Central Berkshire lakes during fall migration (and you should), you will likely see the following: common loon, pied-billed grebe, Canada goose, wood duck, American black duck, mallard, common goldeneye, bufflehead, hooded and common mergansers, and American coot.

A considerable variety of other species passes through each year in lesser numbers, including the red-throated loon, horned grebe, red-necked grebe, double-crested cormorant, snow goose, green-winged teal, blue-winged teal, gadwall, northern pintail, American wigeon, canvasback, ring-necked duck, lesser and greater scaup, oldsquaw, black, white-winged, and surf scoters, red-breasted merganser, and ruddy duck. From time to time the lakes produce some unusual or uncommon birds for this area, such as mute swan, northern shoveler, and brant, and even a rarity such as tundra swan. And once in a while the birding community is electrified by a sighting. On May 5, 1991, a flock of twelve king eider, an arctic species never before known to stop off here on its way to coastal waters, was found at Pontoosuc Lake. Unfortunately, they were beheld by only one observer with a camera.

If you visit the lakes from late October until just before freeze-up (generally from the end of November to mid-December in Central Berkshire), your chances of finding many of these species will be very good. A spotting telescope will aid your efforts greatly.

Waterfowl are by no means the only birds that seek out the lakes. Small numbers of a variety of species annually stop off here on their long journeys to the tropics. Although the annual lake draw-downs (which may be prohibited in the future by local conservation commissions) occur too late in the season to benefit many species that pass through as early as August and September, they do provide the mud-flat habitat in late fall that sandpipers and plovers are likely to search out. At places such as the north end of Pontoosuc Lake, where Town Brook, its major source, enters, and sometimes the area around the boat ramp at Richmond Pond, you will find killdeer, greater yellowlegs, pectoral sandpiper, and dunlin, provided you come often enough. Less frequently you'll encounter white-rumped sandpipers or black-bellied plovers. During November 1991 a Hudsonian godwit even stopped by for a week along what was then a marshy channel flowing into Richmond Pond at its south end. The motto here is: Be prepared, as you never know what might come your way!

The lake shores and marshes are also fine places to find the magnificent great blue heron, and you might get really lucky and spot a black-crowned night heron perched in a tree. Swamp sparrows nest in the marsh vegetation. Belted kingfishers are usually present at Onota, and migrating ospreys also search for fish over the lakes in fall.

Gulls, both ring-billed and herring (please don't call them sea gulls!) have become far more numerous in recent years. In the past they were a rare sight indeed at any season except winter. Ring-billed gulls, which breed to the north, are most numerous. Herring gulls are common enough, and the great black-backed gull, the largest, is becoming more so. A few Bonaparte's gulls show up each fall, and occasionally an Iceland or even glaucous gull puts in an appearance. There are even two sightings of lesser black-backed gulls on the books. During one outing at Onota, our birding group spied an immature ring-billed gull wearing a bird band around its right ankle. We later found that this bird had been banded as a chick on an island in Lake Champlain five months earlier — an interesting clue to the origins of our winter ring-billeds.

The mud flats and beaches are where you should go to find snow bunting and horned lark in November, and Richmond Pond is a reliable spot for rusty blackbird in October and November. Fall is the only time of year that they are true to their name. Merlins and sharp-shinned hawks sometimes stop off briefly in search of a bird meal on their way south. For swallows, try the utility wires at the Onota causeway (Dan Casey Drive); in spring and fall they are sometimes festooned with several swallow species, including the northern rough-winged.

Reptiles: You may find the common turtles of the area, snapping and eastern painted, in the less disturbed portions of the lakes. Look also for painted turtles in a small pond just south of Dan Casey Drive at the north end of Onota. I once came upon a tiny hatchling snapper on a graveled road adjacent to Richmond Pond in early September; it seemed to be headed for the lake.

Certainly the common garter snake, northern water snake, and other species occur at the lakes, but seeing one casually is an unusual occurrence.

Amphibians: As with the reptiles, the marshy and wooded portions of the lakes provide the requisite food and cover for amphibians. You will find most of the usual species here, including spring peeper, bull, pickerel, and green frogs, and the American toad. Likewise, the most common species of salamanders, red-backed (in woodlands) and red-spotted newt (in shallow portions of the lakes and their backwaters), have sizable populations.

Fishes: All three lakes contain significant fish populations, with Onota having the greatest variety. Such game species as largemouth bass, chain pickerel (its sides have a dark, chainlike pattern), northern pike, and tiger muskellunge (Pontoosuc) sometimes reach record proportions in these lakes. Tiger muskies, as they're known, are specifically managed by the Massachusetts Division of Fisheries and Wildlife. Smaller types such as bluegill, pumpkinseed, and yellow perch are also present in large numbers.

A variety of other fish species lives in the lakes, including golden shiner, common shiner, and white sucker. As you stand looking out over Pontoosuc Lake, for instance, you may see numerous silvery fish leaping out of the water. These are white suckers. An unusual species in this area, yellow bullhead, has been found in Pontoosuc, and white catfish are found only in Onota.

Notably, Town Brook, which empties into Pontoosuc at its north end, is the only place in the state that has all three species of trout reproducing; but only the brook trout is native to Berkshire.

Seasonal draw-downs of Richmond Pond have adversely affected the fishery, according to Leo Daly, fisheries manager, Region 7 of the MDF&W. In the future, such draw-downs will be allowed only for flood control, not weed control, thereby improving the conditions for many species of fish life.

A large percentage of fish that now call these lakes home are not native. MDF&W stocking programs are responsible for some of them, while people simply releasing their bait fish into these waters are the causes of other, inadvertent introductions. As an example, a bowfin, an odd-looking and primitive fish with a long dorsal (top) fin, turned up in Onota once! Check with the local people at the lake edge to find out what's biting.

Seasonal Highlights

In spring, waterfowl pass through Berkshire and stop off on area lakes to rest and feed. Don't expect to see the numbers or variety of ducks that show up in fall, however. Some species are reliable here even in spring (March and early April). These include American wigeon, ring-necked duck, lesser and greater scaup, common goldeneye, buffle-head, and common merganser (a fish eater). Others are possible. You can always count on seeing the nesting spe-cies: American black duck, mallard, and of course Canada goose, whose population has grown tremendously here as elsewhere in the Northeast. There was a time when these big birds didn't nest south of James Bay in Canada. How times change!

Summer is a relatively quiet time. Except for the local nesters, waterfowl activity on the lakes comes to a virtual standstill after April. You can still find plenty of beautiful wood ducks at Onota Lake, though. If you park along the causeway at the north end, they will likely swim right up to you, making for excellent photo opportunities. Not sport-ing, perhaps, but effective. One word of advice, however: Don't feed the wildlife (unfortunately, too many people do so already).

Fall migrant waterfowl activity begins in early October and builds throughout the month, peaking in early to mid-November. It then declines to just before freeze-up. The lakes are sometimes teeming with waterfowl at this season; but it can be feast or famine, depending largely upon the passage of weather fronts and other variables. In any event, you should visit early in the day, before fishing and other human activities have had a chance to frighten away the more timid among the flocks. Each year, on a weekend day in early November, the local Hoffmann Bird Club conducts its annual waterfowl census. It's a lot of fun and a wonder-ful opportunity to learn from people who can tell apart lesser and greater scaups! The census includes these three lakes, as well as a number of others in the county. While you're out there, don't neglect to search for other feathered migrants on shores and in woodlands. A beautiful white flock of snow buntings is always a memorable sight. Bartlett's Orchard on Pittsfield Road, near Richmond Pond, is a great place to warm up and fortify one's self on a cold day.

When mild weather delays the freeze-up, your search for waterfowl can last well into December, which was the case in 1990 and 1991. Even after the ice takes hold, the views of the hills across the frozen expanses will make your visit to the lakes worthwhile. Just be sure to dress for the north winds.

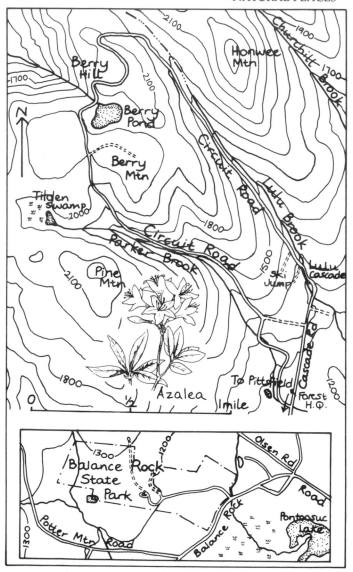

PITTSFIELD S.F. & BALANCE ROCK S.P.

✤ 18 ✤

PITTSFIELD STATE FOREST AND
BALANCE ROCK STATE PARK
Pittsfield, Lanesborough, Hancock

Managed by DEM.

Acreage: 10,960.

Elevation: 1,115—2,313 ft.

Trails: 45 mi.

Hours: Year-round; office hours, 8-5.

Admission: Hikers free; camping $5 per night per vehicle.

Facilities/Other: Pittsfield State Forest campgrounds situated near main entrance and at Berry Pond; interpretive materials and information available at office beyond entrance gate. Phone: 413-442-8992. Rest rooms available at both locations. Public programs conducted July to Sept.

Directions: For main entrance to Pittsfield State Forest: From Park Square in Pittsfield, take West St. W. for 2.7 mi. to Churchill St. Turn right onto Churchill and proceed N. for 1.7 mi. to Cascade St. Turn left onto Cascade and follow it, staying right, to the forest entrance in 0.7 mi. After stopping at gatehouse, proceed straight ahead. This becomes the one-way Berry Pond Circuit Road (at Lulu Day Use Area). To reach Balance Rock State Park in Lanesborough, included within state forest, take Rte. 7 from Park Square in Pittsfield N. for approx. 2.3 mi. to Hancock Road at the light. Turn left onto Hancock Road and proceed W. for approx. 1.5 mi. to Pecks Road. Turn right onto Pecks (which becomes Balance Rock Rd. — stay left where road splits) and follow it N. for 1.75 mi. from the split to park entrance on left.

This is one of Massachusetts' larger state forests and contains an extensive tract of northern hardwoods, overlying the peaks of the Taconic Range (Honwee Mountain, capped by a tower, is the highest at 2,313 ft.) along the Massachusetts-New York border. Highlights include Berry Pond (15 acres, and the highest natural water body in the state at 2,050 ft.), mountain azalea blooms that are noted for their beauty in early June (can vary) along the upper end of Berry Pond Circuit Road, and an easily accessible summit: Berry Hill (2,150 ft.), a well-known hawk-watching site. Balance Rock State Park in Lanesborough features a large glacial erratic that is also worth a visit. This 165-ton marble boulder was left here by the retreating ice sheet thousands of years ago. Since then, soil and loose rock have been removed by the forces of erosion, leaving the boulder in a seemingly precariously balanced position. The original source of the boulder and others in the upper reaches of the Housatonic Valley is probably close by, since this location is at the western edge of the lime belt that runs north-south through the central valleys of Berkshire. As you walk around Balance Rock, observe how nearly horizontal grooves have been weathered into it through the solution action of water. It is unfortunate that the rock itself is covered largely with graffiti (some dating from the 19th century) despite periodic removal by forest staff.

Views and Vistas

A panorama of neighboring New York state, including the tall office buildings of its capital, Albany, is available from the hawk watch site, just above the informal parking area at the highest point of the road. You can park off the road here on the right. If you take the path up the hillside, you will reward yourself with other impressive views to the north and west, including the Helderberg Escarpment in New York. (To find out about a fine view of the northern Taconic Range from the valley, see Ch. 17.)

Plant Communities

Berry Pond Circuit Road will take you up through about 1,000 feet or so of elevation, enabling you to see the variety of trees found in the northern hardwood forest: sugar maple, yellow birch, American beech, and eastern hemlock, to mention a few. Understory trees characteristically include striped maple, ironwood, and shadbush, which blooms in late April. The shrub layer is dominated by hobblebush (large white flower heads in May resembling hydrangea) and mountain laurel. The moist forest floor in many spots is covered with partridgeberry, goldthread, wood sorrel, and a multitude of early blooming spring wild-flowers including dutchman's breeches, painted trillium, wild ginger, and sharp-lobed hepatica. Mountain azaleas line upper portions of the road and produce a gorgeous spectacle of fragrant pink blossoms in late May and early June (call office for peak dates).

On summits, trees tend to be of smaller stature. Mountain ash is a small tree that will charm you in fall with its large clusters of bright red berries. Pleasing to the palate as well as the eye is highbush blueberry, which forms dense stands near the summit. The delicious berries ripen in August. Not so tasty are the fruits of abundant chokeberry shrubs that form thickets here.

Studies of the Berry Pond bottom sediments have opened a fascinating botanical history book of sorts, shedding light on vegetation and climate since the glaciers melted some 12,000 years ago. Fossilized pollen grains in these sediments reveal that, first, sedges were present, then spruces, and as the climate warmed, birches and pines became dominant, followed in succession by hemlock, maples, oaks, hickories, and American chestnut. The common trees now are northern red oak, red maple, American beech, and yellow and white birches.

You'll find the remnants of an unusual and interesting natural community at Tilden Swamp, located at the 2,000-foot elevation. It can be reached from Taconic Skyline Trail off Berry Pond Road or from the Parker Brook Trail. After you pass Berry Pond on the Circuit Road and start downhill, look for a gravel road on the left; 800 feet farther down the Circuit Road on the right is the start of the trail. At a fork bear left, and left again at the blue triangles. The actions over the past few years of North America's largest rodent, the beaver, have nearly obliterated, at least for now, the former bog community. The animals, which reside in three lodges (two of which are bank lodges), have constructed a formidable dam at the southeastern end of the swamp, now actually a pond. It is one of the highest I have seen anywhere! Beavers have felled virtually all pole-sized understory trees — American beech (which sprouts profusely), witch hazel, red maple, and even some tough red oaks, from a concentric ring 80 to 100 feet wide around the pond. They have also created two tiny ponds above Tilden Swamp where the source stream enters it.

The rising water inundated most of the bog plants. Pitcher plant and round-leaved sundew once grew abundantly along the boggy swamp margins. A few pitcher plants still remain on a small islet of sphagnum moss between two of the lodges. These plants are unmistakable, with their upturned green-and-red pitchers. Downward-pointing bristles line the interior; unsuspecting insects that enter rarely escape. The pitchers often contain water that includes compounds which set quickly to work digesting unfortunate captives. A few sundews, which are small and less conspicuous than the larger pitcher plants, also remain. The sundew's *modus operandi* is different but equally effective. Its leaves have numerous projections covered with a sweet but very sticky substance; insects that come to feast are held fast. Both plants have evolved carnivorous habits in order to obtain needed minerals not available to them in the nutrient-poor, acidic soil. Another holdover from the swamp is leatherleaf, a shrub of the shallow pond margins.

Blue swamp (marsh) skullcap blossoms, and water smartweed produces handsome bright-pink flower clubs six inches above the water surface in July. You may see the massive dug-up rootstock of yellow pond-lily (as thick as your forearm), a favorite beaver food, floating near the dam. When the amphibious rodents eventually abandon this site, after exhausting their food plants, the water level will drop as their dam falls into disrepair. The bog community, a relict of the ice ages, may eventually flourish again.

Wildlife

Mammals: Black bear, coyote, and bobcat occur here. All have been recorded near the office in summer. As with other large heavily wooded tracts in Berkshire, Pittsfield State Forest is home to many species, including but not limited to porcupine, gray fox, mink, striped skunk, raccoon, opossum, and the very common white-tailed deer. Bishops Field across from the picnic area is a good place to see deer. Although you may see only rabbits, squirrels, and chipmunks, the thrill of sighting one of the less often encountered species is worth the extra time and effort; spending the night in the campground will give you a head start. You might be rewarded by hearing the yips, barks, and howls of a coyote family.

Birds: Watch for eastern bluebirds and tree swallows in late spring and early summer in the farm fields just outside the entrance. The forest supports a rich bird life. In summer you may encounter ruffed grouse, winter wren, wood thrush, veery, red-eyed vireo, yellow-bellied sapsucker, eastern wood pewee, black-throated green and black-throated blue warbler (the last especially in laurel thickets), and scarlet tanager, among others. At higher elevations you might find a Swainson's thrush. At Tilden Swamp, spotted sandpiper and common yellowthroat (a warbler with a black mask) are sometimes seen. At Berry Pond look for Canada geese and wood ducks in early October. The belted kingfisher is possible, too. It gets its name from the blue band across its white breast; females have a chestnut-colored band in addition to the blue one.

But without doubt the birding highlight of the year here takes place from the end of August through the first half of November, when numerous southbound raptors (predatory birds) are seen from the traditional hawk-watching site. If you're able to make several visits during the fall, you will no doubt see broad-winged, Cooper's, sharp-shinned, and red-tailed hawks, as well as American kestrel, merlin, northern harrier, turkey vulture, and flocks of com-

mon ravens. Each season a few peregrine falcons and bald
eagles are seen from this vantage point. The super-fast per-
egrines are among the most sought-after birds. Late in the
season, beginning at the end of October, even a small number of magnificent golden eagles pay their respects. One
reason this spot is so good for hawk watching is its unobstructed views (kept open by forest staff) to the east, north,
and west. At times you may actually be looking down on
the birds. Hawks follow the Taconic Range because it enables them to take advantage of updrafts created when
southbound air currents strike the ridge. Hawks also utilize
rising warm air thermals by spiraling up (sometimes in
large groups called kettles) and then setting their wings for
a rapid downward glide toward the southwest, only to pick
up another thermal there that enables them to repeat the
maneuver. This type of nearly effortless flight saves much
energy.

In the shrubbery surrounding the exposed watch site
you can also find many species of smaller migrating birds,
including vireos, warblers, kinglets, and flycatchers. This is
in fact the most reliable spot I know of for finding the
Philadelphia vireo in fall (try mid-September). If the hawk
watching is slow, there are plenty of eastern (formerly rufous-sided) towhees, northern flickers, gray catbirds, and
white-throated sparrows in addition to migrating monarch
butterflies to entertain you. More than 300 of these large
insects were counted during one day from this spot.

A few suggestions: Hawk watching is usually best
when fall winds are out of the northwest; bring a lawn chair
if you are planning to stay for awhile, and dress for the
weather. The exposed site is often much windier, and as a
result much colder, than the valley below.

Reptiles: Painted turtles and big rough-shelled snapping turtles live in Tilden Swamp, where you might find
one or more basking on a log. Exposed bedrock on the
summit of Berry Mountain and the sunny shores of Tilden
Swamp are where you are most likely to see a snake. They
take advantage of the sun-warmed rock to transfer some of

Vernal Pools

Small, isolated woodland ponds known as vernal pools are the only type of breeding site for tan-colored wood frogs and the large (yellow) spotted and Jefferson salamanders. A number of these critical nurseries exist within Pittsfield State Forest. One can be found not far from the ski jump and is easy to reach on foot. If you follow the trail up the slope to the left of the jump, you'll come to the small pool. In late March and April these frogs and salamanders make the long (for them) trek from burrows in the leaf litter to such temporary pools during evening rains. It is one of nature's most fascinating yet little-known annual events. After courtship and mating, the female salamanders attach their eggs to submerged sticks. The gelatinous egg masses, about the size of a human fist, are readily visible in the clear, shallow water. The animal's entire life cycle must be completed before the ponds dry up in late summer. In future years the amphibians hatched here will return to the same pool to breed (if it is still here). Pools such as this one are extremely important to the creatures that depend upon them. Do your part to protect them from abuse.

---

the stone's stored radiant energy into their bodies. The common garter snake is most often found by chance, but the small northern brown, red-bellied, and ringneck snakes are possible to locate, if you search for them. You might see a milk snake in open areas along the road. It's unlikely that you would find a northern black racer, but this is the most northerly location in Berkshire where the species has been recorded.

Amphibians: Tilden Swamp and the other water bodies support a variety of frog species, including bull, green, and pickerel frogs and the elfin spring peeper. We counted some three dozen green frogs at Tilden, as they comically shrieked and leapt into the water ahead of our approach. In midsummer while walking a woodland trail you might come upon a host of half-inch-long American toads that have just transformed from aquatic tadpoles into air-breathing creatures.

Other water bodies in the forest contain the red-spotted newt, and fast-flowing brooks provide habitat for dusky and two-lined salamanders. Red-backed salamanders, which have been called the most common vertebrate by weight in eastern forests, spend the daylight hours under logs and leaf litter. If you roll a log to search for them, be sure to return it to its original position. On one visit we found two all-red individuals among a total of five redbacks in beech and oak woods. These are thought to mimic the poisonous red eft.

Fishes: The fast-flowing streams of the state forest contain brook trout. Lulu Brook, which parallels the uphill portion of the Circuit Road, is spring-fed and flows except during the driest part of summer. The waters of Tilden Swamp are home to such species as bluegill and brown bullhead. Berry Pond contains brown and brook trout (stocked each May), yellow perch, pumpkinseed, creek chub, golden shiner, brown bullhead, and even goldfish.

Seasonal Highlights

April is a good month to seek out the inhabitants of vernal pools. Woodland wildflowers peak in late April and early May, while migrating songbirds peak in mid-May. Fragrant and lovely mountain azalea blooms in early June along the Berry Pond Circuit Road.

From mid-June to early July, mountain laurel shrubs are covered with large clusters of gorgeous white-and-pink flowers along the Circuit Road and in sunny openings. Purple-fringed orchis and the white-flowered turtlehead, looking very much like their names, bloom around Berry Pond in July, and fragrant and yellow pond lilies cover the water's surface. The woodlands, too, are alive with sweet-voiced avian songsters such as the wood thrush and white-throated sparrow. Butterflies visit the sunny open spaces of ponds, fields, and mountaintops. Lovely pink fireweed flowers near the summit pull-over.

In fall, take some food and drink and a lawn chair to the summit of Berry Hill to do some hawk watching. In early October you will also be rewarded by spectacular fall colors. The Berry Pond Circuit Road is one of the nicest ways to do some leaf peeping if a woodland walk is out of the question for you.

In winter, the entire state forest is open for cross-country skiing (see *Skiing*). Many miles of trails are also used by snowmobilers. Skiing is a peaceful and healthful means of personal propulsion. If the snow lies deep, a pair of snowshoes may be just the ticket. Try your skills at tracking. Perhaps you'll come upon a porcupine in a stand of conifers. Look for tiny black insects called springtails ("snow fleas") jumping about on top of the snow during warm spells in late winter.

Comments

The half-mile-long paved Tranquility Trail was constructed near the office in 1985 in order to give persons with mobility impairments an opportunity to experience the out-of-doors. An interpretive leaflet keyed to marked points along the trail is available from the office. Wheelchair accessible toilets are also present here.

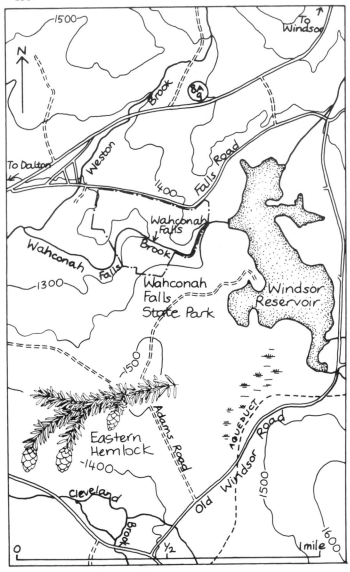

WAHCONAH FALLS STATE PARK

◆§ 19 §◆

WAHCONAH FALLS STATE PARK
Dalton, Hinsdale, Windsor

Managed by DEM.

Acreage: 650.

Elevation: 1,260—1,450 ft.

Trails: 1 mi.

Hours: Year-round. Closes at sunset.

Admission: None posted.

Facilities/Other: Information available at DEM regional office, Pittsfield. Phone: 413-442-8992. Composting toilet available. No camping. Fishing and picnicking permitted; swimming prohibited.

Directions: From jct. of Rtes. 8 and 9 in Dalton, bear left (N.) on Rte. 9 for 2.3 mi. to North Rd. on the right. Turn right and continue straight where road splits, following gravel Wahconah Falls Rd. for 0.4 mi. to parking on right. Park off road if gates to paved lot are closed.

The falls, which lie in Windsor, tumble commandingly down a rocky decline, widening as they spill toward you. More accurately they are a series of falls, each drop paired with a lovely, clear pool beneath it.

Wahconah Falls Brook, a tributary of the Housatonic River, flows through a shaded hemlock gorge, a breach of the Berkshire Plateau. The falls have formed in what is known as Becket gneiss, an ancient rock that recrystallized under extreme heat and pressure. Be sure to follow the trail to the top of the frothy cascade, where you'll be able to view several types of rocks, one of which is called talc schist. It is greenish-gray in color and so soft that you can easily scratch it with your fingernail. Across the stream, near the top of the falls, is the remains of a talc-producing mine shaft, which was active around the turn of the century.

The outstanding feature here, however, is the tremendous volume of water that flows over the falls — perhaps the greatest of any in Berkshire. The source of this water is

Windsor Reservoir, just a short distance upstream. You can follow a trail paralleling the lovely cascading stream through shaded hemlock woods to reach it.

Views and Vistas

There are no panoramic views, given the site within a narrow gorge; but the views of the cascade, the pools beneath, and the gurgling brook are quite beautiful.

Plant Communities

The characteristic trees of the northern hardwood forest grow in the park, including yellow birch, white ash, American beech, sugar maple, and some red maple. The ashes and maples grow in the sunnier areas nearer the parking lot. The rocky gorge itself has a vigorous growth of eastern hemlock, a shallow-rooted species that does well even in thin, rocky soils. Little else grows within the shade cast by these large evergreens.

On the rocks of the gorge you'll find the common rock-loving ferns: marginal wood fern and common polypody, both of which remain green throughout the year, as well as long beech fern. Mosses, too, grow on the damp, shaded rock surfaces, trapping and helping to create soil that often serves as a bed for seedling hemlocks. Spring wildflowers here include Canada mayflower, red trillium (wake robin), painted trillium, and false Solomon's seal.

Wildlife

Mammals: The common northern hardwood forest mammals exist in the park and surrounding lands. They include the gray squirrel (also occurs in an all-black phase), southern flying squirrel, porcupine, eastern chipmunk, gray fox, bobcat, coyote, black bear, long-tailed weasel, white-footed mouse, short-tailed shrew, and white-tailed deer. You will seldom be fortunate enough to see most of these during daylight hours. Your chances do improve early and late in the day, as well as on cloudy days. More likely, though, you will find tracks, scat (droppings), food items, gnawed branches, or other signs of their presence.

Birds: The roar of the falls makes hearing bird song difficult, at least in the cataract's vicinity. Common resident birds here include ruffed grouse, black-capped chickadee, brown creeper (which creeps up tree trunks), and white-breasted nuthatch. Red-tailed hawks, which require a mixture of open (for hunting) and wooded country (for nest sites), patrol the skies in search of their rodent prey.

During the summer, veeries and wood and hermit thrushes, plus the usual variety of vireos, warblers (black and white, black-throated blue, black-throated green, and ovenbird), and flycatchers, nest in the woodlands. Of the flycatchers, the eastern phoebe is an engaging little olive-gray bird that repeats its name quite emphatically — not to be confused with the whistled *fee-be* song of the chickadee! The phoebe usually returns to our area in late March and builds its mud nest (always covered with green mosses) on a ledge, be it natural or artificial.

Reptiles: The wood turtle, a state-listed species that spends a large part of its time wandering about on dry land in search of food, may live within the park. Other turtles are probably absent owing to the lack of ponds here. Eastern painted and snapping turtles do reside in the reservoir above the falls. The common garter snake, which grows to a length of about 2.5 feet (and sometimes up to 4 feet), is probably the only species of serpent you could hope to observe here.

Amphibians: The absence of marshes, swamps, and standing water precludes the presence of many frog types. Wood frogs and perhaps spring peepers occur in the park. Early spring would be an opportune time to search for vernal pools, which wood frogs (and several salamanders) require for breeding. (For more about vernal pools, see Ch.

18.) Tailed amphibians, the salamanders, likewise are represented by only a few species, among them the red-backed, dusky, and two-lined salamanders, the latter two along streams. If vernal pools are present, two additional species, the Jefferson and the yellow-polka-dot-patterned spotted, would occur here as well. Near the reservoir you might encounter a red eft walking over the leaf litter, and in the reservoir you might see the red-spotted newt, the adult aquatic stage of the eft, on the bottom.

Fish: Within the cold, clear, turbulent and therefore oxygen-rich waters of Wahconah Falls Brook are brook trout (trout are also stocked here), slimy sculpin, blacknose and longnose dace, creek chub, yellow perch, white sucker, and brown bullhead. All are native, and in these cold waters none attains great size. Most are common to other permanent Berkshire streams.

Seasonal Highlights

Spring rains and snow-melt combine forces to send a tremendous volume of water over the falls. The flow is greatest in spring, but this falls has the distinction of having a considerable flow all year long, because of the presence of Windsor Reservoir. Spring wildflowers grace the forest floor, and bird migrants and returning summer residents are arriving.

In summer this is a refreshing spot to escape the heat, although temperatures in Berkshire never quite equal those of lower-lying areas like the Connecticut Valley. The woods shelter nesting birds, but you'll have an easier time hearing and identifying their songs and calls away from the falls.

The woods are certainly beautiful during the foliage season, but even afterward, the grandeur of the falls is undiminished. The hemlocks are as green as ever and show off their foliage to better advantage once the broad-leaved trees have discarded their worn-out leaves.

Even in winter the falls are easily reachable, *but take care, since ice and snow can make for dangerous footing on the way down the slope. Likewise watch your footing along the water's edge.* The freezing temperatures create ever-changing ice sculptures on the rocks and vegetation.

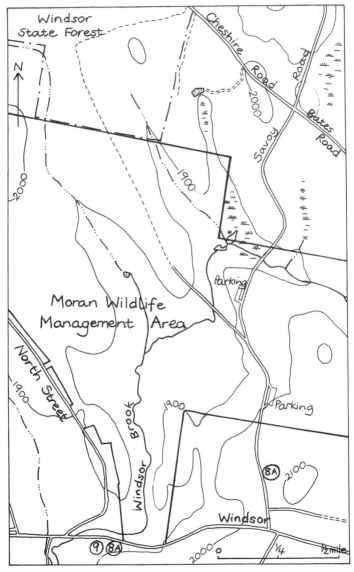

EUGENE D. MORAN W.M.A.

✺ 20 ✺

EUGENE D. MORAN WILDLIFE MANAGEMENT AREA
Windsor

Managed by MDF&W.

Acreage: 1,147.

Elevation: 1,400—2,297 ft.

Trails: 2 mi. (includes trail in adjacent Windsor State Forest).

Hours: None posted.

Admission: None.

Facilities/Other: Map available from district office. Phone: 413-447-9789. No rest rooms or camping.

Directions: From Windsor center, at jct. of Rtes. 8A and 9, take 8A, N. for 0.75 mi. to parking area on left.

This is a fairly remote yet easily accessible area of open grasslands, wetlands, and woodlands, including boreal (northern) forest, that boasts an impressive bird life. Rapidly dwindling grassland habitat is a great cause for concern across New England. Moran provides increasingly scarce grassland bird species crucial nesting habitat. In addition, over-wintering birds such as northern shrike, red and white crossbills, pine grosbeak, and even boreal chickadee on occasion, have made this area famous among local birders. This is probably the most reliable place in Berkshire to find some of these northern species. The spacious fields, dense evergreen stands, and boreal ambiance make for an invigorating experience whether wildlife observation happens to be productive during your visit or not.

This former dairy farm has a mystique and charm that make it one of my favorite places. On many occasions you may be the only person on the property, adding markedly to the adventure. A visit here can be combined with excursions to Tannery Falls and Spruce Hill (Ch. 24), Notchview Reservation (Ch. 21), Wahconah Falls (Ch. 19), or Windsor Jambs (Ch. 22).

Views and Vistas

The property lies so high, much of it at or above 2,000 feet, that there are few promontories to behold. Nevertheless, the rolling topography and open fields bordered by spruce forest may well make you think you're walking through a scene from *Dr. Zhivago*, especially in winter. From the vicinity of the parking area you can get a good if moderately distant view to the north of the state's highest peak, Mount Greylock (3,491 ft.).

Plant Communities

The plant communities are quite varied; you will find large (by Berkshire standards) grass and sedge meadows, pastures, deciduous woods, northern hardwoods, boreal forest pockets of red spruce and balsam fir, beaver pond communities, and other wetlands. Brushy swamps contain speckled alder and red maple. Of greatest interest to the naturalist are the open habitats, which include shrubby pastures with scattered small trees, and the dark, dank evergreen forest.

The spruce and fir stands are intermingled with the more prevalent deciduous forest species such as sugar maple and white birch. Little is able to grow in the dense shade of the conifers, and so the moist, spongy forest floor is virtually devoid of other plant life.

The wet meadows contain reed canary grass and various sedges (which have triangular stems, rather than round ones, as grasses do) that require moist soils. In addition to native species in the old pastures, there are the characteristic aliens such as thistle. There was once a farmstead here, and cultivated species such as apple are still very much in evidence along the roadway. These trees provide fruit in fall and winter for numerous mammals and birds, as do the cranberry viburnum shrubs. These tall bushes are heavily weighted down with bright red, almost translucent fruit in fall and winter.

Wildlife

Mammals: White-tailed deer are abundant in the mosaic of woodlands, open fields, and wetlands. Even moose, New England's largest native land mammal, have been found here. The meadows and pastures are home to many species of small rodents, of which the most numerous is probably the meadow vole. This dark-brown mouse with a short tail maintains a circuitous system of runways through the grass thatch. It is the favorite prey of many predators, both bird and mammal. Red foxes and coyotes pounce on them with great relish. Red-tailed hawks and, in migration, northern harriers (which actually fly low over the ground, listening for the little creatures) and big rough-legged hawks in winter hunt them by day, while owls seek them out by night. Also in the thick grass are meadow jumping mice, which use their tremendous jumping ability to evade capture.

Within the woodlands are snowshoe hare, porcupine, gray squirrel, red squirrel (more common in the mixed and conifer stands), red-backed vole, and of course eastern chipmunk. Along the field and forest edges you will find evidence of cottontail rabbit, white-footed mouse, and short-tailed shrew.

Although wetlands are not extensive on the property, they do host beaver, muskrat, and mink. Watch for tracks and other signs of these animals as you walk down the old graveled roadway to and across Windsor Brook. Beaver have dammed the brook to create the ponds you see. Black bear, whose populations have been steadily increasing, are seen here on occasion.

Birds: The relatively large variety of vegetative communities results in a diversified bird fauna; at least 180 species have been recorded here since 1977.

Moran's major claim to fame is its grassland birdlife. The very uncommon sedge wren has nested recently in the wet meadows, and the rare Henslow's sparrow and the unusual grasshopper sparrow, all grassland specialists, have been found here. Lincoln's sparrow, a northern breeder, has nested in sedge tussocks among the alder stands. In spring 1996, an out-of-range male dickcissel put in a lengthy appearance. Far more regular are the bobolinks that build nests on the ground among the meadow grasses. You might flush a ring-necked pheasant in late fall. These Asian game birds are regularly stocked by MDF&W staff.

Although the actual numbers and variety of birds you will see in winter here will be sparse (this is one of the very few places I know of where sighting six species during a morning's outing can be cause for celebration!), the species that *are* present may be among the most sought-after. Quality rather than quantity is the motto at Moran. Birds that seem to gravitate here from late fall to early spring include the rough-legged hawk, northern shrike, pine and evening grosbeaks, pine siskin, red and white-winged crossbills, common raven, and rarely even boreal chickadees, whose call is a less musical and more nasal rendition of that of the familiar and common black-capped chickadee.

As you walk down the graveled road, keep your ears and eyes open for a flock of pine grosbeaks eating the shiny red viburnum fruit in the shrubs along the road and near the brook. These are handsome, reddish (adult males), robin-sized birds that can often be approached quite closely; and this is the most reliable spot I know of in Berkshire for finding this erratically occurring species.

While strolling through the upper pasture check the tops of the small trees for a perched northern shrike or "butcher bird." The shrike, a black-and-gray robin-sized predator, has a hooked beak but not the curved talons required to hold and tear prey; thus it has the interesting habit of impaling its prey — mice, small birds, or large insects — upon thorns or even barbed-wire fences!

Follow the path through the dense spruce stands into a weedy clearing beyond. This is a good spot in winter from which to test your screech owl call in an attempt to attract the attention of any boreal chickadee that might be present. Listen for the calls of finch flocks as they travel about the forest feasting on the bounty of the conifer seeds, and watch the tops of the spruces for perched finches and other northern types. You'll almost certainly hear the nasal *yank-yank* of the active red-breasted nuthatch, a common denizen of the evergreen forest.

Beyond the spruce and fir stands are fairly extensive deciduous woods where ruffed grouse and wild turkey nest, as well as a wide range of deciduous forest birds found in other similar locations. In all, about 20 species of warblers nest on the property.

Reptiles: Species to be expected here include wood turtle and eastern painted turtle in the beaver ponds. Snakes are represented mainly by the ubiquitous common garter. Other species that dwell here include the milk, smooth green, northern brown, and red-bellied snakes.

Amphibians: The most common frogs here are the spring peeper, wood frog, and pickerel frog. The lack of larger, deep-water bodies is the reason other frog species are absent; the shallow water would make them vulnerable during a deep freeze as they rested in the mud. A few salamanders, however, are present. In the deciduous woods, you might find red-backed (under logs) and spotted salamanders.

Fishes: A few native species, including brook trout, are found in Windsor Brook. The small beaver ponds contain yellow perch and brown bullhead.

Seasonal Highlights

Spring comes late to this high plateau, and snow may lie under the evergreens much longer than in the lowlands. The deciduous and mixed woodlands produce a very respectable early spring wildflower show in late April and early May. Watch for eastern bluebirds in the meadows. The beautiful males usually return by the beginning of March, when snowstorms still pose a threat to their survival.

In summer, the wildflowers of fields and pastures take their turn to show off. Check the meadows for unusual grassland specialty birds. Woodland birds are nesting, too, and included in this number are yellow-rumped, Blackburnian, and Canada warblers.

Beginning in late October, watch for the arrival of the winter resident birds such as northern shrike, pine grosbeak, and evening grosbeak. Scan the skies for migrating hawks as well.

Winter, when the mercury falls well below freezing and the winds kick up swirls of snow, is the time to bundle up and head for Moran. Search for northern shrike, boreal chickadee, and other northern birds. Even if you see only black-capped chickadees and a common raven, walking through the fields and spruce woods on a crisp blue day can be exhilarating. The fragrance of spruce and balsam fir alone is worth the price of admission. This is also a fine place to try out snowshoes. Even if the snow cover is only moderate elsewhere in Berkshire, it will likely lie deeper at this elevation.

⊰ 21 ⊱

NOTCHVIEW RESERVATION
Windsor

Owned and managed by TTOR.

Acreage: 3,090.

Elevation: 1,440—2,297 ft.

Trails: 25+ mi.

Hours: Year-round, dawn to 4:30.

Admission: Adults $2; children (12 and under) free. Winter: Adults $7 ($4 after 2 p.m.), children $2. Programs and special events have different fees.

Facilities/Other: Rest rooms, self-guiding interpretive trail leaflet, and trail map (small fee) available. Some trails may be difficult to locate; a map is recommended. There are facilities for skiers as well. No camping. Mountain bikes and motorized vehicles prohibited. Phone: 413-684-0148, (TTOR regional office) 413-298-3239.

Directions: From the intersection of Rtes. 8A and 9 in Windsor center, take Rte. 9, E. for 1 mi. to entrance and parking on left.

Notchview is one of the largest privately owned pieces of conservation land in Berkshire. This relatively wild property is situated at high elevation on the Berkshire Plateau and contains pockets of boreal forest, three clear brooks, open meadows with panoramic views, and abundant plant and animal life. Judges Hill (2,297 ft.) is the highest point in Windsor. The extensive trail system makes this a favorite destination for cross-country skiers (see *Skiing*). Notchview borders Windsor State Forest and Windsor Jambs State Park (Ch. 22) and the Moran Wildlife Management Area (Ch. 20).

Views and Vistas

There is a beautiful view of the Westfield River notch (hence the name Notchview) from a high meadow at the General Bates Homesite. From here you'll be treated to a panoramic view eastward, down the Berkshire Trail, to the hills in the town of Cummington. Given the considerable elevation of the property, reaching this viewpoint does not demand a great climb. The views from the trail-head near the office, while not as panoramic, are nonetheless bucolic.

Plant Communities

There is definitely a boreal, or northern, look and feel to this place. You'll see it in the vegetation — red spruce, balsam fir, and other species indicative of a cool, moist climate — while some trails will take you through ravines and moist low spots where the sweet aroma of the ever-greens can instill in you a feeling of euphoria. You'll also find the characteristic northern hardwood trees, such as yellow birch, sugar maple, and American beech, and other species including white ash and black cherry. The two prominent understory maples are here — striped (moosewood) and mountain (with velvety twigs). The area's common shady ravine tree, eastern hemlock, borders the small gorges cut by the three streams on the reservation.

The cool forest's herb layer has Christmas, spinulose, and marginal wood ferns, long beech (its two bottom leaf-lets point down at 45-degree angles), lady fern, rattlesnake fern, and patches of shining clubmoss.

Among the many flowering plants that you're likely to encounter are painted trillium, clintonia (also called bluebead lily because of its fruit), Indian cucumber root (the root itself is edible), bunchberry (a six-inch-tall dogwood), and cloverlike wood sorrel.

Wildlife

Mammals: Black bear (notice claw mark scars on beech and aspen trunks), bobcat, and coyote roam these forests. On one of our summer walks we surprised a young nap-ping coyote! The smaller carnivores include red and gray foxes, striped skunk, raccoon, and a variety of weasels,

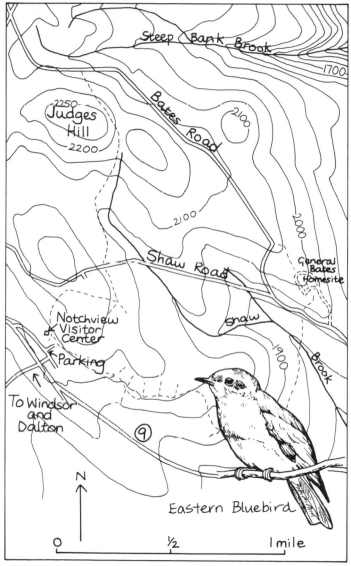

Steep Bank Brook

1700

Bates Road

2250
Judges
Hill
2200

2100

2100

Shaw Road

2000

General
Bates
Homesite

Notchview
Visitor
Center

Parking

Shaw

1900

Brook

To Windsor
and
Dalton

⑨

N

Eastern Bluebird

0   ½   1 mile

NOTCHVIEW RESERVATION

including river otter, mink, and the large, dark-brown fisher. Snowshoe hares, larger than cottontails and beautifully outfitted for the snow with enormous hind feet and white fur, are common at these higher elevations. They have been stocked by the MDF&W throughout Berkshire in suitable habitat and are seemingly prospering. Among the many rodent species to be found are beaver (two large populations, neither of which is readily accessible), porcupine, red-backed mouse, deer mouse, meadow vole, flying squirrels, gray squirrel, eastern chipmunk, and the usually vocal red squirrel.

New England's largest native land mammal, the moose, is being reported from this and neighboring lands with increasing frequency, but your chances of encountering one of these magnificent animals is still very slim. State wildlife officials estimated in 1996 that 200 of these big browsers resided in the state. White-tailed deer, on the other hand, are common here.

Several species of shrews, which superficially resemble mice but have very different teeth (for tackling insects), live in the forests and fields, including the masked, short-tailed, and smoky (similar to the short-tailed but smaller). The frenetic shrews are nearly always on the move, often just below the leaf litter, searching for snails, grubs, worms, insects, and other edibles in order to satiate their tiny bodies' nearly constant need for fuel. They venture above ground largely by night, when owls often feed upon them.

Birds: The deep woodlands are home to wild turkey, ruffed grouse, great horned owl, northern saw-whet owl (at eight inches, our smallest), northern goshawk, Cooper's hawk, broad-winged hawk, all the woodpeckers native to the area, winter wren, golden-crowned kinglet, brown creeper, red-breasted nuthatch, eastern wood pewee, dark-eyed junco, red-eyed and solitary vireos, and Canada, black-throated blue, black-throated green, magnolia, ovenbird, and Blackburnian warblers, among others.

Pastures, hayfields, and other open areas are suitable for the American kestrel (our smallest hawk), eastern king-

bird, American goldfinch, bobolink, killdeer, tree swallow
(which is bright white beneath), and eastern bluebird.

Berkshire Bluebirds

You'll see many bluebird nest boxes on the fence
surrounding the pasture near the office. Each year the
beautiful blue, orange, and white males return by the
beginning of March to claim nesting territories, with
older birds usually returning to the same box they've
occupied before. About two weeks later the paler females return and choose a nest site, and thereby the
male that holds it. She lays between three and six pale-
blue eggs (usually four or five) in a grassy nest placed in
the box or a natural cavity. In two weeks or so the young
hatch, and the adults spend most of their time bringing
food to them. The young leave the nest at an average of
18 days. The female usually begins a second clutch after
these young have fledged. The young of this first brood
have been known to help feed the young of the second!

In late summer bluebirds begin flocking in preparation for the fall migration. This gives the young a chance
to search out some potential territories that they might
use upon their return the following spring.

Most of our bluebirds probably winter in the mid-
Atlantic states. Some that breed north of Berkshire winter in our area, and so it's possible for you to see bluebirds year-round in some low-elevation south Berkshire
locales.

This comely species once suffered great population
declines because of pesticide poisoning, competition
with European starlings for nest sites (the 1.5-inch-di-
ameter entry hole excludes the larger starling), and the
loss of the open habitat they need. The dedicated participation of hundreds of volunteers over the years has
made this much-loved bird a regular member once again
of our summer bird life.

Because of the sizable stands of cone-producing spruce and fir, Notchview is an excellent place to search for winter finches such as the pine siskin, evening grosbeak (which looks a bit like a huge goldfinch), pine grosbeak, and red and white-winged crossbills

Reptiles: The wood turtle may be the only turtle found here. Painted turtles may inhabit the beaver ponds, but this has not been confirmed.

Among the resident snakes are most of the common species, with common garter, a hardy species, being the most numerous. You may find milk (especially near the visitor center), northern brown, red-bellied, and perhaps smooth green snakes — all species characteristic of the higher, cooler Berkshire uplands.

Amphibians: In addition to the American toad, tailless amphibians (all have tails as larvae and are commonly known as tadpoles) here include wood and green frogs and spring peepers. Red-backed salamanders inhabit these woodlands, while dusky and two-lined salamanders live in brookside habitats. One July we found a three-inch-long two-lined salamander near her cluster of several dozen gelatinous eggs, which she had attached to the underside of a flat stone in the clear brook. A spotted salamander has been found in the basement of one of the reservation buildings.

Fish: Notchview includes a 2,500-foot section of the Westfield River, which contains brook trout and other coldwater species. The three brooks — Hume, Shaw, and Steep Bank — are intermittent in flow and thus largely without fish.

Seasonal Highlights

In springtime this is a good place to seek out some of the boreal wildflowers, such as bunchberry, which has pretty white flowers with four petals. The ripe berries are in bright-red clusters, as are so many other wild fruits. Presumably this makes them more noticeable to birds, which have excellent color vision. In May many species of birds, including thrushes, warblers, vireos, and flycatchers, return from their wintering grounds in the tropics to breed. Bluebirds are usually feeding nestlings near the visitor center by early June.

In summer, check the meadows for wildflowers and the insect life that they harbor. Bluebirds are usually beginning their second broods by early July, and tree swallows have fledged their one and only brood by then. Bobolinks, which winter in southern South America, nest in the hayfields.

In fall, you'll appreciate the lovely colors from the high meadows and the scenic view of the notch. Migrant birds actually begin moving through the area in August, and by leaf-fall the vast majority of perching birds have passed through. No wonder, since many of these birds depend upon the rapidly decreasing supply of insects. The winter finches usually arrive by November, and area birders consider this to be one of the better locations for finding them.

At this elevation the snows come early and winter lasts six months, more or less. That is fine with skiers, who take advantage of the many trails for ski touring. Be on the lookout for the tracks of snowshoe hares and fishers. Although the number of birds you'll find is quite low, it might include one of the sought-after types such as the rose-colored pine grosbeak. The sound of the wind through the spruces adds a touch of wilderness atmosphere to Notchview at this season.

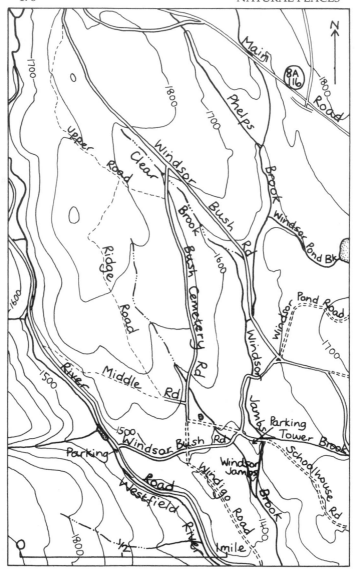

WINDSOR S.F. & WINDSOR JAMBS S.A.

❧ 22 ❧

WINDSOR STATE FOREST AND
WINDSOR JAMBS SCENIC AREA
Windsor

Managed by DEM.

Acreage: 1,743.

Elevation: 1,380—1,900 ft.

Trails: 7 mi.

Hours: Year-round. Parking areas close at 8 p.m.

Admission: None posted. Fee for camping.

Facilities/Other: Phone: 413-684-0948 (summer), 442-8928 (winter). Rest rooms, camping available summer. Map available from office in summer.

Directions: To Windsor Jambs: From the jct. of Rtes. 8A and 9 in Windsor, travel E. on Rte. 9 for 5.2 mi. to W. Main St. on the left in W. Cummington. Take W. Main St. for 0.2 mi. to River Rd. on the left. Follow River Rd. for 3.1 mi. to Windsor Bush Rd. (graveled) at the camping and picnic sites. Turn right onto Windsor Bush Rd. and proceed for 0.7 mi. to School House Rd. at the second intersection (graveled, no sign). Turn right and proceed 0.1 mi. to paved parking area on right. Park off road, if gate is closed. This site can also be reached from the jct. of Rtes. 116 and 8A in Savoy. Take Rtes. 116/8A, E. for 1.9 mi. to Windsor Bush Rd. on the right. Windsor Bush Rd. goes S. into the state forest.

This is a place of significant geological interest and scenic beauty. Boisterous Windsor Jambs Brook, a tributary of the Westfield River, gushes through a fissure (fault) in the bedrock, a mere 25 feet wide in places, to cascade over a long series of low falls. Mica-rich gray schist walls towering 80 feet contain the rushing torrent, giving it a loud, reverberating voice. The rocks, some of which contain white quartz veins, are set on nearly a vertical plane, something you can observe as you look south down the gorge. You'll probably agree that "jambs" is an apt name for the tight squeeze the brook experiences here. The entire production, about a quarter mile long, is set in a lovely conifer grove of large eastern hemlock and red spruce.

You may want to combine a visit to this picturesque spot (camera recommended) with a trip to Wahconah Falls State Park (Ch. 19), Notchview Reservation (Ch. 21), or Moran Wildlife Management Area (Ch. 20). The Westfield River, the major stream of eastern Berkshire, flows through the state forest on its way to the mighty Connecticut River. Here, near its headwaters, the Westfield is an attractive, fast-flowing trout stream with a rocky, graveled bottom.

Views and Vistas

Although lying at a considerable elevation, Windsor State Forest lacks the high promontory that is a prerequisite for panoramic views. Rather, the view to be savored here is at your feet, as you look down the picturesque crevice in the earth's crust.

Plant Communities

The Berkshire Plateau is clothed in general by northern hardwood forest, with the notable addition of red spruce. Under the maturing spruce trees adjacent to the gorge is a lilliputian forest of red spruce seedlings that adds a fairy-tale atmosphere to the setting. Other tree species growing in the vicinity of the Jambs are eastern hemlock and red maple. American beech, obvious by its smooth, light-gray bark, is the small understory tree here. Hobblebush, a white-flowered viburnum, blooms here in May. A few yellow birches line the gorge itself. Around the parking lot are tall Norway spruces that were planted.

The thick coniferous growth around the Jambs precludes a lavish forest floor community, but a number of evergreen herbs are visible year-round. You will notice that the ground under your feet, near the edge of the gorge walls, is covered by mosses; the most common of these is white cushion moss. This attractive, non-flowering plant forms a soft, thick mat on acid soils. It can grow here because of the dependable supply of water in the form of spray from the falls and the shading effect of the hemlocks and spruces.

Among the low-growing flowering plants is partridge-berry, which has small, paired, roundish leaves growing along a creeping stem. Its tubular flowers are white, and its berries are bright red. Another low-growing plant that sports red berries is the flavorful wintergreen, with its two shiny leaves. Both the leaves and the edible red fruits contain oil of wintergreen, a familiar flavor to anyone who uses toothpaste and a host of other products.

Ferns grow in the moist soil, and even on the scant soil on top of rocks. One is common polypody, which is encountered county-wide on boulders. On the forest floor you'll see the larger spinulose wood fern, the quintessential lacy fern. Both species are evergreen, so you'll find them here at all seasons.

Even the bark of tree trunks supports a community of plants. Lichens are actually a mutually beneficial partnership between an alga and a fungus. The alga contains chlorophyll, a necessary ingredient, along with sunlight and water, for the manufacture of sugar; the fungus supplies the physical support for the venture. The moist, shaded conditions along and above the gorge promote the growth of this often overlooked group of organisms. Many types of lichen grow on rocks as well, and you can see these here also. The acids produced by the life processes of the lichen actually etch away at the rock. Over many millennia, the rock is slowly broken down, becoming one of the ingredients of soil.

Wildlife

Mammals: The forests here contain the same array of mammals you would expect to find in many other wooded uplands of the Berkshire Plateau. The northern species naturally tend to be better represented here than in the valley areas. The most conspicuous mammal at the Jambs is the diminutive red squirrel. The presence of large Norway spruce trees heavy with cones amounts to a bountiful pantry for this rodent. The ground below the trees is littered with the scales of spruce cones gnawed by the squirrels in their quest for seeds. Since they don't hibernate, these animals cache supplies of seeds and nuts for the cold, lean days of winter. Their loud chattering is a common and bemusing sound of the shaded evergreen forest. Your presence in its haunts may in all likelihood be the cause of the squirrel's unease.

Birds: Of the year-round residents, the pileated woodpecker is notable because of its large size and striking appearance. Both sexes have a bright-red crest. You won't often have the pleasure of seeing one, but the deep rectangular excavations it makes while probing for big, black carpenter ants in standing or fallen timber are in great evidence in most forested areas in Berkshire. You are much more likely to see the nearly robin-sized hairy woodpecker hitching up the trunk of a large maple or other tree in search of beetle grubs below the bark. Summer residents include black-throated green, stunning Blackburnian, and magnolia warblers in the conifers, and the fine-singing purple finch (actually raspberry red), wood thrush, and veery.

Among the conifers at any time of year you will encounter the acrobatic and inquisitive black-capped chickadee, the Massachusetts state bird. From late fall through early spring listen for the high-pitched, usually three-note calls of foraging golden-crowned kinglets as they search the conifer needles for insects, spiders, and their eggs.

The interior forests are inhabited by fast-flying Cooper's hawks that dart through the thick growth in pursuit of birds. These hawks are about the size of a crow and posses a long, banded tail and relatively short wings — adaptations for rapid flight through dense cover. Over the more open areas of the state forest you may see a soaring red-tailed hawk, one of our largest and most attractive species. These birds of prey hunt rodents primarily. The reddish tail of the adult is a striking sight against a bright blue sky.

Reptiles: This group of animals is not particularly well represented in this cool area. Few ponds are present to provide habitat for turtles, though wood turtles may live along stretches of the Westfield River.

The common garter snake is probably the only reptile you will see, but other snakes, usually less obvious, are present: milk (once thought to suck milk from cows!), northern brown, ringneck, and red-bellied.

Amphibians: Wood frogs, which breed in small temporary woodland ponds known as vernal pools, are present here, but the absence of significant marshlands, sluggish streams, or larger ponds means that the variety of frog life is necessarily smaller. Tiny spring peepers, each with an X-shaped mark on its back, do occur in the woodlands.

Salamanders are represented by all the common woodland species, and the cold, clear brooks provide just the right conditions for two-lined and dusky salamanders, both of which seek out hiding places under stones and logs along streams. The less common and large spring salamander, orange-brown in color, may dwell in the springs and streams, too.

Fishes: The MDF&W has stocked the Westfield River with juvenile Atlantic salmon. These fish normally live the majority of their lives in salt water, returning when mature to their streams of hatching to spawn. Because of the many dams now situated along the river's route, these salmon will never be able to return here.

Another cold-water fish in the Westfield and the other, smaller streams is the brook trout, which grows to a maximum of only seven inches here. The Westfield also contains brown trout (non-native), creek chub, and white sucker. Another resident of the fast-flowing brooks is the slimy sculpin, an odd, three-inch-long fish that you may spy out in the less turbulent pools along brook edges. These fish are nearly invisible because of their protective coloration and their habit of lying quite still on the stream bottom. The brooks also contain two other small species — bluntnose dace and longnose dace.

Seasonal Highlights

Spring rains and the snow-melt combine to create an impressive spectacle within the confining gorge of Windsor Jambs. This is the season of greatest water flow, and the roar can be deafening. The views of the brook and its cascades are least obstructed before leaves emerge. Painted trillium, trout lily, Canada mayflower, clintonia, and wood anemone (the last near the brook) show off their blossoms in May.

By midsummer the torrent has long since diminished, but the setting is nonetheless beautiful. Away from the rush of Windsor Jambs Brook you'll hear the melodic voices of the hermit thrush and winter wren, among others. Look for the paired white tubular flowers of partridgeberry on the forest floor beneath the conifers in June and July.

The autumnal rains unleash the water necessary to once again produce the roaring surge that echoes off the steep-sided walls of the gorge. After leaf-fall, the views are enhanced. The turning foliage in early October along the Westfield River is lovely.

In winter, the tumbling water produces fantastic shapes in ice as it coats the vegetation near the edge of each falls. The footing above the gorge can be very slippery, so considerable caution is called for. A sturdy metal fence runs the length of the escarpment and provides a level of safety. State forest trails are open to cross-country skiers.

✌ 23 ✌

HOOSAC LAKE
Cheshire

Formerly known as Cheshire Reservoir, Hoosac Lake, its water
rights, and most abutting properties are privately owned.
Rest area owned and managed by town of Cheshire.

Acreage: (Water surface) 500.

Elevation: (Water surface) 970 ft.

Hours: None posted.

Admission: None.

Facilities/Other: No rest rooms or camping.
Phone: 413-743-1690 (town hall).

Directions: From the jct. of Rtes. 8 and 9 in Pittsfield, take Rte.
8, N. for 5.2 mi. to Farnams Rd. on the left. Turn left onto
Farnams Rd. and proceed for short distance; park off the
paved surface on the right near the lake shore. Roadside
rest area is 1.7 mi. farther N. along Rte. 8, on the left.

This is the northernmost of the large Berkshire lakes
and also the longest, at slightly over 3.5 miles. Like all the
other larger area lakes, its trend is north-south, indicative of
the movement of the glacial ice that scoured out the lake
basins in the soft limestone. The now-defunct limestone
quarries and processing plant at Farnams serve as a reminder of the limestone bedrock found in the Hoosic River
Valley. From here the Hoosic River flows northward, eventually emptying into the Hudson. In spring and especially
fall, this is a good place to observe migrant waterfowl.
Hoosac Lake can be a quick, pleasant stop while you are on
your way somewhere else, and if ducks are on the water, so
much the better. The Farnams Road causeway is the best
vantage point. Sheer cliffs near its western shore have been
the site in the past of a common raven nest. The upper end
of this long, narrow impoundment has many cabins along
its shore, but it is still a scenic lake from a number of
vantage points.

Views and Vistas

From the causeway at Farnams Road you will see, to
the right as you look northward along the lake, North Mountain (2,211 ft.), and north of that a rock outcrop along the
Appalachian Trail known as the Cobbles (1,850 ft.). The
Cobbles are, conversely, a wonderful spot from which to
view the entire lake from above. If you look straight north
along the lake from the causeway you can make out Spruce
Hill (2,566 ft.). Closer and somewhat to the left is the
rounded form of Cole Mountain (2,133 ft.).

Plant Communities

Much of the natural vegetation around the lake has
been altered over the years. White birch is one visually
dominant species that you'll see growing on the several
tiny islands of the lake's northern end, as well as along the
shoreline. Other trees around the lake's perimeter include
northern red oak, quaking aspen, and red maple. The surrounding steep uplands have characteristic northern hardwood forest trees. In fall and winter the white pines and
eastern hemlocks stand out like green islands within a drab
gray-brown hardwood sea.

In the marshlands at the south end, where Muddy
Brook flows into the lake, there is an extensive cattail
growth, and along the less altered shores wetland shrubs
such as speckled alder, winterberry, and red-osier dogwood
still prosper. The sluggish waters of this end of the lake also
have considerable amounts of aquatic vegetation, including
common reed (*Phragmites*) and yellow-flowered pond-lilies.
The prolific growth of invasive aquatic weeds such as Eurasian milfoil have recently caused consternation to residents and other recreational users of the lake.

Wildlife

Mammals: As would be expected, aquatic mammals
are at home here. Beaver, muskrat, mink, and river otter are

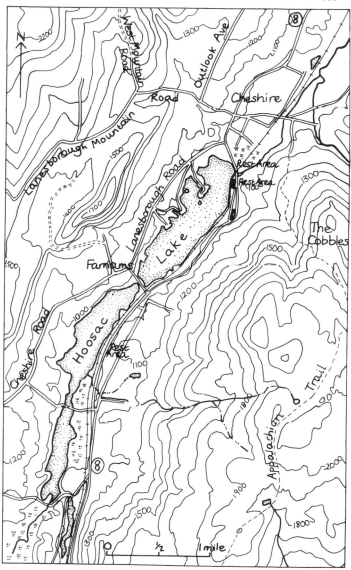

HOOSAC LAKE

found in the marshes at the south end of the lake. Muskrat lodges are sometimes visible just south of the causeway. White-tailed deer are occasionally spotted in the woodlands around the lake. Raccoon, opossum, and striped skunk are common and thrive in proximity to humans. These animals are opportunistic feeders — they will consume almost anything edible.

Birds: A few of the year-round residents are the pileated woodpecker, blue jay, black-capped chickadee, and northern cardinal. Other species are present as long as open water is available to them; these include belted kingfisher, American black duck, mallard, and Canada goose. Ring-billed and herring gulls are now nearly year-round residents, too.

During early spring and late fall, the lake plays host to a variety of waterbirds passing through the area. They use the lake to rest up and feed before continuing on toward the Atlantic coast. The pied-billed grebe, hooded merganser, and wood duck are here in the spring; look for them after the ice goes out. In fall, a greater variety are present, and I have seen large numbers of common merganser (130 on one occasion), hooded merganser (the male with an astonishingly bright white crest, edged with black), ring-necked duck, green-winged teal, lesser scaup, Canada goose (sometimes hundreds), and common goldeneye, an attractive diving duck with a small white spot on the side of its greenish head (male only). Other species, such as ruddy duck, show up in smaller numbers.

Unusual or downright rare birds have also been spotted in recent years: A greater white-fronted goose traveled with a flock of Canadas for a time during late March of 1991, sparking great excitement within the local birding community. A brant, a small blackish goose, made an appearance during the first week of November during the same year.

One of the more exciting birds you may see over the lake in fall is the osprey, sometimes called a fish hawk because of its exclusive fish menu. Also of special note are the pair of big common ravens that have nested on the east-facing cliff near the causeway. The birds located their nest on an inaccessible ledge, as is their custom. Ravens are reputedly the most intelligent birds in the world and display wonderfully intriguing social behaviors. Until about 1983 they were extirpated in Massachusetts, not having bred within the state's borders for more than 100 years. The regeneration of the forests following agricultural abandonment has made their resurgence possible. You can tell ravens from crows by their much larger size (about that of a red-tailed hawk), their wedge-shaped rather than rounded tails (in flight) and, if you're fortunate enough to hear them call, by their deep, hoarse, guttural croaks. Ravens also tend to soar much more often than crows. They are opportunists like their smaller relatives and will methodically patrol sections of roadways in early morning searching for road kills. Seeing one of these great birds is always a great pleasure.

Reptiles: Painted turtles are common in the marshlands at the north and south ends of the lake. They are often visible in summer as they sun themselves upon the old tree stumps that protrude above the water at the north end near the highway rest area. Snapping turtles are likewise common but less often seen.

The usual Berkshire snakes occur in the woods and wetlands bordering the lake — the milk, common garter, northern brown, and ribbon — but this is not an especially propitious place to observe them.

Amphibians: The extensive cattail marsh at the south end of the lake is where you can expect to find, usually by ear rather than by eye, such common species as pickerel, bull, and green frogs and spring peepers. Spotted and Jefferson salamanders inhabit the woodlands surrounding the lake and are dependent upon temporary pools for breeding.

Fishes: Hoosac Lake contains northern pike, chain pickerel, largemouth bass, black crappie, rock bass, bluegill, pumpkinseed, golden shiner, yellow perch, white sucker, brown bullhead, and even channel catfish. As with the other large area water bodies, this lake contains many non-native species such as carp.

Seasonal Highlights

The lake is always worth a brief visit in early spring in order to seek out migrant waterfowl. Scan the cliff face with your binoculars as well to search for possible nesting common ravens.

In summer there's not much to see with regard to ducks and geese, but the views are always pleasant. You might want to hike the Appalachian Trail to the Cobbles to get a raven's-eye view of the lake.

Fall is the best time to view the waterfowl. Make several visits during late October to early December if possible. You may see very little, and then again you may find a large number of ducks, geese, and other visitors. The morning light is best, as it allows you to have the sun at your back as you scan northward up the lake. As at the other lakes, a spotting scope is of great help.

Winter here is not for the waterfowl — they're away until the ice leaves the lake for good next April. You might see a muskrat atop the ice near a hole or, if you're extraordinarily lucky, an otter.

⌐ 24 ⌐

SAVOY MOUNTAIN STATE FOREST
Adams, Florida, North Adams, Savoy

Includes Spruce Hill and Tannery Falls. Managed by DEM.

Acreage: 10,357.

Elevation: 1,200—2,566 ft.

Trails: 49 mi.

Hours: Year-round. Office, 8-4:30. Camping May-Oct.

Admission: None posted. At North Pond (Jun.-Aug.) $2.

Facilities/Other: Trail maps and information available at
   Central Shaft Rd. (Florida) office. Rest rooms, camping
   available May to Oct. $6 a night. Rustic cabins available
   year-round. Phone: 413-663-8469; camping area
   413-664-9567.

Directions: To Spruce Hill: From Rte. 2 (Mohawk Trail) and
   Rte. 8 intersection in N. Adams, proceed E. (N.) on Rte. 2
   for approx. 5.7 mi. (past the Hairpin Turn) to Central Shaft
   Rd. on the right; follow Central Shaft Rd. to where it splits
   off from S. County Rd. Continue S. on Central Shaft Rd. for
   approx. 1 mi. to graveled pull-off on right. From Savoy
   (village), on Rtes. 8A/116, take Center Rd. N. for approx.
   2.9 mi. to Adams Rd. Go left on Adams Rd. for 0.2 mi. to
   New State Rd.; turn right on New State Rd. and go N. for
   approx. 1.5 mi. to Burnett Rd. Turn left onto Burnett Rd. and
   continue for 0.5 mi. to Florida Rd. Turn right and proceed N.
   for approx. 1.8 mi. (past the campground) to Central Shaft
   Rd. trail-head on left. To Tannery Falls: From jct. of Rtes.
   8A and 116 in Savoy, turn right onto Rte. 116 and travel E.
   for 1.7 mi. to Loop Rd. on left. Follow Loop Rd. for 1.4 mi. to
   Chapel Rd. and turn left onto Chapel Rd. Follow it for 4 mi.
   to Tannery Rd. (gravel) on left. Follow Tannery Rd. for 0.3
   mi. and park along roadside, unless you have a high-
   clearance vehicle. A walk (or drive) of approx. 0.5 mi. brings
   you to falls parking area on right.

This is one of the largest state forests in Massachusetts, encompassing portions of four towns, and also one of the most remote. Much of the property is at or above 2,000 feet elevation, and so the feel here is distinctly boreal and wild. There are large expanses of red spruce and balsam fir forest. Spruce Hill, the highest point, is reached by a 1.3-mile hike (see *Hikes & Walks*), provides outstanding views, and also serves as an excellent hawk-watch lookout.

Tannery Falls is the highest and one of the most beautiful of Berkshire waterfalls. Ross Brook has cut a steep-sided, often narrow chasm on its way through 400-million-year-old bedrock and then free-falls fully 100 feet into a pool below. Only a hundred feet or so away, the tumbling cascade of Parker Brook flows through its own scenic cleft at a less acute angle, to merge with Ross Brook below Tannery Falls. Thus united, the brooks flow off together as one — Tannery Brook. This is a feast for all your senses — except perhaps taste!

Views and Vistas

A truly spectacular view is awaiting you at the top of Spruce Hill, the highest point of the Hoosac Range (2,566 ft.), although it takes some effort to reach it. A 1.3-mile-long trail from Central Shaft Road (at 1,900 ft. elev.) leads to the summit. The last portion consists of a steep but safe scramble up rocks.

From this high point you will literally have a 360-degree view that encompasses portions of three states besides Massachusetts. The imposing Greylock Range is visible in its entirety to the west, with the Taconic Range beyond it. Far below, between you and Greylock, are the towns of Adams to the left and North Adams to the right in the Hoosic River Valley. The river and the limestone quarry just west of it are clearly visible. The valley with its limestone floor presents a graphic contrast to the schist and gneiss rocks of the ridges, such as the one upon which you are standing. The gash on Greylock's east face is the result of a 1990 rock slide.

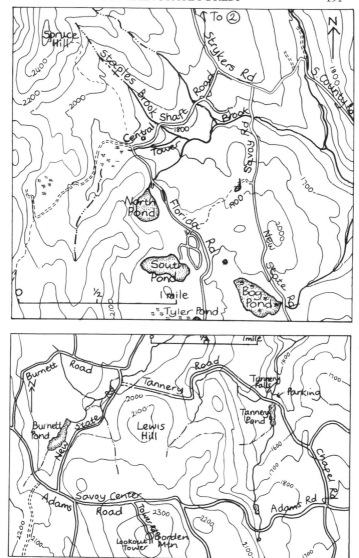

SAVOY MOUNTAIN STATE FOREST

The southern summits of the Adirondack Forest Preserve in New York appear as a bluish ridge far to the northwest. The peaks of Vermont's Green Mountains lie nearby to the north, and to the east you'll see the relatively pointed profile of Mount Monadnock in New Hampshire. Nearby to the southeast is the summit of Borden Mountain, capped by a lookout tower, and to the south, Cheshire Reservoir and Lenox Mountain are visible. What a view!

Plant Communities

This forest has a decidely northern aspect. The sweet smell of balsam fir here will make you think you're in northern Canada. Stands of towering spruces abound (both planted Norway spruce and the native red spruce), while shaded ravines are clothed in eastern hemlock. The hardwood forest is composed of sugar maple, yellow birch, white birch, and American beech; understory trees include mountain maple and striped maple (moosewood), with its smooth, green-and-white striped bark. Shrubs include hobblebush, which has large, heart-shaped leaves, and mountain laurel. The forest floor nearly everywhere hosts a good selection of ferns.

Along the trail to Spruce Hill look for painted trillium and trout lily (adder's tongue) in spring. Skunk currant, a low shrub, is found near the summit. Crush a leaf to fully appreciate the appropriateness of this name. An upper-elevation fern, the mountain wood fern, is also found here. There is a prolific growth of the state flower, trailing arbutus (mayflower) along the last rocky stretch of the trail. Look for its pretty white blossoms in May, as you might expect.

At the summit of Spruce Hill you'll find a short-statured growth of mountain ash, shadbush, black chokeberry, and hobblebush. All have attractive white flowers in spring. The fragrant and lovely pink mountain azaleas bloom here in mid-June, since at this elevation everything is delayed relative to the valley.

North and South ponds are almost unspoiled examples of northern ponds. South Pond contains many interesting water plants, including water lobelia, pipewort, wild celery, and arrowhead. A bog along the far shore holds sundews, green woodland orchid, and the unusual lance-leaved violet. Sweet gale, mountain laurel, elderberry, winterberry, high bush blueberry, and wild raisin line the shore. South Pond is surrounded by a growth of eastern hemlock, red spruce, red maple, and white birch.

The short and steep but lovely trail to Tannery Falls wends its way through a cool, dark forest of eastern hemlock that allows very little undergrowth, apart from marginal (evergreen) wood fern. Some of the trees are magnificent specimens supported by huge trunks covered with deeply furrowed brown bark. There are also large red spruces. The accumulated needle fall from the conifers gives the ground a spongy feel underfoot. At the bottom of the gorge you'll find the usual northern hardwood species, including yellow birch, red maple, and the understory striped maple.

Tannery Pond above the falls has a peaty shore, with many yellow-flowered St. John's-worts, sedges, and nodding ladies tresses (a small white orchid) along small streams. Floating in the pond are bladderwort and, on the surface, yellow pond-lily and water shield, which has flat, football-shaped leaves.

One of the most interesting natural communities in the state forest is Bog Pond. (To find it, travel south from the Spruce Hill parking area on Central Shaft Rd. (Florida Rd. in Florida) for 2.3 mi. to Burnett Rd. Follow Burnett Rd. left for 0.6 mi. and bear left onto New State Rd. Go north for 1.2 miles; pond is visible on left.) This is a relatively unspoiled pond that was created in the 1930s when a bog was flooded. The mat of sphagnum, sedges, and shrubs floats in the center of the pond, rather than along its edges. This is an ideal place to explore bog vegetation from a canoe.

In late May the bog is pink with bog laurel. Pitcher plant, round-leaved and spatulate-leaved sundews, and the delicate orchid, rose pogonia, edge the mat. Bladderwort, another carnivorous plant, traps small aquatic animals in its submerged bladders to supplement the scarce nitrogen supply in these acidic waters (see also Ch. 11). One species floats on the surface, with radiating inflated "branches" like the spokes of a wheel to support the stem of a lovely yellow flower. Buckbean, another aquatic plant, has fuzzy white flowers and three-parted leaves. Both the large cranberry, identical with our commercial variety, and the wren's egg cranberry twine about the bog mat, showing off their tiny but elegant reflexed flowers in early June to early July.

Sweet gale and leatherleaf shrubs and beech, birch, balsam fir, red spruce, red maple, and sugar maple trees surround the pond. There are also a few northern white cedars (arborvitae) that may have escaped from plantings. Look also for the low-growing American yew, an attractive native evergreen shrub.

Wildlife

Mammals: The mammal fauna is very similar to what is found on the Greylock Reservation. Black bear, bobcat, coyote, fisher, porcupine (one of the fisher's favorite foods), white-tailed deer, snowshoe hare, and beaver are found here, too. A beaver dam and lodge are located at Tannery Pond, above the falls. Other beaver dams are located at Bog, Burnett, North, and South ponds. River otter and mink are known to occur in the vicinity of South Pond. There have even been sightings of moose and mountain lion. The existence of mountain lions in this region is still a hotly debated issue among biologists and the public alike, and so far no irrefutable evidence of their presence has come to light. The mammals that you are most likely to encounter along the trails, however, are red squirrel and eastern chipmunk.

Birds: The forests are likewise home to many of the same species that you will find on Mount Greylock. Blue jays, black-capped chickadees, and hairy and pileated woodpeckers are among the common permanent residents. Two species that prefer to nest in the spruce groves are the dark-eyed junco (known to some as snowbird) and white-throated sparrow. During late fall and winter you should look for flocks of the large, yellow-and-white evening gros-beaks and the two types of crossbills, red and white-winged. The crossbills' oddly shaped bills are perfectly designed for the task of extracting seeds from fir and spruce cones.

The hemlock gorge at Tannery Falls was the site of a nesting pair of Acadian flycatchers during 1990. This small bird, which has an unusually explosive call that sounds a bit like a sneeze, is very uncommon in Berkshire. It is a southern species that has been extending its range north-ward. Two rare nesters from the north have also bred here: Rusty blackbirds have nested at South Pond, and Lincoln's sparrow once nested in the bog north of North Pond.

Spruce Hill is renowned as a hawk-watching site, like Berry Hill in Hancock (see Ch. 18). From the end of August until early or mid-November, flight after flight of hawks, eagles, and other birds pass by this point on their way south. Broad-winged hawks, the most numerous, make up the great majority of the first contingent in September. When the winds are out of the northwest, flights of several hun-dred or more per day are possible. Along with them are the smaller sharp-shinned hawks. Other species in September and October include Cooper's hawk, osprey, peregrine fal-con, merlin, American kestrel, northern harrier, and an oc-casional bald eagle. Late migrants in the latter half of Octo-ber and early November are the red-tailed hawk and, the biggest treat of all, the magnificent golden eagle, one or more of which are spotted most years. Other birds that you may well see as you munch on some trail mix are various species of migrant geese, ducks, loons, gulls, turkey vul-tures, and resident common ravens.

Reptiles: High, cold areas such as this generally have few reptile species. The hardy eastern painted turtle does live in the larger ponds of the state forest, as does the bigger snapping turtle.

As for snakes, the common garter is, as usual, the only one you are likely to encounter. A diligent search might

reveal a little red-bellied snake sunning on a warm rock
outcrop; or perhaps a larger brown-patterned milk snake
might reward you.

Amphibians: The various species of common frogs
dwell in the woodlands and wetlands here. Wet areas provide many suitable habitats for wood frogs (the topography
is conducive to vernal pools), spring peepers, green frogs,
pickerel frogs, and others.

Salamander life in the pool below Tannery Falls consists of the dusky and two-lined species, both of which are
common along the area's cold, clear streams. You might spy
the red-spotted newts that reside in Tannery Pond above
the falls, on the other side of the road, and at the larger
South Pond. In the woodlands live red-backed salamanders,
and the newt's land-dwelling stage, called the red eft, might
be common during warm, wet days.

Fish: A number of reasonably large water bodies exist
within the forest. Bog Pond, Burnett Pond, North Pond, and
South Pond have fish, as do many of the clear, cold mountain brooks that feed them. North Pond is stocked with
brook, brown, and rainbow trouts (the last is now considered a salmon), while you will find largemouth bass, brown
bullhead, pickerel, and yellow perch in Bog Pond. Tannery
Falls Brook has brook trout, longnose dace, blacknose dace,
common shiner, and pumpkinseed.

Seasonal Highlights

Snow melt and seasonal rains combine in late March
and early April to produce the thunderous spectacle of
Tannery Falls. Spring comes late to this high, cool plateau,
with early spring wildflowers not blooming here until May.
The campground is situated in an old apple orchard, and in
May the trees burst forth with fragrant blossoms, which
attract bees and hummingbirds.

By summer water flow over the falls has diminished, but bird nesting is underway, and many species of warblers, such as the fiery orange Blackburnian, black-throated green, and black-throated blue, should be looked and listened for. Pink ladyslipper blooms in the acidic duff under conifers in June. Many plants bloom well into the summer months, two or three weeks later than their counterparts in the lowlands. Look for mountain azalea in mid-June on the summit. Mid-June is also an auspicious time to visit Bog Pond to behold bog plants in bloom. Mountain laurel thickets around North Pond fill with blossoms in late June and early July.

Fall is the season that hawk watchers wait for with eager anticipation all year long. If you ascend Spruce Hill to do a bit of your own observing, you may well meet two engaging fellows who spend hundreds of hours on this summit each fall, recording all that flies by. They will probably be happy to help you identify what you're seeing. The conifer woodlands provide food for crossbills, species that make unpredictable forays southward from their usually more northern haunts when food supplies there are wanting. Next to springtime, the water flow at Tannery Falls is heaviest in fall. But no matter during what season you visit, you won't be disappointed.

Winter's snow comes sooner, lies deeper, and tends to melt correspondingly later here than in the valley, 1,300 feet below. Cross-country skiing is popular (see *Skiing*), and it certainly helps to have a four-wheel-drive vehicle to get you to the trail-head. Snow-mobiling, ice fishing, and snowshoeing are also popular pursuits here.

Comments

Savoy Mountain State Forest is a wild and beautiful place that entertains relatively few visitors. Public programs are presented at the camping area during the summer months. Check with forest staff about upcoming events.

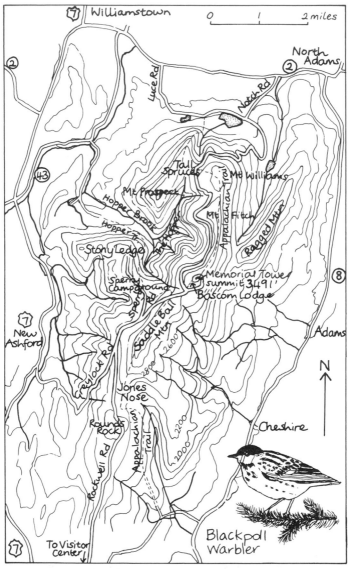

MOUNT GREYLOCK STATE RESERVATION

✺ 25 ✺

MOUNT GREYLOCK STATE RESERVATION

Adams, Cheshire, Lanesborough, New Ashford,
North Adams, Williamstown

Managed by DEM.

Acreage: 12,496.

Elevation: 1,160—3,491 ft.

Trails: 68 mi., including 13 mi. of AT.

Hours: Reservation lands open year-round; Visitor Center
open 9-5 daily. Notch and Rockwell Rds. to summit close in
mid-Dec. Bascom Lodge operated by the AMC on summit
is open from May to mid-Oct.

Admission: None. Fee for camping.

Facilities/Other: Lodging, meals, rest rooms available at
Bascom Lodge at summit. Rest rooms, information at
Visitor Center. Camping, toilets at Sperry Campground.
Phones: 413-499-4262 (Visitor Center), 743-1591 (Bascom
Lodge), 499-4263 (headquarters).

Directions: The summit is 9 mi. by road from downtown N.
Adams and 16 miles from downtown Pittsfield. From N.
Adams, take Notch Rd. S. off Rte. 2, just over 1 mi. W. of
downtown N. Adams. The road turns sharply left at the Mt.
Williams Reservoir. Follow Notch Rd. into the reservation
(boundary marked) and continue to its intersection with
paved Summit Rd. Turn left and continue ascent to the
summit. From Pittsfield, take Rte. 7, N. to N. Main St. (note
reservation sign) in Lanesborough. Turn right and follow the
paved surface 10 miles to summit. To reach the Hopper
Trail, follow Hopper Rd. south from Rte. 43 (Green River
Rd.) past Bressett Rd. and continue on Hopper Rd. as it
bears left; follow it to the end and park on the right.
Reservation roads close to automobiles in mid-Dec.
because of the harsh winter weather on the mountain's
upper reaches.

At 3,491 feet, Mount Greylock is the state's loftiest peak. In geological terms, it is a monadnock — a residual mountain mass that stands alone and above the surrounding terrain. As you walk around the summit, notice the rocks under your feet. They are greenish-gray chlorite and mica-rich schists. Here and there are "knobs" and irregular "stringers" of milky-white quartz that stick up an inch or two above the softer schist. This very hard quartz is why the mountain has been able to endure millions of years of weathering and erosion.

By virtue of the elevation, the mountain's climate is cool and damp. Greylock's upper reaches are reminiscent of Canada's boreal (northern) forests and thus are home to an array of plants and animals not found in numbers anywhere else in the state, or in southern New England, for that matter. The summit area, with clusters of stunted balsam fir trees, is unique in Massachusetts. The sheer size of the reservation, one of the state's largest, coupled with its elevation and relatively undisturbed red spruce and balsam fir forests, gives this area a near wilderness look and feel. It is understandably a mecca for naturalists and outdoor enthusiasts.

The Appalachian National Scenic Trail traverses the reservation, primarily along the ridge line, and a substantial network of other trails winds through the property (see *Hikes & Walks*).

Views and Vistas

These are abundant within the reservation. On the way up Rockwell Road, at 2,400 feet elevation, is Jones Nose, a former hillside pasture regenerating to small trees and shrubs. A graveled parking area is situated off the road on the right. The "Nose" represents the southern end of the Saddleball ridge. If you take the short walk from the parking area along the blue-blazed trail up the lower portion of the hillside, you will be rewarded with spectacular views to the west and south, including the Catskill Mountains in New York state. To the south, the valley of the Housatonic

River is readily apparent, and the lakes of Central Berkshire (see Ch. 17) stand out brightly as they reflect the sun's rays. Closer at hand is the Taconic Range due west and the farmland of rural Lanesborough and New Ashford, Massachusetts. These views, virtually uncluttered by humanity's structures, are among the finest to be had within the reservation.

Most breathtaking, however, is the view from Stony Ledge, an outcropping of Berkshire schist perched high above a bowl-shaped valley known as the Hopper on the west side of Greylock. Stony Ledge is easily accessible by way of Sperry Campground Road, which ends at this point, and offers arguably the most spectacular view in the entire commonwealth. From the ledge, the world drops some 1,400 feet to the valley below, through which Hopper and Money brooks flow. Straight across from you is the Greylock summit, and to your left are Mount Fitch (3,110 ft.), Mount Williams (2,951 ft.), and Mount Prospect (2,690 ft.), the highest set of peaks in Massachusetts. The peaks and valleys are covered with a thick, almost unbroken growth of northern hardwoods and stands of red spruce and balsam fir on the ridges, with eastern hemlock in the ravines. The evergreens stand out distinctly, especially after leaf fall. When you visit Greylock, don't miss this view.

For a look at the ledge itself you'll need to travel down Notch Road a short distance toward North Adams. From here the views back across the valley to Stony Ledge are spectacular.

Then there's the other side of the mountain. Along Summit Road, at the Adams Overlook, a paved parking area adjacent to the roadway, you'll have breathtaking views to the east: the town of Adams in the Hoosic River Valley below, with Ragged Mountain lower and in the near distance. The forested, slightly undulating Berkshire Plateau seems to stretch on endlessly beyond the valley to the east.

From the summit itself, the views are truly spectacular, extending to near 100 miles. Four states in addition to Massachusetts are visible from this vantage point. To the north sit the rounded summits of the Green Mountains in

Vermont. To the northeast is the prominent pyramid of New Hampshire's Mount Monadnock. To the south are Pontoosuc and Onota lakes in Pittsfield, Lenox Mountain, and beyond, Mount Everett, the "Dome of the Taconics" in southwest Berkshire near the Connecticut line. At the top of the 92-foot-high War Memorial Tower on the very summit is a 360-degree map identifying these and other prominent features and giving their distances. Even the southerly views from the dining room and enclosed porch of Bascom Lodge (built by the Civilian Conservation Corps in 1937) are inspirational. There are many other views available to the energetic, including a fine vista of Vermont's Mount Haystack from the Appalachian Trail atop the summit of Mount Williams.

Plant Communities

The lower slopes of the Greylock range are covered by sugar maple, American beech, northern red oak (prefers south-facing slopes), yellow, black, and white birches, white ash, and black cherry. Eastern hemlocks tend to grow in the ravines and on shady north-facing slopes.

Nearly 200-year-old stands of red spruce, protected within a 1,600-acre area designated by the federal government as a National Natural Landmark, are situated in the area known as the Hopper. This area is a rare natural laboratory of old-growth red spruce forest. The forest floor here is made up of years of accumulated needle fall, resulting in a thick, spongy, and acidic layer with a ground cover of wood sorrel, goldthread, and bunchberry. The latter's attractive white blossoms come into being in June and by late summer have transformed into bright-red berries.

To reach the giant three-sided valley on foot use the trail that begins at the end of Hopper Road in Williamstown (see "Directions"). Walk to the right up through the pastures along the Hopper Trail. You'll be walking through a forest of northern hardwoods and basswood, with a few spruce as the trail rises. Take the Hopper Cutoff Trail that leads back down toward the Money Brook Trail. In early

Boreal Greylock

It is the upper 800-900 feet of elevation that sets Greylock apart from any other place in southern New England. It is generally accepted that the 2,600-foot elevation marks the low-end boundary of the boreal forest community here. Increasingly, in this zone and above, the characteristic trees, red spruce and balsam fir, are reminiscent of areas far to the north in Canada. As a rule of thumb, every 400 feet that you ascend is the equivalent of traveling 100 miles north. It is this northern aspect to the flora and fauna that makes Greylock so tantalizing to naturalists.

spring, hepaticas and many other flowers bloom here, and maidenhair fern unfurls its delicate fronds. The trees are large and stately, and the underlying carpet of spring beauties can be as thick as a late snow in these rich woods. To return, make a left onto the Money Brook Trail.

You will find an easily accessible stand of spruces known as the Tall Spruces — although not true old growth — where the Appalachian Trail crosses Notch Road (the road to North Adams) at about the 2,600-foot level. Here the trail leads northward through very large spruces that impart an unmistakable boreal atmosphere. A thick growth of regenerating spruce borders the narrow trail through this area. In early summer, this cool, shady forest is often alive with bird song.

Within this northern community are a number of wet pockets characterized by very absorbent sphagnum moss and other plants tolerant of very acidic conditions. One such pocket is easily accessible on foot along the Appalachian Trail at about the 3,000-foot elevation, from the point at which the trail passes Rockwell Road at the upper hairpin turn. Park along the wide graveled shoulder and proceed to the right, southward along the trail for approximately a quarter mile to where split-log bridges cross the wetland.

East of the trail are boglike areas, not with a floating mat, but covered with sphagnum moss. Small streams originate here in peaty swamps and then form the rushing brooks that accelerate down the mountainsides. Among the spruces and firs is heart-leaved birch, closely related to our white birch but a tree of boreal forests. Bartram's shad and mountain holly grow along the trail. You might find creeping snowberry covering a rotted, mossy log, or notice shining clubmoss as a ground cover here. Bunchberry plants are set in the mossy banks. The white, pink-striped wood sorrel with shamrocklike leaves blooms in early July. Rose twisted-stalk has pink bells under its branching stems. The large mountain wood fern grows only in these higher, cooler altitudes.

On the west side of Saddleball Mountain, a trail called the CCC Dynamite Trail begins at the junction of Rockwell and Sperry roads and travels south, high (at 2,700 ft.) on the west flank of Saddleball. After passing through spruce-fir and hardwood forest, the trail enters a wide terrace where tall sugar maples form an open woods. These "rich" woods have an abundance of spring wildflowers: large patches of wild leek, wild ginger (the liver-red flowers are pollinated by carrion beetles), waterleaf, blue cohosh, Canada violet, Goldie's fern (up to 4 ft. tall), silvery spleenwort, bristly black currant, and small marshes with swamp saxifrage and native grasses.

The summit itself, although greatly altered, is still clothed with a growth of wind-battered and stunted balsam fir. The shiny, flat, one-inch-long needles distinguish the fir from spruce or hemlock. Many of the firs growing on the more exposed sites of the summit lack branches on their windward sides. High winds blast this side of the trees with ice crystals, making growth nearly impossible, while lower branches are protected by a sheltering blanket of snow. In spring, northern and American mountain ashes provide pretty displays of white flower clusters, and the delicate shrub Bartram's shadbush flowers in late May near the parking lot. At the edges of the remaining woods you may find red trillium, the yellow bells of clintonia, white patches

of spring beauty, and skunk currant. Look later in the season for the tiny eyebright, hidden among the grasses of the
summit, and in the fall the large-leaved goldenrod blooms
along trails and edges. Only here and on a few other
mountaintops in Massachusetts will you see this northern
species; it's quite a handsome plant.

Much of the southern end of the reservation is former
farmland regenerating with a cover of birches, oak, black
cherry, pin cherry, and blackberries. Only a small percentage consists of open land, such as the Jones Nose area. Here
mountain ash, chokecherry, shadbush, blueberry, and *Spiraea* shrubs (meadowsweet and steeplebush) cover the
rocky, sloping meadows. Numerous species of colorful
wildflowers blossom here throughout the summer, including the dainty maiden pink. The *Spiraea* shrubs put forth
their showy pink flower clusters in early July, as does the
larger-flowered pink fireweed, at the lower end of the trail.
The profusion of flowering plants in this sunny open area
makes this one of the best places for observing butterflies
and other insects on the mountain.

Wildlife

Mammals: All the characteristic northern hardwood
forest mammals are present within the reservation. One of
the more visible mammals of the upper reaches of Greylock
is the aptly named snowshoe (varying) hare. This hare's fur
turns white to match its background in winter. You might
see one during daylight hours at the campground and along
Summit Road. Porcupines, which consume tender plant
shoots and the inner bark of trees, are also quite commonly
seen as they lumber along roadways.

Greylock may be one of the best places to catch a
glimpse, albeit fleeting, of the nocturnal and elusive bobcat.
A momentary flash of tawny fur in the beams of your car's
headlights will probably be all that you see. This is precisely how I saw my first "wildcat" in Berkshire late one
July evening as my wife and I descended the mountain.

Certainly other predators such as coyote and fisher are present, as are black bear. Red squirrels and red-backed mice are common throughout the area, along with a wide variety of other rodents and shrews. Raccoons and skunks especially may be unwelcome visitors to unattended food and refuse at the Sperry Road Campground.

Birds: The boreal forest community on Greylock includes some of the most sought-after species in Massachusetts. A few, such as the blackpoll warbler, nest nowhere else in the state. Others, such as the mourning warbler, are found here and in a few other cut-over, regenerating uplands in Berkshire. Certain northern species such as the yellow-rumped (myrtle) warbler, white-throated sparrow, and dark-eyed junco are common nesting birds on Greylock. Swainson's thrush, another northener, has recently become a very scarce breeder within the mountain's upper-elevation woodlands. You may yet hear the ascending flutelike song of this thrush, a shy, retiring bird, in the vicinity of Saddleball bog.

The musical trill of the junco and the plaintive whistled *old Sam Peabody Peabody Peabody* of the white-throated sparrow are evocative natural sounds of the summit area. The loud, bubbling song of the tiny winter wren is often heard in moist, shaded ravines. Fifteen species of wood warblers regularly breed on the upper reaches of the reservation. In addition to the blackpoll, which is most readily seen in spruces along the upper reaches of Notch Road, and the mourning warbler, which is found in brushy areas such as below the Appalachian Trail crossing of Summit Road and at the junction of Sperry and Rockwell roads, are the Blackburnian (Tall Spruces), yellow-rumped (summit area), and Canada warbler (Saddleball bog). Magnolia, black-throated blue, black-throated green, black and white, American redstart, and ovenbird are common warblers in many wooded portions of the reservation. You will find the Louisiana waterthrush along mountain brooks.

Species characteristic of more open communities include the chestnut-sided warbler, common yellowthroat, and blue-winged warbler (all at Jones Nose), indigo bunting (at the summit, Stony Ledge, and Jones Nose), and field sparrow, which can sometimes be found nesting at the latter site. In the spacious meadows near the Visitor Center, at the base of the mountain, such open-country birds as the eastern meadowlark, bobolink, and eastern bluebird nest in spring and summer.

Another Greylock specialty is the olive-sided flycatcher, a boreal species that is sometimes found in summer in a wet area near Wilbur's Clearing along the Appalachian Trail, just beyond the Tall Spruces. Very occasionally another northern flycatcher, the yellow-bellied, has been found along the Appalachian Trail on Saddleball Mountain, approximately one mile south of the point where the trail passes by Summit Road at the upper hairpin turn. The area is wet, with stunted red spruces, a favorite habitat of the species. Recent nesting has been suspected. The common raven is becoming just that on Greylock. With increasing frequency, their low, guttural croaks can be heard throughout the higher reaches of the reservation. Stony Ledge is a good spot from which to look for them. This is also a fairly reliable location to hear calls of barred owls during the breeding season in June. Other selected species that breed on the mountain include the purple finch, golden-crowned kinglet, yellow-bellied sapsucker, solitary vireo, and perhaps the evening grosbeak.

A hike up Greylock is an excellent way to experience the changes in birdlife as you move from the northern hardwood forest into the boreal forest community. Hikes over the Appalachian Trail, the Bellows Pipe Trail, and Hopper Trail (see *Hikes & Walks*) can accomplish this, as will a drive from the Visitor Center to Bascom Lodge. Pull off the roadway periodically, at designated areas, to listen for bird song. The thrushes are a good example: The veery nests in the valley up to perhaps 1,500 feet elevation. As you travel upward (and "northward"), this species is replaced by the wood thrush. From approximately 1,800 to 2,500 feet, the hermit thrush holds sway, and beyond that, in the boreal forest zone, is found the Swainson's, the least common (and becoming rare in fact) of the group on Greylock. The Bicknell's thrush used to nest on the summit, but it has not been found breeding there since 1979, despite annual searches.

The peak time for bird nesting activity on the upper reaches of Greylock is late June to early July.

Reptiles: Exposed rock outcrops are where you might occasionally see snakes sunning themselves. The common garter snake is by far the one most often observed. Other species are present, such as the small ringneck, red-bellied, smooth green, and northern brown snakes. You are most likely to find some of them in the sunny blueberry fields at Jones Nose and at Rounds Rock, about one-half mile due south.

Amphibians: The most common species of frog on the reservation are probably the wood frog and American toad. Green frogs live in the small pond near where the Appalachian Trail crosses the Rockwell Road-Notch Road junction.

Salamander diversity is very good. In addition to the more abundant species that you might expect to find in northern hardwood forest, such as the red-backed under logs, are the spotted (near the summit) and Jefferson (lower elevations) salamanders. Water-loving animals such as two-lined, dusky, and spring salamanders are found in and along mountain brooks. A reliable place to find the large yellowish-orange spring salamander (a state-listed Species of Special Concern) is Deer Hill Falls.

Fish: The reservation has few bodies of water. A number of small cold-water species do inhabit the brooks. These include brook trout, blacknose dace, and longnose dace. The Appalachian brook crayfish, an endangered species, is found in some of the brooks.

Seasonal Highlights

Bird migration is at its colorful best in spring. Mid-May to early June will yield the greatest diversity. Woodland wildflowers, as elsewhere in Berkshire, are at their peak before the trees leaf out, but this is several weeks later on upper Greylock than in the valleys below. The trout lily, with its brown-blotched leaves, and spring beauty — both early spring species — are still in bloom on the summit in mid-May, as are many other plants. The lovely white flower clusters of hobblebush, a common understory shrub, open a bit later in May under the forest canopy. In May, too, both low- and highbush blueberries flower at Rounds Rock.

In summer, Greylock's forests are alive with bird music during the breeding season. A visit to a variety of sites, such as the meadows near the Visitor Center, the shrubby fields of Jones Nose, the mixed forest from the Sperry Campground to Stony Ledge, the cool, shaded Tall Spruces, the Saddleball bog, the Adams Overlook, and, of course, the summit, will provide plenty of opportunities to experience the varied breeding bird life in late June or early July.

The meadows especially offer a profusion of summer wildflowers. *Spiraea* shrubs bloom in early July at Jones Nose, as do the colorful yellow and orange varieties of hawkweed. Don't overlook the insect life, including many species of colorful butterflies, such as the tiger swallowtail, red admiral, and red-spotted purple (a species that includes white admiral). During 1989 the early hairstreak, a species thought to be extinct in the state for a century, was rediscovered by an enterprising Berkshire amateur! For a tasty treat, revisit Rounds Rock, where the blueberries ripen in July. Also look for the tiny flowers of mountain holly in June.

The summit, too, is at its most exuberant in summer. An early morning bird walk from Bascom Lodge to the Adams Overlook is an experience I highly recommend. This is also the hour when your chances of catching a glimpse of a snowshoe hare or porcupine are best.

The fall foliage season brings hordes of visitors to the mountain. Most drive to the summit, but unless you happen to be present during a major annual event such as the Greylock Ramble on Columbus Day, when thousands of hikers ascend the peak on foot from Adams, you'll probably find few people on the trails. The southward migration of birds is underway; it actually has been since late summer. Look for goldenrods, asters, and gentians blooming in such open areas as Jones Nose.

Winter on Greylock is for the hearty. But for those willing to put on snowshoes or cross-country skis, it can be an exhilarating time of year to explore the reservation. Bird diversity is low, but the conifer-clothed slopes are excellent places to find the erratic red and white-winged crossbills, pine siskins, and evening grosbeaks. Mammal tracking in the snow can also be enjoyable. Be aware that the reservation's roads and a few of its trails, like those elsewhere in the state park system, are designated for snowmobiles.

Comments

Greylock is the crown jewel of the park system in Massachusetts. Don't miss it, if at all possible. Employees of the Department of Environmental Management, Appalachian Mountain Club, and guest naturalists present a wide variety of public programs on the reservation from mid-May through mid-October. The weekly Tuesday evening barbecue and public program is a special treat, but you must call ahead. Check with the Visitor Center and Bascom Lodge staff about program schedules.

✒ 26 ✑

FIELD FARM
Williamstown

Owned and managed by TTOR.

Acreage: 294.

Elevation: 960—1,095 ft.

Trails: 3 mi.

Hours: Dawn to dusk.

Admission: Donation requested. TTOR members free.
Programs and special events have separate fees.

Facilities/Other: Lodging available at Field Farm Guest
House. Rest rooms available at main house. Phone: (office,
554 Sloan Road) 413-458-3144, (guest house) 413-458-
3135. Fishing, picnicking permitted. No motorized vehicles,
camping, fires, or hunting allowed.

Directions: From Rtes. 7 and 43 in S. Williamstown, follow
Rte. 43, W. (left, when approaching from the S.) and almost
immediately turn right onto Sloan Rd. Follow Sloan Rd. for
1 mi. to entrance on right. Keep right for trail-head parking.

Field Farm is a scenic, largely open property of agricultural fields, pastures, forests, and wetlands. This combination of plant communities results in varied flora and fauna.
It is also one of the best and most accessible places from
which to view the picturesque western flanks of the
Greylock Range.

Views and Vistas

The views alone are enough to recommend Field Farm.
From just northwest of the guest house, along the North
Trail, there are dramatic views of virtually the entire
Greylock Range. This is perhaps the best non-roadside vantage point from which to observe the part of Mount Greylock
known as the Hopper; the view over the cornfields is idyllic. Within the Hopper you'll be able to discern the narrow
gash created by a 1990 landslide. To the left and in front of

the Greylock summit (3,491 ft., topped by the War Memorial Tower and communications antennas) is Mount Prospect (2,690 ft.). The hill on the right side of the Hopper is the
site of Stony Ledge; but the ledge is on the side away from
you.

To the north the views encompass the Green Moun-
tains of Vermont. Immediately to the west, straddling the
New York border, is the formidable barrier of the Taconic
Range, best viewed from the eastern side of the property.
Berlin Mountain (2,798 ft.) is the highest point visible.

Plant Communities

Your first impression of Field Farm may be that it is
aptly named (actually it was named after the Field family).
The majority of this rectangular property is devoid of large
trees, much of it in fact still actively farmed; it consists of
cornfields, hayfields, and pastureland. The extensive pastured areas are dotted with Japanese barberry and creamy-
white flowering multiflora rose, two alien species that
thrive, since the more palatable plants are grazed by cattle.
Another woody plant here is buckthorn, a shrub or small
tree that bears large quantities of dark blue berries eaten by
birds. It, too, is an invasive foreigner that quickly overruns
abandoned fields. It takes its name from the sharp, almost
thornlike branch tips. In summer, shrubby cinquefoil
blooms yellow in the meadows.

Boundaries between fields are delineated by apple
trees, and old orchards of this species provide a considerable bounty for the resident wildlife. Such places also contain black cherry, a native tree that is one of the first to
colonize open land. Birds are the eager, if unwitting, dis-
persers for black cherry and many other species of fruit-
bearing trees, shrubs, and vines, such as wild grape.

The forest at the north end of the property contains
smooth-barked, silvery American beech, (which retains its
tan-colored leaves well into winter), white ash, white, yellow, and black birches, sugar maple, bitternut hickory, basswood, and northern red oak. Many of the oaks especially

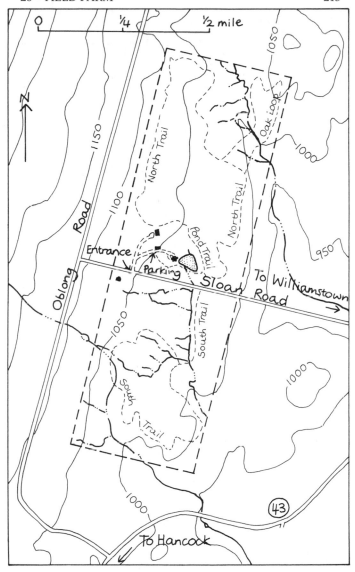

FIELD FARM

are quite sizable and imposing. Under these large trees grows a small understory tree, eastern hophornbeam, the fruit of which bears a superficial resemblance to brewery hops. On the forest floor are Christmas fern, maidenhair fern, spinulose wood fern, and hay-scented fern, among others.

In the springtime, exquisite wildflower shows occur along the Oak Loop Trail in the North Woods, where a happy combination of marble outcrops and ample moisture produces fertile soil. In mid-April to early May, before the trees have fully leafed out, a walk through this wood will reveal sharp-lobed hepatica near the bridge, first unfurling its white or pink flowers and then its hairy leaves. Here also is the attractive plantain-leaved sedge, its red-banded stems crowned with yellow stamens. As you walk on, notice blue cohosh with its ghostly blue leaves unfurling, red trillium (wake robin), long-spurred violet, downy, yellow, and early yellow violets, white toothworts (the food plant for the native mustard white and West Virginia white butterflies), lovely bloodroot (which has an orange sap), the uncommon large-flowered bellwort, and delicate miterwort (examine this one with a hand lens).

Farther along the trail, some of the marble boulders are crowned with miterwort and unrolling fronds of bulblet fern, one of the most unusual. The "bulblets" are produced on the undersides of the subleaflets and drop off to germinate into new plants. An interesting treelike shrub called leatherwood also grows here. Its bark is so tough it can barely be broken by hand (but don't try it). Native Americans used the bark for bow strings, fish lines, and baskets. Boulders under the huge oaks support walking fern, another unusual species. This one spreads by rooting at the tips of its long, tapering leaves.

The small pond near the house and the wetlands adjacent to it are bordered by quaking aspen, speckled alder, and cattail—all plants adapted to wet soil conditions. Aspen, of course, is a culinary favorite of beavers. In summer a light green mat of tiny duckweed plants covers the surface of the wooded swamps.

Wildlife

Mammals: Given the cornucopia of cultivated and accidentally introduced plant species here such as corn and apple, a wide range of mammal life is present to take advantage of the bounty. White-tailed deer are common, and the sight of these beautiful animals bounding across a cornfield in fall with their warning "flags" stiffly erect is always a treat. Other open country and woodland-edge species occurring here are red fox, raccoon, striped skunk, cottontail rabbit, meadow vole, masked shrew, short-tailed shrew, and white-footed mouse. The woodlands shelter red and gray squirrels, southern flying squirrel (actually a glider), opossum, and eastern chipmunk. Coyotes feast on the abundant rodents and rabbits.

The most obvious wetland species is beaver. They are perpetually attempting to plug the outflow of the pond near the house with pole-sized trees they have cut nearby; enterprising humans have just as eagerly created a considerable pile of beaver-cut branches they have removed from the outflow. Freshly downed aspens, stripped of their nutritious green inner bark by the animals, litter the area below the pond.

Birds: Since the property has a varied mix of natural and altered communities, the bird fauna is quite diverse. So far, 111 species have been recorded, and no doubt others will be added. Species adapted to open and edge habitats are numerous here, as you might expect. Among these are the American kestrel, eastern bluebird, American goldfinch, brown thrasher, gray catbird, eastern kingbird, field sparrow, and eastern meadowlark. Bluebirds are especially fond of old, unsprayed apple orchards that provide nesting cavities within the gnarled trunks. This lovely and winsome bird adds a welcome splash of color at any season (see Ch. 21 for details of their biology).

During late fall, winter, and early spring, watch for the reddish-capped American tree sparrow, on holiday in our area from the edge of the tundra. It has a single black spot

on its otherwise unmarked breast. You might very well see
a flock of horned larks, water pipits, or beautiful snow
buntings at this time of year as you wander along the field
edges. Ring-necked pheasant, an introduced game bird,
finds suitable habitat here, and you will often see its single-
file tracks, usually about eight inches apart, in the mud or
snow of the fields and paths.

Among the resident woodland birds are wild turkey,
ruffed grouse, pileated, hairy, and downy woodpeckers,
white-breasted nuthatch, brown creeper, blue jay, black-
capped chickadee, and its more southern cousin, tufted
titmouse. The northern flicker nests at Field Farm, and you
might see one during winter, too. Roving bands of crested,
tan cedar waxwings seek out fruit, and you'll probably spot
this elegant species during your visit.

The woodlands, although not extensive on the property itself, host such colorful breeders as the rose-breasted
grosbeak, scarlet tanager, and Baltimore oriole. You'll also
see or hear in summer the somewhat raucous great crested
flycatcher, the little least flycatcher, and three species of
vireos: red-eyed, solitary, and warbling. Thirteen warblers
have been recorded so far, among them ovenbird, yellow,
chestnut-sided, American redstart, and black and white.

The wet places provide the requisite habitat for the
common yellowthroat, alder flycatcher, swamp sparrow,
red-winged blackbird (one of the earliest spring arrivals),
and tree swallow. Swallows nest in the boxes near the pond
in late spring. The small pond has also hosted great blue
and green herons, blue-winged teal, ring-necked duck, and
hooded merganser. Even great egrets have stopped off here.
Wood ducks nest in the swamp's nest boxes.

Reptiles: Eastern painted turtles live in the swamp.
The state-listed wood turtle may also occur, since a brook in
the southern part of the property is bordered by wet meadows, and woodlands are nearby — the kind of habitat mix
these turtles require.

Among snakes, the common garter is the most numerous and observable. The smooth green and the three small

northern hardwood forest species, northern brown, ring-neck, and red-bellied, all occur on the property. The larger milk snake may be found in the fields, where they hunt rodents, frogs, fish, earthworms, and even smaller snakes.

Amphibians: The common species of Berkshire frogs reside in the relatively limited marshes and swamps of the property, as well as in the small pond. You can expect to find in spring and summer the spring peeper, green frog, bullfrog, American toad, and perhaps a pickerel frog.

Among the salamanders, the red-backed is the most common in the oak woodlands. The pond is home not only to frogs but also to the aquatic red-spotted newt, which is not eaten by fish because it is poisonous. Likewise, the newt's land phase, the red eft, will be found wandering about during the three to five years that these brightly colored creatures spend on land prior to returning to water as adult newts for the remainder of their existence.

Fish: Yellow perch, brown bullhead, and introduced pumpkinseed, large-mouth bass, and huge goldfish live in the pond. Pumkinseeds guard their gravel-scrape nests along the pond margin in summer. There is only one per-manent stream (on the southern part of the property), thus limiting the diversity of cold-water species.

Seasonal Highlights

Woodland wildflowers bloom in April and early May before the tree leaves develop and cast their shade upon the forest floor (see description of Oak Loop Trail above). Apple trees blossom in May; their pinkish-white flowers attract numerous insect species and ruby-throated hummingbirds, which arrive around the beginning of the month. A walk along the trails through pastures, hayfields, wetlands, and woodlands will show you a goodly number of migrant and resident birds. Bluebirds are nesting by late April; watch and listen for them in trees bordering the pastures.

By late June the bluebirds are sitting on their second clutches of three to five eggs. Listen for the fledgling young of the first brood calling for handouts from their father; while the female incubates the second clutch, he tends to the first batch of young. These fledglings have mottled breasts, a clue to their thrush family relations. Many other birds are in the midst of raising nestlings that demand nearly constant feeding for two to three weeks. American goldfinches wait until thistles ripen and line their nests with its down in August and even September.

A rich diversity of wildflowers bloom in the meadows, pastures, and woodlands, attended by an equally rich insect life, the most colorful of which are the butterflies.

The riot of fall color on the Greylock Range is at its peak in early October, and this is one of the best places from which to view it. In late fall, after the corn harvest, the fields are visited by flocks of Canada geese, and deer spend time harvesting forgotten apples and waste corn.

In winter, Field Farm is a wonderful place to cross-country ski through the open meadows (see *Skiing*), examining bird and mammal tracks in the snow and gazing with appreciation at the white-mantled Mount Greylock to the east. The openness of this property and its relative flatness make for good accessibility for birding and other pursuits year-round.

ঌ 27 ঌ

NATURAL BRIDGE STATE PARK
North Adams

Managed by DEM.

Acreage: 47.

Elevation: 850—1,018 ft.

Trails: Less than 1 mi.

Hours: 10-6, Memorial Day to Columbus Day. Closed in winter.

Admission: $2 a vehicle.

Facilities/Other: Public programs conducted by park interpreters during summer months. Phone: 413-663-6392 (May-Oct.), 413-663-6312 (Nov.-Apr.). Rest rooms, picnicking available. No camping.

Directions: From intersection of Rtes. 2/8 and 8A in N. Adams, follow Eagle St. (Rte. 2) E. for 0.1 mi. to flashing yellow signal (Rte. 8). Turn left onto Rte. 8 and proceed N. for 0.5 mi. to road on left (just past red factory building). This is McCauley Rd. Follow McCauley Rd. to the right and uphill to old quarry and continue on to parking area above quarry.

Natural Bridge is truly a geologic wonder. It is, in fact, the only marble bridge in North America that was formed by water erosion. The nearly white Stockbridge marble (named after the town where it was first extensively studied) is 500 million years old, making it one of the oldest rock types in Berkshire. The formation of the bridge and chasm, however, occurred much more recently, taking shape over the course of the Ice Ages, beginning two million years ago. By the glacier's last retreat—13,000 years ago—the formations may have been nearly complete. Some geologists, in contrast, believe that the chasm formed after the last Ice Age.

But how did it happen? Hudson Brook, a tributary of the North Branch of the Hoosic River, flowed in almost overlapping switchbacks so that at one point it folded back upon itself, thereby cutting both downward (to a depth of 60 ft.) and laterally. Eventually this lateral erosion cut through the rock to form today's 30-foot long bridge within a 475-foot-long chasm. Although the flow of Hudson Brook has been somewhat altered, this slow but steady process continues even now.

Adjacent to the bridge and chasm is an abandoned marble quarry, the walls of which will also enable you to see this exposed bedrock. Marble was quarried for use in construction and agricultural products for 110 years, until 1947. In some parts of Berkshire this marble layer is more than 940 feet thick!

The quarry floor has two rare plant species growing upon it: fringed gentian and variegated horsetail. Recently, non-native wildflowers have been planted. Dwarf horsetail, another unusual species, has been found in the ravine.

Although not imposing in sheer size, the narrow cleft through which the roaring waters of Hudson Brook flow is nonetheless an impressive sight, testifying to the amazing ability of moving water to cut through tough rock, given enough time. Granite boulders, acting as giant pestles powered by meltwater, have scoured out round potholes in the chasm marble.

Views and Vistas

From atop the chasm, you will have pleasant views of the hills to the east, where Route 2 ascends to the well-known Hairpin Turn. The elevation of the highest point within view, West Summit (with radio tower) is 2,018 feet.

Plant Communities

The soils here, as elsewhere, are in large measure a product of their underlying bedrock, in this case marble. Marble is heat-altered limestone, rock laid down by the death of countless marine creatures that lived in warm, shallow seas one-half billion years ago. The entire Hoosic Valley of North Berkshire, in fact, is underlain with marble.

Soils of limestone origin, because of their alkaline qualities, often have unusual plants associated with them, and

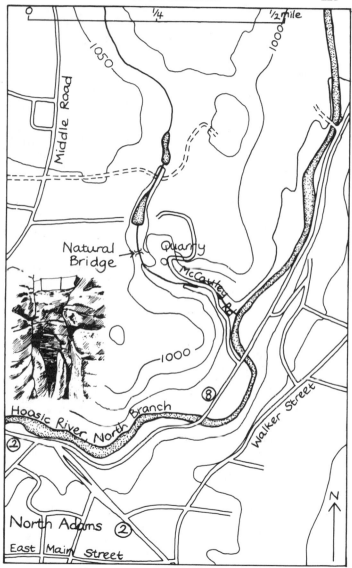

NATURAL BRIDGE STATE PARK

this site is no exception. Three rare plant species within the park are an example. Two are horsetails, primitive plants that have a 300-million-year-old lineage. Today's species closely resemble those of the distant past that grew to huge size in the "coal forests" of the Carboniferous age. The horsetails (scouring rushes) resemble small, green stems of bamboo, although they have no leaves. The green stalks contain chlorophyll and conduct photosynthesis. These stems also contain large amounts of silica (the prime ingredient of glass), making them very raspy to the touch. Early settlers used them to scour pots and pans.

Other plants on the old quarry floor that indicate limey conditions are shrubby cinquefoil, with small yellow flowers; grass of Parnassus, which is not a grass at all, but puts out beautifully veined white flowers in fall; and the unique blue fringed gentian.

On the marble rock of the chasm itself grow other lime-loving species, including maidenhair spleenwort, a dainty evergreen species that favors moist outcroppings. Also present on the chasm walls is bulblet fern, a lacy, delicate, non-evergreen species that also requires rock of limestone origin. It is the only fern that has tiny roundish "bulblets" at the bases of its leaflets. These bulblets drop off and germinate into fern plants.

The woodland atop the quarry and along Hudson Brook below the chasm contains white pine, eastern hemlock, northern red oak, white birch, cottonwood, basswood, and red maple. The tiny wetland near the marble dam above the quarry has characteristic wetland plants such as cattail and speckled alder.

Wildlife

Mammals: The common species of human-influenced and disturbed areas are found here, including gray and red squirrels, eastern chipmunk, cottontail rabbit, raccoon, opossum, striped skunk, short-tailed shrew, hairy-tailed mole, big and little brown bats, and white-footed mouse. Others visit the park on occasion.

Birds: Common year-round residents in the park and its environs include the northern cardinal, blue jay, black-capped chickadee, tufted titmouse, and American crow. Wood thrush and red-eyed vireo are summer residents that nest in the adjacent woodland. Red-tailed hawks patrol the skies in search of rodents.

Reptiles: Don't expect to find many turtles here, for there are few suitable ponds. Wood turtles might find the exposed, gravelly soil of the quarry floor suitable for egg-laying and the brook below the chasm fine for over-wintering.

The abundance of exposed rock provides many suitable basking sites for snakes, which absorb the radiant energy of the sun directly and from the rocks upon which they lie. Species found here include the common garter, red-bellied, northern brown, milk, and smooth green snakes.

Amphibians: You'll find the ubiquitous and warty American toad here and a few other species of frogs as well, including the spotted pickerel frog (the spots are rectangular). You might also a encounter a wood frog in the forested areas. Spring peepers call from the vegetation of the tiny wetland above the quarry in early spring.

Salamanders are not numerous, but the woods do contain red-backed salamanders, which are two to three inches long and have a broad reddish band the length of their backs. Along the brook there may be species that require wetter conditions and stones for concealment during daylight hours, such as dusky and two-lined salamanders. The spring salamander is also a possibility.

Fish: The fast, clear, and cold waters of Hudson Brook are home to several small species requiring oxygen-rich water, including brook trout and slimy sculpin. Above the chasm is a small impoundment created by a marble dam across the brook. This pool also contains fish.

Seasonal Highlights

Spring is the season of high water flow. The network of fenced walkways makes it possible for you to get right into the upper reaches of the chasm for an intimate yet safe look at the tremendous power of flowing water.

Although the volume of water diminishes in summer, the impoundment just upstream of the bridge guarantees that there will almost always be a considerable flow through the chasm. You might want to take part in an interpretive program; check with park staff for a schedule of upcoming events.

In fall, water volume tends to pick up again. The walkways allow you to examine the marble, darkened by growths of algae, lichens, and mosses, from very close at hand. The fringed gentian, a lovely four-petaled, violet-blue flower, blooms in fall upon the moist floor of the quarry. Care should be taken not to trample the gentians and the variegated horsetails, both uncommon, state-listed species.

The park is closed during the winter months, when the footing on the walkways often is icy and treacherous. In addition, the entrance road to the park is not plowed.

✍ 28 ✍

EPH'S POND AND HOOSIC RIVER
Williamstown

Owned and managed by Williams College.

Elevation: 580—600 ft.

Trails: 1 mi.

Hours: None posted.

Admission: None posted.

Facilities/Other: None.

Directions: From jct. of Rte. 2 and Park St. in Williamstown, turn onto Park St. and follow N. for 0.3 mi. to Lynde Lane (sign missing) on right. Turn onto Lynde Lane and follow E. for 0.1 mi. to Stetson Rd. (at tennis courts). Turn left (N.) onto Stetson Rd. (no sign) and follow it for 0.4 mi., eventually downhill and curving right. Eph's Pond is on right. Park left off road along barrier near gate. Be sure not to block gate. To access river, walk down paved lane bordered by light poles between playing fields. Follow paved path to right and take first woodland path on the left. Trail proceeds past a shallow pond, through overgrown fields, and then turns right, down to and along river.

This floodplain area, within the glaciated Hoosic Valley, sits at one of the lowest elevations in Berkshire. While little here is still in a truly natural state, it is an excellent place to observe birds, especially during migration periods. This is also one of the few places where it is possible to gain access to the Hoosic River, which flows briskly here, with riffles produced by a stony bottom. There is also fine wildlife viewing (especially birds) along Eph's Pond (named for the college's founder, Ephraim Williams).

Views and Vistas

By walking around the perimeter of the Williams College playing fields, you'll achieve virtually 360-degree views of the surrounding hills. Perhaps the most picturesque sight is to the southeast, where the peaks of Mount Williams (2,951 ft.) and Mount Prospect (2,690 ft.) in the Greylock Range are clearly visible. The rock outcrop of Pine Cobble (1,894 ft.) is due east (see Ch. 29), while the Taconic Range is to the west. To gain a view of what lies north of the floodplain, take a brief walk back up Stetson Road for a fine look at the Dome (2,748 ft.) due north in Vermont.

Plant Communities

While the entire area is within the floodplain of the Hoosic River, much has been altered. To experience the floodplain forest, walk the trail along the river. You'll find yourself in an area of huge cottonwood trees and other typical floodplain vegetation, including box elder (actually a maple, as its winged seeds attest) and beautiful American sycamore. You'll instantly recognize the sycamore by its splotched, multicolored trunk. Shades of brown, green, and off-white give this tree a distinctive dappled appearance. Look also for the round seed heads that, like ornaments, hang from its limbs. Other species of trees here are black willow and big-tooth aspen. In the slightly drier soils, you'll find many black locust trees. This tree's seed pods often litter the ground below it.

The shrub layer under the floodplain giants is dominated by introduced Morrow's honeysuckle (red berries) and buckthorn (blue-black fruits), both readily spread by American robins and cedar waxwings. There is also a thick growth of another alien plant, Japanese bamboo (Japanese knotweed). This invasive plant is not actually a bamboo, but does have hollow, jointed stems and grows to a height of seven feet. In late summer it has stalks of tiny white flowers. Ostrich fern is the abundant tall fern that forms a thick growth in these wet soils. These plants impart an almost junglelike atmosphere in summer.

In the old fields near the river grow Queen Anne's lace, staghorn sumac (with clusters of fuzzy red berries and branches that look like deer antlers in velvet), goldenrods, and sunflowers — all common in disturbed soils — and

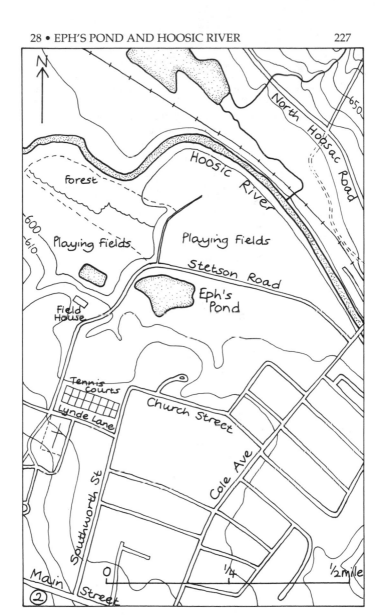

EPH'S POND AND HOOSIC RIVER

various grasses. In the wetter spots, reed canary grass, cat-tail, common reed (*Phragmites*), and various sedges are common. You can distinguish the latter from grasses by their triangular (rather than round) stems. Draped over many trees along the field edges are vines of wild grape, the fruits of which are sought after by birds and mammals alike.

The borders of Eph's Pond are lined with cattails, sedges, bulrushes, and grasses, and red-osier dogwood shrubs, box elders, and cottonwoods.

Wildlife

Mammals: Aquatic species dominate. The former include beaver, muskrat (lodges visible at Eph's Pond), mink, and river otter. As you walk along the river banks, look for washed-up twigs stripped of their bark by beavers; and you will doubtless find raccoon tracks on the muddy banks. The large sycamores and cottonwoods provide fine den trees where raccoons pass the daylight hours.

Mammals more at home in fields and woodland edges are white-tailed deer, opossum, striped skunk, red fox, short-tailed shrew, meadow vole, white-footed mouse, eastern cottontail, and woodchuck (look for the entrances of large burrows). Gray squirrels (in oaks above the flood-plain) are abundant, and red squirrels also occur here, although less common. Mounds of soil atop the playing field lawns are signs that the odd star-nosed mole (with a fleshy snout sporting 22 sensitive tentacles used for feeling for earthworms) has been active in its search for food below the surface. Every so often, the animal must push the soil it has accumulated out of the way and up to the surface. These mole hills don't really wreck a lawn, as many people think, since all that one need do is rake out the dirt. The mole actually aerates the soil, and the grass prospers as a result.

Birds: Over the years, at least 175 species of birds have been recorded within this small area! The river serves as a migratory corridor for many species, augmenting the annual diversity. Among the year-round residents here are the red-tailed hawk, the almost dainty American kestrel, downy woodpecker, blue jay, black-capped chickadee, the closely related tufted titmouse (also a cavity nester), white-breasted nuthatch, and American goldfinch. In winter, American black duck, common merganser (a fish-eating duck with a sawlike bill), and belted kingfisher may be seen along the river.

During the breeding season, the spotted sandpiper, green heron, and common yellowthroat are among the water-loving birds that you may find. The *witchity witchity witch* song of the yellowthroat is a much-heard wetland refrain. The spotted sandpiper, almost always in teetering motion, is a regular along the rocky river shores.

Reptiles: During the warm months look for painted turtles in Eph's Pond. Snapping turtles live here, too. Wood turtles frequent the woods and fields along the river, although you would be quite fortunate to encounter one.

The fields and wetlands are home also to the common garter, ribbon, northern water, ringneck, redbelly, northern brown, smooth green, and milk snakes. Finding most of these can take some deliberate searching, but even disturbed areas like this provide habitat for these interesting and non-poisonous snakes. Look under old boards and other pieces of litter during the warm seasons, but be sure to return the snake and its cover to their original positions.

Amphibians: Because of the presence of ponds and associated wetlands, this group of vertebrates is well represented. You can expect to find bull, green, and pickerel frogs, the American toad, and spring peepers in and around Eph's Pond, which is also known locally as Frog Pond. Visiting herons, bitterns, and egrets are drawn by the cover and food in the way of frogs and fish that the pond provides them. You may also encounter wood frogs here, although they require vernal pools for breeding. Check the upland woods for this yellowish-pinkish frog with the black mask.

Among the salamanders here are the red-spotted newt and the red-backed salamander (in the oak woods). Spotted and Jefferson salamanders, both of which, like the wood frog, depend solely upon vernal pools for procreation, may be found traversing the area during their early spring nocturnal migrations. Two-lined and dusky salamanders may reside along the shaded portions of the Hoosic, where they would spend the daylight hours under flat stones along the shore.

Fishes: The Hoosic is the major river draining North Berkshire, and it is one of the few streams in New England that flows northward. The Hoosic from Williamstown flows north into Vermont, then northwest into New York, where it empties into the Hudson some 35 miles north of Albany.

In this part of Williamstown, it is a moderately fast, cold stream that has cut several meanders along its course. Its bottom is lined mostly with rock, and it harbors cold-water species such as brook trout (native), rainbow trout (now considered a species of salmon), and to a lesser extent brown trout. Brook and brown trout and perhaps also rainbows have naturally reproducing populations. Cold-water fish depend upon riverbank vegetation to shade the stream and moderate its temperature during the hot summer months; development along portions of the river has eliminated much of this vegetation.

Other species that live in this portion of the river are both largemouth and smallmouth bass, white sucker, bluegill, pumpkinseed, longnose dace, and the occasional northern pike. Since the river is contaminated with PCBs, people are urged not to eat fish taken from the Hoosic. The river is a fairly popular "catch and release" trout stream, however.

Seasonal Highlights

In late March, the playing fields are often covered with returning American robins and killdeer, searching for edibles. The killdeer is well-known to many for its broken-wing act. This attention-getting device is used strategically by birds to draw predators away from their nests. Check the shrubs and treetops for migrating warblers and vireos in late April and May.

Summer is an excellent season to seek out aquatic birds at Eph's Pond. If you arrive early (this is a popular location, with many people walking dogs) you may be treated to the sight of a stalking great blue heron, a crow-sized green heron, various species of ducks, sora (a small rail that is much more often heard than seen), belted kingfisher, and marsh wren.

Some unusual species found here over the years include black tern, little blue heron, and American bittern. There have even been occurrences of such mouth-watering species as tricolored heron and red-necked phalarope (a sea bird). In migration, which begins in late summer for hawks, you may well see a beautiful brown and white osprey gliding overhead on bent wings, searching the river or pond for fish. This is also the time to look the pond over for the occasional great egret, an impressive white species that breeds along the coast and then frequently wanders northward following nesting.

By fall, bird migration is in full swing. Shorebirds such as sandpipers and plovers pass through the valley as early as late July; August and September is the time for many songbirds; late August to early November for hawks; and late October and November for waterfowl. This is also a good spot for panoramic views of the surrounding hills during fall foliage season. Peak color is usually in early October.

In winter, a walk along the river banks can be rewarding, especially if there is a light snow cover. The nightly comings and goings of raccoon, mink, river otter, opossum, striped skunk, mice, and other creatures may be laid out like a book waiting to be read. Although birding may be on the dull side in wooded, upland areas, there is still a surprising amount of activity to be found in floodplain com-

munities such as this; and the open water of the Hoosic
provides habitat for American black duck, common merganser, and other waterfowl.

Comments

You can easily spend a leisurely couple of hours birding
here, especially in spring and fall, and then make an excursion to nearby Pine Cobble if you wish to do some serious
walking.

❧ 29 ❧

PINE COBBLE AND EAST MOUNTAIN
Williamstown

Various portions owned by Williams College, Williamstown
  Rural Lands Foundation (WRLF), DEM, and private owners.

Acreage: 80 (WRLF), plus privately held land.

Elevation: 720—2,100 ft.

Trails: 2.1 mi (maintained by Williams College Outing Club) to
  jct. with AT.

Hours: None posted.

Admission: None posted.

Facilities/Other: Camping available along AT in Clarksburg
  State Forest (see *Hikes & Walks*). No rest rooms.

Directions: From the traffic signal at jct. of Rte. 2 and Cole
  Ave. in Williamstown, take Cole Ave., N. for 0.8 mi.,
  crossing the Hoosic River, to N. Hoosic Rd. Turn right (E.)
  onto N. Hoosic and drive for 0.4 mi. (not 0.25 mi. as
  indicated by small brown sign) to Pine Cobble Rd. on left.
  Turn left onto paved Pine Cobble Rd. and follow uphill for
  just over 0.1 mi. to gravel parking area on left. Trail-head is
  on opposite side of road.

The blue-blazed Pine Cobble Trail will take you from
the Hoosic River Valley abruptly up the south-facing slope
of East Mountain for 1.6 miles through a forest reminiscent
more of Cape Cod than Northern Berkshire. After reaching
a quartzite promontory known as Pine Cobble at the 1.6
mile mark, several hundred feet right of the main trail, the
trail continues for another half mile to a junction, at 2,100
feet elevation, with the Appalachian Trail. The partially
exposed summits of East Mountain are covered with 600-
million-year-old grayish-white quartzite slabs, among
which grow stunted pitch pines. This rock, banded with
shades of pink and brown, is known to geologists as
Cheshire quartzite and probably began as beach sand deposited in a shallow lagoon. Several points along the trail
offer outstanding views in all directions.

Views and Vistas

These are some of the best to be found anywhere in Berkshire. You will already get some idea of what's in store as you begin the hike paralleling Pine Cobble Road. Even from here there are fine views of Mount Prospect (2,690 ft.) and Mount Williams (2,951 ft.) to the south, and the views of the Taconic Range to the west aren't bad, either. But the best is yet to come.

From the promontory of Pine Cobble (1,894 ft.) you'll appreciate the grandeur of the entire Greylock Range, with the summit of Mount Greylock (3,491 ft., the highest point in Massachusetts) directly to the south, just over nine miles away. The war memorial and communications towers are clearly visible. Below, and in front of the summit, is the three-sided bowl known as the Hopper. From your vantage point you'll be looking across the north rim of the bowl, which opens toward the west.

Far below and to the west of Greylock stretch the farms and woodlots of the Green River Valley. Continuing to pan clockwise, your eyes will fall upon Brodie Mountain (2,168 ft.) and then the long, jagged line of the Taconic Mountains, which parallel the border with New York. To the north, 180 degrees from Greylock, is the rounded peak of the Dome (2,748 ft.) in Vermont, seemingly just beyond the oak-covered hill in the foreground. Pine Cobble is actually the southernmost extension of Vermont's Green Mountains. As you gaze beyond the extensive oak woods that stretch below you in the distance to the east, you'll be able to make out the wall of the Hoosac Range. Everywhere you turn, the view is delightful and even inspirational.

If you backtrack and then continue up the main trail (turn right at the junction after leaving the Cobble) for a half mile and another 200 feet in elevation, to just short of where it joins the Appalachian Trail, you'll find yourself at another excellent vantage point. If you're up to it, this extra climb is worth the effort, since the views are even more expansive. You may in fact never want to come down!

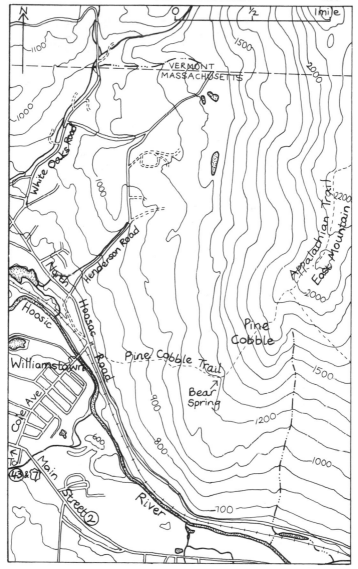

PINE COBBLE AND EAST MOUNTAIN

Plant Communities

The lower portions of the mountain are clothed in cut-over oak woods, with white and red oaks predominating. There are also quite a few black locust and black cherry trees, the former recognizable by their deeply furrowed bark. You'll also find red maples and some American chestnut sprouts along the trail, but the chestnut blight (a fungus that chokes the tree's circulatory system) generally kills the tree before it can achieve any size. You might notice the cankers caused by the fungus on the trunks of the chestnuts. Before the 1930s this tree was one of the most important species in Berkshire.

On the forest floor are many spinulose wood ferns and an occasional Christmas fern. Some trees are wrapped with poison ivy vines (which appear hairy), and among the major understory trees you'll find eastern hophornbeam and witch hazel, the latter blooming in the fall. At a point where the trail levels out, approximately halfway to Pine Cobble, look for a blue-blazed side trail to your right. This short, slightly downhill path will take you to the base of a sheer, west-facing cliff, topped by dark-green eastern hemlocks. Below the cliff, near the trail, is little Bear Spring. You'll see the slight up-welling of water and the trickle of a brook that originates at this spot. Opposite the cliff is a more gradual slope that prevents as much sunlight from reaching this site as the rest of the mountain.

This cool woods is in stark contrast to the rest of the woodland you have been walking through. The common northern hardwood forest trees that favor cool, moist conditions — yellow birch, sugar maple, and striped maple — grow here, and below these you'll find Christmas fern, spinulose wood fern, and shining clubmoss. Obviously, exposure is very important. There is some speculation that this small plateau was once the shoreline of a glacial lake that existed during the last retreat and melting of the glacier about twelve thousand years ago. The glacier's ice was nearly one mile thick!

As you continue to ascend the main trail, you'll probably recognize that this open forest differs from many others you might have experienced in Berkshire. Below the short northern red oaks, chestnut oaks, and now more common black oaks is sassafras, a small, primarily southern species, with greenish bark and mitten-shaped leaves. The crushed leaves and bark are very aromatic, smelling of citrus. It is one of the few food plants of the very uncommon spicebush swallowtail butterfly caterpillar; the adult is a gorgeous blue-and-black insect, which I've had the pleasure of seeing here. Flowering dogwood, another southern species, occurs here, too. Its beautiful four-petaled white flowers bloom in spring before its leaves emerge.

The shrub layer consists of low-bush blueberry and some mountain azalea, a shrub that has lovely and fragrant pink flowers. This warm southern exposure is covered with sheep laurel (poisonous to sheep), a shrub of much smaller stature than the mountain laurel. You'll find only a few mountain laurel shrubs here. This dense growth of sheep laurel is about two feet high and covered with pretty, dark-pink blossoms in early summer.

A fern characteristic of dry, sterile soils is the large, coarse bracken fern, and you'll find it in large numbers on this slope. The shiny green leaves (and red berries on female plants) of wintergreen are common on the forest floor. Its fruit and leaves contain the aromatic oil of wintergreen. In a few spots you may see the low-growing trailing arbutus or mayflower, the state flower. Its white blossoms open in May, but the foliage is evergreen among the brown oak leaves in winter.

As you climb higher, a few pitch pines will appear, and you'll also see white pines. The latter have five soft needles per bundle, while pitch pine has three rather stiff needles in each bundle. On the quartzite-strewn summits both pines are present, as are blueberry, black huckleberry, purple chokeberry, sheep laurel, red maple, and mountain ash, an attractive small tree that sports large clusters of bright red berries in fall. Small white birches, another tree that likes sunny conditions, is also common at these heights. Up here there are even a few red spruce.

The rocks, composed of the same material as Monument Mountain (Ch. 8) and perhaps of the same age, are also covered with gray-green lichens. Some also have common polypody fern growing in the thin soils atop them.

Wildlife

Mammals: Among the common species in the woodlands here are white-tailed deer, snowshoe hare (higher elevations), gray and red squirrels, eastern chipmunk, white-footed mouse, and masked shrew. Predators include coyote, gray fox (the species that inhabits woodlands), and bobcat. Black bear are becoming increasingly common throughout Berkshire, and this area is no exception. Some are drawn to the abundance of berry-producing shrubs in late summer.

Birds: Both species of large game birds, wild turkey (very fond of acorns) and ruffed grouse, are common on the oak slopes. Other year-round residents include tufted titmouse (basically a southern species), black-capped chickadee, white-breasted nuthatch, blue jay, hairy woodpecker, and downy woodpecker. Among the pines along the Appalachian Trail is where you'll find the little golden-crowned kinglet, and in some years red-breasted nuthatches search the trunks and branches of pines for insect larvae, pupae, and eggs.

Summer residents include the hermit thrush, veery, American robin, red-eyed vireo (a fairly accomplished if monotonous singer that can be difficult to spot in the foliage), American redstart, black-throated blue warbler, ovenbird, eastern wood pewee, eastern (formerly rufous-sided) towhee (on the shrubby summits), cedar waxwing, and dark-eyed junco. The latter move to lower elevations in Berkshire for the winter. In wet areas along the Appalachian Trail you may encounter the lovely Canada warbler. It has a black "necklace" across its bright yellow breast.

Reptiles: Plenty of southern exposure with rocky outcrops for basking and den sites make this a good place to find and observe snakes. Besides the ubiquitous common garter, inhabitants include smooth green, ringneck, red-bellied, northern brown, and milk snakes. Rattlesnakes have not been reported, as far as I know, although the habitat may be suitable. The garter is the species that is most often seen. Its ability to tolerate temperature extremes and to eat almost anything makes it one of the most adaptable snakes in the world.

I was thrilled once to find a beautiful 16-inch-long smooth green snake (so called because of its smooth scales) on one of the quartzite summits in August. The light-green coloration serves to camouflage this serpent as it crawls through vegetation. Its diet consists largely of insects, snails, and spiders.

Amphibians: The woodlands are home to the wood frog, American toad, and spring peeper. Bear Spring is a good place to search for these and green frogs, as are wet, boggy pockets on the mountain's summit.

Salamanders include the numerous red-backed, red eft (land stage of red-spotted newt), spotted, and Jefferson. Along with the wood frog, these last two depend for egg-laying on woodland depressions that fill with water from rain and snow-melt and retain that water until late summer. Such temporary water bodies are known as vernal pools (see also Ch. 18). These pools have received increasing attention from biologists and conservationists in recent years. The state of Massachusetts has a certification program that affords some of these important habitats at least a measure of protection. Anyone may submit the necessary paperwork in order to have a pool certified by the state Natural Heritage Program.

Fishes: The lack of permanent streams and ponds precludes fish from occurring here.

Seasonal Highlights

A walk through the oak forests to Pine Cobble in early spring will show you woodland wildflowers such as trailing arbutus. The large white blossoms of flowering dogwood brighten up the woods in mid-May. Mountain azalea shrubs put forth fragrant and beautiful blossoms from late May to early June. In sunny spots on the summits and elsewhere, pink lady's-slipper (an orchid), mountain ash, and purple chokeberry are in bloom. Along the trail you might also find an unusual orchid, large-whorled pogonia, with greenish flowers that have three tentaclelike projections, called sepals. Migrant and returning songbirds fill the trees and shrubs of the south-facing slope.

Summer is one of the best seasons to visit, since sheep laurel blooms in June. During late summer the blueberry and black huckleberry bushes are heavily laden with sweet, ripe, dark-blue fruit. In mid-August the berries may be so abundant that you find yourself spending more time on the rocky summit than you had planned. Look for sunning snakes and, where there is sassafras, the lovely and uncommon spicebush swallowtail butterfly.

In the fall, blueberry and huckleberry leaves turn red and put on quite a show among the almost white boulders. Sassafras leaves turn yellow, as do those of white birch and mountain ash, which isn't really an ash at all. Its clusters of bright-red berries are eagerly consumed by songbirds. Of course the views of Greylock and other peaks, bedecked in fall colors, are a highlight of a fall pilgrimage to Pine Cobble and East Mountain. In September and October, keep an eye out for southbound hawks passing overhead.

In winter, pick a sunny day with a clear blue sky and strike out for the rocky summits. Unless the snow lies very deep (which is infrequent on this south-facing hillside) or there has just been an ice storm, you'll probably find the mountain accessible. Watch for the tracks of turkey, grouse, deer, snowshoe hare, squirrels, mice, and shrews in light snow. If the day is mild, say around 40 degrees, you may see myriads of tiny black flecks hopping about on the snow. These very primitive insects, which possess a sort of spring-loaded lever under their abdomens, are known as spring-tails. They are among the most abundant insects on the planet, and each square foot may have hundreds or even thousands of these interesting little creatures. A look through a 10x hand lens will give you an up-close and personal perspective.

You might also notice small, fuzzy, tan-colored clumps on the south sides of oak trunks. These are gypsy moth egg masses. This imported insect is a major defoliator of trees, especially oaks, in the Northeast. Along with the eggs, the brown, bristly, discarded skins of the gypsy moth cocoons still cling to the trees.

COMMON AND SCIENTIFIC NAMES OF SPECIES MENTIONED IN TEXT

Plants

Common name	Scientific name
Alder, speckled	*Alnus rugosa*
Arbutus, trailing	*Epigaea repens*
Arrowhead	*Sagittaria latifolia*
Arrowhead, grass-leaved	*Sagittaria graminea*
Arrowwood, smooth	*Viburnum recognitum*
Ash, black	*Fraxinus nigra*
Ash, green	*Fraxinus pennsylvanica*
Ash, white	*Fraxinus americana*
Aspen, bigtooth	*Populus grandidentata*
Aspen, quaking	*Populus tremuloides*
Aster, flat-topped	*Aster umbellatus*
Aster, white wood	*Aster divaricatus*
Azalea, mountain	*Rhododendron roseum*
Bamboo, Japanese	*Polygonum cuspidatum*
Barberry, Japanese	*Berberis thunbergii*
Basswood, American	*Tilia americana*
Bearberry	*Arctostaphylos uva-ursi*
Bedstraw	*Galium mollugo*
Beech, American	*Fagus grandifolia*
Beechdrops	*Epifagus virginiana*
Bellwort, large-flowered	*Uvularia grandiflora*
Bellwort, sessile-leaved	*Uvularia sessilifolia*
Bergamot, wild	*Monarda fistulosa*
Birch, gray	*Betula populifolia*
Birch, heart-leaved	*Betula cordifolia*
Birch, paper	*Betula papyrifera*
Birch, black	*Betula lenta*
Birch, yellow	*Betula alleghaniensis*
Bittersweet, Oriental	*Celastrus orbiculatus*
Black-eyed Susan	*Rudbeckia hirta*
Bladderwort, horned	*Utricularia cornuta*
Bloodroot	*Sanguinaria canadensis*
Blueberry, highbush	*Vaccinium corymbosum*
Blueberry, low-bush	*Vaccinium angustifolium*
Box elder	*Acer negundo*
Buckbean	*Menyanthes trifoliata*
Buckthorn	*Rhamnus spp.*
Bulrush, tall	*Scirpus tabernaemontanii*
Bunchberry	*Cornus canadensis*
Bur-reed	*Sparganium eurycarpum*
Buttonbush	*Cephalanthus occidentalis*
Cabbage, skunk	*Symplocarpus foetidus*
Calla, wild	*Calla palustris*
Cardinal flower	*Lobelia cardinalis*
Cattail	*Typha latifolia*
Celery, wild	*Vallisneria americana*
Cherry, black	*Prunus serotina*
Cherry, choke	*Prunus virginiana*
Cherry, fire	*Prunus pensylvanica*
Chestnut, American	*Castanea dentata*
Chokeberry, black	*Aronia melanocarpa*

— Cinquefoil, marsh	*Potentilla palustris*
— Cinquefoil, shrubby	*Potentilla fruticosa*
— Columbine	*Aquilegia canadensis*
— Cliffbrake, purple-stemmed	*Pellaea atropurpurea*
— Clintonia	*Clintonia borealis*
— Clubmoss, shining	*Lycopodium lucidulum*
— Clubmoss, tree	*Lycopodium obscurum*
— Cohosh, blue	*Caulophyllum thalictroides*
— Coontail	*Ceratophyllum demersum*
— Cottonwood, eastern	*Populus deltoides*
— Cow-vetch	*Vicia cracca*
— Cranberry, large	*Vaccinium macrocarpon*
— Cranberry, wren's egg	*Vaccinium oxycoccus*
— Cucumber, wild	*Echinocystis lobata*
— Cucumber root, Indian	*Medeola virginiana*
— Cup plant	*Silphium perfoliatum*
— Currant, bristly black	*Ribes lacustre*
— Currant, skunk	*Ribes glandulosum*
— Dewberry, bristly	*Rubus hispidus*
— Dogwood, flowering	*Cornus florida*
— Dogwood, gray	*Cornus foemina*
— Dogwood, red-osier	*Cornus sericea*
— Dogwood, silky	*Cornus amomum*
— Duckweed	*Lemna minor*
— Dutchman's breeches	*Dicentra cucullaria*
— Elder, red-berried	*Sambucus racemosa*
— Elm, American	*Ulmus americana*
— Elodea	*Elodea canadensis*
— Eyebright	*Euphrasia nemorosa*

— False foxglove	*Aureolaria* spp.
— False Solomon's seal	*Smilacina racemosa*
— Fern, bracken	*Pteridium aquilinum*
— Fern, bulblet	*Cystopteris bulbifera*
— Fern, Christmas	*Polystichum acrostichoides*
— Fern, cinnamon	*Osmunda cinnamomea*
— Fern, fragile	*Cystopteris tenuis*
— Fern, Goldie's	*Dryopteris goldiana*
— Fern, hay-scented	*Dennstaedtia punctilobula*
— Fern, interrupted	*Osmunda claytoniana*
— Fern, lady	*Athyrium filix-femina*
— Fern, long beech	*Thelypteris phegopteris*
— Fern, maidenhair	*Adiantum pedatum*
— Fern, ostrich	*Matteuccia struthiopteris*
— Fern, rattlesnake	*Botrychium virginianum*
— Fern, royal	*Osmunda regalis*
— Fern, sensitive	*Onoclea sensibilis*
— Fern, walking	*Camptosorus rhizophyllus*
— Fir, balsam	*Abies balsamea*
— Fireweed	*Epilobium angustifolium*
— Foamflower	*Tiarella cordifolia*
— Gentian, bottle	*Gentiana clausa*
— Gentian, fringed	*Gentianopsis crinita*
— Geranium, wild	*Geranium maculatum*
— Ginger, wild	*Asarum canadense*
— Ginseng	*Panax quinquefolius*
— Ginseng, dwarf	*Panax trifolius*
— Goldenrod, large-leaved	*Solidago macrophylla*
— Goldthread	*Coptis groenlandica*

243

— Grape, wild	*Vitis* spp.
— Grass, reed canary	*Phalaris arundinacea*
— Grass of Parnassus	*Parnassia glauca*
— Hackberry	*Celtis occidentalis*
— Harebell	*Campanula rotundifolia*
— Hawkweed, orange	*Hieracium aurantiacum*
— Hazelnut	*Corylus cornuta*
— Heal-all	*Prunella vulgaris*
— Hellebore, false	*Veratrum viride*
— Hemlock, eastern	*Tsuga canadensis*
— Hepatica, blunt-lobed	*Hepatica americana*
— Hepatica, sharp-lobed	*Hepatica acutiloba*
— Hickory, bitternut	*Carya cordiformis*
— Hickory, pignut	*Carya glabra*
— Hickory, shagbark	*Carya ovata*
— Hobblebush	*Viburnum alnifolium*
— Holly, mountain	*Nemopanthus mucronatus*
— Honeysuckle	*Lonicera morrowii*
— Hophornbeam, eastern	*Carpinus caroliniana*
— Horsetail, dwarf	*Equisetum scirpoides*
— Horsetail, river	*Equisetum fluviatile*
— Horsetail, variegated	*Equisetum variegatum*
— Huckleberry, black	*Gaylussacia baccata*
— Indian pipe	*Monotropa uniflora*
— Indian poke	*Phytolacca americana*
— Iris, wild	*Iris versicolor*
— Iris, yellow	*Iris pseudacorus*
— Ironwood	*Carpinus caroliniana*

— Jack-in-the-pulpit	*Arisaema triphyllum*
— Joe-pye weed, spotted	*Eupatorium maculatum*
— Juniper, common	*Juniperus communis*
— Ladies' tresses, nodding	*Spiranthes cernua*
— Lady's-slipper, pink	*Cypripedium acaule*
— Larch, Japanese	*Larix leptolepis*
— Laurel, bog	*Kalmia polifolia*
— Laurel, mountain	*Kalmia latifolia*
— Laurel, sheep	*Kalmia angustifolia*
— Leatherleaf	*Chamaedaphne calyculata*
— Leatherwood	*Dirca palustris*
— Leek, wild	*Allium tricoccum*
— Lily, Canada	*Lilium canadense*
— Lily, trout	*Erythronium americanum*
— Lobelia, great blue	*Lobelia siphilitica*
— Lobelia, water	*Lobelia dortmanna*
— Locust, black	*Robinia pseudoacacia*
— Loosestrife, purple	*Lythrum salicaria*
— Maple, mountain	*Acer spicatum*
— Maple, red	*Acer rubrum*
— Maple, silver	*Acer saccharinum*
— Maple, striped	*Acer pensylvanicum*
— Maple, sugar	*Acer saccharum*
— Marsh marigold	*Caltha palustris*
— Mayapple	*Podophyllum peltatum*
— Mayflower, Canada	*Maianthemum canadense*
— Meadow-sweet	*Spiraea latifolia*
— Milfoil, Eurasian	*Myriophyllum spicatum*

Common name	Scientific name	Common name	Scientific name
Milkweed, common	Asclepias syriaca	Pogonia, large whorled	Isotria verticillata
Milkweed, swamp	Asclepias incarnata	Pogonia, rose	Pogonia ophioglossoides
Miterwort	Mitella diphylla	Poison ivy	Toxicodendron radicans
Moss, haircap	Polytrichum commune	Polypody, common	Polypodium vulgare
Moss, sphagnum	Sphagnum spp.	Pond-lily, yellow	Nuphar variegatum
Moss, white-cushion	Leucobryum glaucum	Poplar, balsam	Populus balsamifera
Mountain ash, American	Sorbus americana	Queen Anne's lace	Daucus carota
Mountain ash, northern	Sorbus decora	Raspberry, flowering	Rubus odoratus
Mulberry, red	Morus rubra	Red cedar, eastern	Juniperus virginiana
Nannyberry	Viburnum lentago	Reed, common	Phragmites australis
Oak, black	Quercus velutina	Rose, multiflora	Rosa multiflora
Oak, chestnut	Quercus montana	Rose, swamp	Rosa palustris
Oak, northern red	Quercus rubra	Rue anemone	Anemonella thalictroides
Oak, pin	Quercus palustris	St. John's-wort, dwarf	Hypericum mutilum
Oak, scrub	Quercus ilicifolia	Sarsaparilla, wild	Aralia nudicaulis
Oak, swamp white	Quercus bicolor	Sassafras	Sassafras albidum
Oak, white	Quercus alba	Saxifrage, early	Saxifraga virginiensis
Orchis, ragged fringed	Platanthera lacera	Saxifrage, swamp	Saxifraga pensylvanica
Orchis, woodland	Platanthera clavellata	Scouring rush, common	Equisetum hiemale
Partridgeberry	Mitchella repens	Sedge, plantain-leaved	Carex plantaginea
Pickerelweed	Pontederia cordata	Sedge, three-way	Dulichium arundinaceum
Pine, pitch	Pinus rigida	Sedge, tussock	Carex stricta
Pine, red	Pinus resinosa	Shadbush, Bartram's	Amelanchier bartramiana
Pine, eastern white	Pinus strobus	Shadbush	Amelanchier arborea
Pink, Deptford	Dianthus armeria	Skullcap, swamp	Scutellaria epilobiifolia
Pink, wild	Silene caroliniana	Snowberry, creeping	Gaultheria hispidula
Pipewort	Eriocaulon pellucidum	Solomon's seal	Polygonatum pubescens
Pipsissewa	Chimaphila umbellata	Solomon's seal, three-leaved	Smilacina trifolia
Pitcher plant	Sarracenia purpurea	Speedwell, common	Veronica officinale

— Spicebush	*Lindera benzoin*	
— Spikenard	*Aralia racemosa*	
— Spikemoss, rock	*Selaginella rupestris*	
— Spleenwort, ebony	*Asplenium platyneuron*	
— Spleenwort, maidenhair	*Asplenium trichomanes*	
— Spleenwort, Scott's	*Asplenosorus ebenoides*	
— Spleenwort, silvery	*Athyrium thelypterioides*	
— Spring beauty	*Claytonia caroliniana*	
— Spring beauty, narrow-leaved	*Claytonia virginica*	
— Spruce, black	*Picea mariana*	
— Spruce, Norway	*Picea abies*	
— Spruce, red	*Picea rubens*	
— Starflower	*Trientalis borealis*	
— Steeplebush	*Spiraea tomentosa*	
— Sumac, staghorn	*Rhus typhina*	
— Sundew, round-leaved	*Drosera rotundifolia*	
— Sundew, spatulate-leaved	*Drosera intermedia*	
— Swamp candles	*Lysimachia terrestris*	
— Sweet gale	*Myrica gale*	
— Sycamore, American	*Platanus occidentalis*	
— Tea, Labrador	*Ledum groenlandicum*	
— Thyme, wild	*Thymus serpyllum*	
— Tamarack	*Larix laricina*	
— Thimbleberry	*Rubus occidentalis*	
— Toothwort, cut-leaved	*Dentaria laciniata*	
— Toothwort, white	*Dentaria diphylla*	
— Touch-me-not	*Impatiens capensis*	
— Trillium, painted	*Trillium undulatum*	
— Trillium, red	*Trillium erectum*	
— Trillium, white	*Trillium grandiflorum*	
— Trout lily	*Erythronium americanum*	
— Tuliptree	*Liriodendron tulipifera*	
— Turtlehead	*Chelone glabra*	
— Twisted-stalk, rose	*Streptopus roseus*	
— Viburnum, cranberry	*Viburnum trilobum*	
— Violet, Canada	*Viola canadensis*	
— Violet, downy yellow	*Viola pubescens*	
— Violet, early yellow	*Viola rotundifolia*	
— Violet, lance-leaved	*Viola lanceolata*	
— Violet, long-spurred	*Viola rostrata*	
— Violet, sweet white	*Viola blanda*	
— Wall rue	*Asplenium ruta-muraria*	
— Water crowfoot, white	*Ranunculus longirostris*	
— Waterleaf	*Hydrophyllum virginianum*	
— Water-lily, fragrant	*Nymphaea odorata*	
— Water shield	*Brasenia schreberi*	
— White cedar, northern	*Thuja occidentalis*	
— Wild raisin, northern	*Viburnum cassinoides*	
— Willow, black	*Salix nigra*	
— Willow, pussy	*Salix discolor*	
— Willow, shining	*Salix lucida*	
— Winterberry	*Ilex verticillata*	
— Wintergreen	*Gaultheria procumbens*	
— Witch hazel	*Hamamelis virginiana*	
— Wood fern, marginal	*Dryopteris marginalis*	
— Wood fern, mountain	*Dryopteris campyloptera*	

— Wood fern, spinulose — *Dryopteris spinulosa*
— Wood sorrel, common — *Oxalis acetosella*
— Yew, American — *Taxus canadensis*

Mammals

— Bat, big brown — *Eptesicus fuscus*
— Bat, little brown — *Myotis lucifugus*
— Bat, red — *Lasiurus borealis*
— Bear, black — *Ursus americanus*
— Beaver — *Castor canadensis*
— Bobcat — *Felis rufus*
— Chipmunk, eastern — *Tamias striatus*
— Cottontail, eastern — *Sylvilagus floridanus*
— Coyote — *Canis latrans*
— Deer, white-tailed — *Odocoileus virginianus*
— Fisher — *Martes pennanti*
— Fox, gray — *Urocyon cinereoargenteus*
— Fox, red — *Vulpes vulpes*
— Flying squirrel, southern — *Glaucomys volans*
— Hare, snowshoe — *Lepus americanus*
— Mink — *Mustela vison*
— Mole, hairy-tailed — *Parascalops breweri*
— Mole, star-nosed — *Condylura cristata*
— Mouse, deer — *Peromyscus maniculatus*
— Mouse, meadow jumping — *Zapus hudsonicus*
— Mouse, white-footed — *Peromyscus leucopus*
— Moose — *Alces alces*
— Muskrat — *Ondatra zibethicus*
— Opossum, Virginia — *Didelphis virginiana*

— Otter, river — *Lutra canadensis*
— Porcupine — *Erithizon dorsatum*
— Raccoon — *Procyon lotor*
— Shrew, masked — *Sorex cinereus*
— Shrew, short-tailed — *Blarina brevicauda*
— Shrew, smoky — *Sorex fumeus*
— Skunk, striped — *Mephitis mephitis*
— Squirrel, gray — *Sciurus carolinensis*
— Squirrel, red — *Tamiasciurus hudsonicus*
— Vole, meadow — *Microtus pennsylvanicus*
— Vole, red-backed — *Clethrionomys gapperi*
— Weasel, long-tailed — *Mustela frenata*
— Weasel, short-tailed — *Mustela erminea*
— Woodchuck — *Marmota monax*

Birds

— Bittern, American — *Botaurus lentiginosus*
— Blackbird, red-winged — *Agelaius phoeniceus*
— Blackbird, rusty — *Euphagus carolinus*
— Bluebird, eastern — *Sialia sialis*
— Bobolink — *Dolichonyx oryzivorus*
— Bufflehead — *Eucephala albeola*
— Bunting, indigo — *Passerina cyanea*
— Bunting, snow — *Plectrophenax nivalis*
— Canvasback — *Aythya valisineria*
— Cardinal, northern — *Cardinalis cardinalis*
— Catbird, gray — *Dumetella carolinensis*
— Chat, yellow-breasted — *Icteria virens*
— Chickadee, black-capped — *Parus atricapillus*

— Chickadee, boreal	*Parus hudsonicus*	
— Coot, American	*Fulica americana*	
— Cormorant, double-crested	*Phalacrocorax auritus*	
— Cowbird, brown-headed	*Molothrus ater*	
— Creeper, brown	*Certhia americana*	
— Crossbill, red	*Loxia curvirostra*	
— Crossbill, white-winged	*Loxia leucoptera*	
— Crow, American	*Corvus brachyrhynchos*	
— Crow, fish	*Corvus ossifragus*	
— Cuckoo, black-billed	*Coccyzus erythropthalmus*	
— Cuckoo, yellow-billed	*Coccyzus americanus*	
— Dickcissel	*Spiza americana*	
— Dove, mourning	*Zenaida macroura*	
— Dove, rock	*Columba livia*	
— Duck, American black	*Anas rubripes*	
— Duck, ring-necked	*Aythya collaris*	
— Duck, ruddy	*Oxyura jamaicensis*	
— Duck, wood	*Aix sponsa*	
— Dunlin	*Calidris alpina*	
— Eagle, bald	*Haliaeetus leucocephalus*	
— Eagle, golden	*Aquila chrysaetos*	
— Egret, great	*Casmerodius albus*	
— Eider, king	*Somateria spectabilis*	
— Falcon, peregrine	*Falco pregrinus*	
— Finch, house	*Carpodacus mexicanus*	
— Finch, purple	*Carpodacus purpureus*	
— Flicker, northern	*Colaptes auratus*	
— Flycatcher, Acadian	*Empidonax virescens*	
— Flycatcher, alder	*Empidonax alnorum*	
— Flycatcher, great crested	*Myiarchus crinitus*	
— Flycatcher, least	*Empidonax minimus*	
— Flycatcher, olive-sided	*Contopus borealis*	
— Flycatcher, willow	*Empidonax traillii*	
— Flycatcher, yellow-bellied	*Empidonax flaviventris*	
— Gadwall	*Anas strepera*	
— Godwit, Hudsonian	*Limosa limosa*	
— Goose, Canada	*Branta canadensis*	
— Goose, greater white-fronted	*Anser albifrons*	
— Goose, snow	*Chen caerulescens*	
— Goshawk, northern	*Accipiter gentilis*	
— Goldeneye, common	*Bucephala clangula*	
— Goldfinch, American	*Carduelis tristis*	
— Gnatcatcher, blue-gray	*Polioptila caerulea*	
— Grackle, common	*Quiscalus quiscula*	
— Grebe, horned	*Podiceps auritus*	
— Grebe, pied-billed	*Podilymbus podiceps*	
— Grebe, red-necked	*Podiceps grisegena*	
— Grosbeak, evening	*Coccothraustes vespertinus*	
— Grosbeak, pine	*Pinicola enucleator*	
— Grosbeak, rose-breasted	*Pheucticus ludovicianus*	
— Grouse, ruffed	*Bonasa umbellus*	
— Gull, Bonaparte's	*Larus philadelphia*	
— Gull, great black-backed	*Larus marinus*	
— Gull, herring	*Larus argentatus*	
— Gull, ring-billed	*Larus delawarensis*	
— Harrier, northern	*Circus cyaneus*	

— Hawk, broad-winged	*Buteo platypterus*	— Nighthawk, common	*Chordeiles minor*
— Hawk, Cooper's	*Accipiter cooperii*	— Night-heron, black-crowned	*Nycticorax nycticorax*
— Hawk, red-shouldered	*Buteo lineatus*	— Night-heron, yellow-crowned	*Nyctanassa violacea*
— Hawk, red-tailed	*Buteo jamaicensis*	— Nuthatch, red-breasted	*Sitta canadensis*
— Hawk, rough-legged	*Buteo lagopus*	— Nuthatch, white-breasted	*Sitta carolinensis*
— Hawk, sharp-shinned	*Accipiter striatus*	— Oldsquaw	*Clangula hyemalis*
— Heron, great blue	*Ardea herodias*	— Oriole, Baltimore	*Icterus galbula*
— Heron, green	*Butorides virescens*	— Osprey	*Pandion haliaetus*
— Hummingbird, ruby-throated	*Archilochus colubris*	— Ovenbird	*Seiurus aurocapillus*
— Jay, blue	*Cyanocitta cristata*	— Owl, barred	*Strix varia*
— Junco, dark-eyed	*Junco hyemalis*	— Owl, great horned	*Bubo virginianus*
— Kestrel, American	*Falco sparverius*	— Owl, northern saw-whet	*Aegolius acadicus*
— Killdeer	*Charadrius vociferus*	— Parula, northern	*Parula americana*
— Kingbird, eastern	*Tyrannus tyrannus*	— Pewee, eastern wood	*Contopus virens*
— Kingfisher, belted	*Ceryle alcyon*	— Pheasant, ring-necked	*Phasianus colchicus*
— Kinglet, golden-crowned	*Regulus satrapa*	— Phoebe, eastern	*Sayornis phoebe*
— Kinglet, ruby-crowned	*Regulus calendula*	— Pintail, northern	*Anas acuta*
— Lark, horned	*Eremophila alpestris*	— Pipit, American	*Anthus rubescens*
— Loon, common	*Gavia immer*	— Plover, black-bellied	*Pluvialis squatarola*
— Loon, red-throated	*Gavia stellata*	— Rail, Virginia	*Rallus limicola*
— Mallard	*Anas platyrhynchos*	— Raven, common	*Corvus corax*
— Martin, purple	*Progne subis*	— Redhead	*Aythya americana*
— Meadowlark, eastern	*Sturnella magna*	— Redpoll, common	*Carduelis flammea*
— Merganser, common	*Mergus merganser*	— Redstart, American	*Setophaga ruticilla*
— Merganser, hooded	*Lophodytes cucullatus*	— Robin, American	*Turdus migratorius*
— Merganser, red-breasted	*Mergus serrator*	— Sandpiper, least	*Calidris minutilla*
— Merlin	*Falco columbarius*	— Sandpiper, pectoral	*Calidris melanotos*
— Mockingbird, northern	*Mimis polyglottos*	— Sandpiper, solitary	*Tringa solitaria*
— Moorhen, common	*Gallinula chloropus*	— Sandpiper, spotted	*Actitis macularia*

__ Sandpiper, white-rumped	*Calidris fuscicollis*	
__ Sapsucker, yellow-bellied	*Sphyrapicus varius*	
__ Scaup, greater	*Aythya marita*	
__ Scaup, lesser	*Aythya affinis*	
__ Scoter, black	*Melanitta nigra*	
__ Scoter, surf	*Melanitta perspicillata*	
__ Scoter, white-winged	*Melanitta fusca*	
__ Shoveler, northern	*Anas clypeata*	
__ Shrike, northern	*Lanius excubitor*	
__ Siskin, pine	*Carduelis pinus*	
__ Sora	*Porzana corolina*	
__ Snipe, common	*Gallinago gallinago*	
__ Sparrow, American tree	*Spizella arborea*	
__ Sparrow, chipping	*Spizella passerina*	
__ Sparrow, clay-colored	*Spizella pallida*	
__ Sparrow, field	*Spizella pusilla*	
__ Sparrow, fox	*Passerella iliaca*	
__ Sparrow, lark	*Chondestes grammacus*	
__ Sparrow, Lincoln's	*Melospiza lincolnii*	
__ Sparrow, Savannah	*Passerculus sandwichensis*	
__ Sparrow, song	*Melospiza melodia*	
__ Sparrow, swamp	*Melospiza georgiana*	
__ Sparrow, white-crowned	*Zonotrichia leucophrys*	
__ Sparrow, white-throated	*Zonotrichia albicollis*	
__ Starling, European	*Sturnus vulgaris*	
__ Swallow, bank	*Riparia riparia*	
__ Swallow, barn	*Hirundo rustica*	
__ Swallow, cliff	*Hirundo pyrrhonata*	
__ Swallow, northern	*Stelgidopteryx serripennis*	

rough-winged		
__ Swallow, tree	*Tachycineta bicolor*	
__ Swan, tundra	*Cygnus columbianus*	
__ Swift, chimney	*Chaetura pelagica*	
__ Tanager, scarlet	*Piranga olivacea*	
__ Teal, blue-winged	*Anas discors*	
__ Teal, green-winged	*Anas crecca*	
__ Thrasher, brown	*Toxostoma rufum*	
__ Tern, black	*Chlidonias niger*	
__ Tern, Caspian	*Sterna caspia*	
__ Tern, common	*Sterna hirunda*	
__ Thrush, Bicknell's	*Catharus bicknelli*	
__ Thrush, gray-cheeked	*Catharus minimus*	
__ Thrush, hermit	*Catharus guttatus*	
__ Thrush, Swainson's	*Catharus ustulatus*	
__ Thrush, wood	*Hylocichla mustelina*	
__ Titmouse, tufted	*Parus bicolor*	
__ Towhee, eastern	*Pipilo erythrophthalmus*	
__ Turkey, wild	*Meleagris gallopavo*	
__ Veery	*Catharus fuscescens*	
__ Vireo, Philadelphia	*Vireo philadelphicus*	
__ Vireo, red-eyed	*Vireo olivaceus*	
__ Vireo, solitary	*Vireo solitarius*	
__ Vireo, warbling	*Vireo gilvus*	
__ Vireo, yellow-throated	*Vireo flavifrons*	
__ Vulture, black	*Coragyps atratus*	
__ Vulture, turkey	*Cathartes aura*	
__ Warbler, black-and-white	*Mniotilta varia*	

— Warbler, Blackburnian	*Dendroica fusca*
— Warbler, blackpoll	*Dendroica striata*
— Warbler, black-throated blue	*Dendroica caerulescens*
— Warbler, black-throated green	*Dendroica virens*
— Warbler, blue-winged	*Vermivora pinus*
— Warbler, Canada	*Wilsonia canadensis*
— Warbler, Cape May	*Dendroica tigrina*
— Warbler, chestnut-sided	*Dendroica pensylvanica*
— Warbler, golden-winged	*Vermivora chrysoptera*
— Warbler, magnolia	*Dendroica magnolia*
— Warbler, mourning	*Oporornis philadelphia*
— Warbler, Nashville	*Vermivora ruficapilla*
— Warbler, palm	*Dendroica palmarum*
— Warbler, pine	*Dendroica pinus*
— Warbler, prairie	*Dendroica discolor*
— Warbler, Tennessee	*Vermivora peregrina*
— Warbler, Wilson's	*Wilsonia pusilla*
— Warbler, yellow	*Dendroica petechia*
— Warbler, yellow-rumped	*Dendroica coronata*
— Waterthrush, Louisiana	*Seiurus motacilla*
— Waterthrush, northern	*Seiurus noveboracensis*
— Waxwing, cedar	*Bombycilla cedrorum*
— Whippoorwill	*Caprimulgus vociferus*
— Wigeon, American	*Anas americana*
— Woodcock, American	*Scolopax minor*
— Woodpecker, downy	*Picoides pubescens*
— Woodpecker, hairy	*Picoides villosus*
— Woodpecker, pileated	*Dryocopus pileatus*
— Woodpecker, red-bellied	*Melanerpes carolinus*

— Wren, Carolina	*Thryothorus ludovicianus*
— Wren, house	*Troglodytes aedon*
— Wren, marsh	*Cistothorus palustris*
— Wren, sedge	*Cistothorus platensis*
— Wren, winter	*Troglodytes troglodytes*
— Yellowlegs, greater	*Tringa melanoleuca*
— Yellowlegs, lesser	*Tringa flavipes*
— Yellowthroat, common	*Geothlypis trichas*

Reptiles

— Racer, eastern black	*Coluber constrictor*
— Rattlesnake, timber	*Crotalus horridus*
— Snake, common garter	*Thamnophis sirtalis*
— Snake, eastern milk	*Lampropeltis triangulum*
— Snake, eastern ribbon	*Thamnophis sauritus*
— Snake, northern brown	*Storeria dekayi*
— Snake, northern water	*Nerodia sipedon*
— Snake, red-bellied	*Storeria occipitomaculata*
— Snake, ringneck	*Diadophis punctatus*
— Snake, smooth green	*Opheodrys vernalis*
— Turtle, bog	*Clemmys muhlenbergi*
— Turtle, musk	*Sternotherus odoratus*
— Turtle, painted	*Chrysemys picta*
— Turtle, snapping	*Chelydra serpentina*
— Turtle, spotted	*Clemmys guttata*
— Turtle, wood	*Clemmys insculpta*

Amphibians

__ Bullfrog	*Rana catesbeiana*
__ Frog, green	*Rana clamitans*
__ Frog, leopard	*Rana pipiens*
__ Frog, pickerel	*Rana palustris*
__ Frog, wood	*Rana sylvatica*
__ Mudpuppy	*Necturus maculosus*
__ Newt, red-spotted	*Notophthalmus viridescens*
__ Peeper, spring	*Pseudacris crucifer*
__ Salamander, dusky	*Desmognathus fuscus*
__ Salamander, four-toed	*Hemidactylium scutatum*
__ Salamander, Jefferson	*Ambystoma jeffersonianum*
__ Salamander, red-backed	*Plethodon cinereus*
__ Salamander, spotted	*Ambystoma maculatum*
__ Salamander, spring	*Gyrinophilus porphyriticus*
__ Salamander, two-lined	*Eurycea bislineata*
__ Toad, American	*Bufo americanus*
__ Treefrog, gray	*Hyla versicolor*

Fishes

__ Bass, largemouth	*Micropterus salmoides*
__ Bass, smallmouth	*Micropterus dolomieui*
__ Bass, rock	*Ambloplites rupestris*
__ Bluegill	*Lepomis macrochirus*
__ Bullhead, brown	*Ictalurus nebulosus*
__ Carp	*Cyprinus carpio*
__ Catfish, channel	*Ictalurus punctatus*
__ Catfish, white	*Ictalurus catus*
__ Chub, creek	*Semotilus atromaculatus*
__ Crappie, black	*Pomoxis nigromaculatus*
__ Dace, long-nosed	*Rhinichthys cataractae*
__ Fallfish	*Semotilus corporalis*
__ Goldfish	*Carrassius auratus*
__ Minnow, bluntnose	*Pimephales notatus*
__ Perch, yellow	*Perca flavescens*
__ Pickerel, chain	*Esox niger*
__ Pike, northern	*Esox lucius*
__ Pumpkinseed	*Lepomis gibbosus*
__ Salmon, Atlantic	*Salmo salar*
__ Sculpin, slimy	*Cottus cognatus*
__ Shiner, bridled	*Notropis bifrenatus*
__ Shiner, common	*Notropis cornutus*
__ Shiner, golden	*Notemigonus crysoleucas*
__ Shiner, spottail	*Notropis hudsonius*
__ Smelt, rainbow	*Osmerus mordax*
__ Sucker, white	*Catostomus commersoni*
__ Trout, brook	*Salvelinus fontinalis*
__ Trout, brown	*Salmo trutta*
__ Trout, rainbow	*Oncorhynchus nykiss*

NATURAL PLACES CATEGORIZED BY AMOUNT OF WALKING REQUIRED

Drive-up	Half Mile or Less	Half Mile or More
Mill Pond	Bash Bish Falls	Mount Everett
Beartown	Bartholomew's Cobble	Sage's Ravine
Stockbridge Bowl	Campbell Falls	Bartholomew's Cobble
Housatonic Valley	Mount Everett	Tyringham Cobble
October Mountain	Tyringham Cobble	Goose Ponds
Central Berkshire Lakes	Beartown	Beartown
Pittsfield State Forest	Ice Glen	Monument Mountain
Hoosac Lake	Pleasant Valley	Ice Glen
Mount Greylock	Housatonic Valley	Pleasant Valley
Natural Bridge	October Mountain	October Mountain
Hoosic River/ Eph's Pond	Canoe Meadows	
	Pittsfield State Forest	Canoe Meadows
	Wahconah Falls	Pittsfield State Forest
	Moran WMA	Moran WMA
	Windsor State Forest	Notchview
	Field Farm	Savoy Mountain
	Natural Bridge	Field Farm
	Hoosic River/ Eph's Pond	Pine Cobble

The above categories refer to "one-way distance" walking required when visiting each natural place. You'll notice that many places are listed under two or even all three categories; this is due to the variety of sites and opportunities at these areas. Places listed in the first column involve virtually no walking and thus are accessible to the disabled from a vehicle.

SELECTED REFERENCES

A Canoeing Guide for the Housatonic River in Berkshire County.
Berkshire Regional Planning Commission and Housatonic
Valley Association, 1996.

Cobb, Boughton. *A Field Guide to the Ferns*. Boston:
Houghton Mifflin Co., 1963.

Conant, Roger. *A Field Guide to Reptiles and Amphibians of
Eastern and Central North America*. Boston: Houghton Mifflin
Co., 1975.

Godin, Alfred. *Wild Mammals of New England*. Baltimore:
The Johns Hopkins University Press, 1977.

Hendricks, Bartlett. *Birds of Berkshire County*. Pittsfield,
Mass.: The Berkshire Museum, 1994.

Jorgensen, Neil. *A Guide to New England's Landscape*. Chester,
Conn.: Globe Pequot Press, 1977.

Jorgensen, Neil. *A Sierra Club Naturalist's Guide; Southern
New England*. San Francisco: Sierra Club Books, 1978.

Kirby, Ed. *Exploring the Berkshire Hills, a Guide to Geology and
Early Industry in the Upper Housatonic Watershed*. Greenfield,
Mass.: Valley Geology Publications, 1995.

Kricher, John. *A Field Guide to Eastern Forests*. Boston:
Houghton Mifflin Co., 1988.

Massachusetts and Rhode Island Trail Guide. Boston: Appalachian Mountain Club Books, 1995.

Murie, Olaus, *A Field Guide to Animal Tracks*. Boston:
Houghton Mifflin Co., 1975.

Newcomb, Lawrence. *Newcomb's Wildflower Guide*. Boston: Little, Brown and Co., 1977.

Opler, Paul A. *Eastern Butterflies*. Boston: Houghton Mifflin Co., 1992.

Peterson, Roger. *A Field Guide to Bird Songs of Eastern and Central North America*. Boston: Houghton Mifflin Co., 1975.

Peterson, Roger. *A Field Guide to Eastern Birds*. Boston: Houghton Mifflin Co., 1980.

Peterson, Roger and Margaret McKenney. *A Field Guide to Wildflowers*. Boston: Houghton Mifflin Co., 1968.

Petrides, George. *A Field Guide to Trees and Shrubs*. Boston: Houghton Mifflin Co., 1972.

Pyle, Robert. *The Audubon Society Field Guide to North American Butterflies*. New York: Alfred A. Knopf, Inc., 1986.

Scott, Shirley L., ed. *A Field Guide to the Birds of North America*. Washington: National Geographic Society, 1987.

Sternfield, Jonathan. *The Berkshire Book: A Complete Guide*. Lee, Mass.: Berkshire House Publishers, 1997.

Stevens, Lauren. *Hikes & Walks in the Berkshire Hills*. Lee, Mass.: Berkshire House Publishers, 1992.

Stevens, Lauren and Lewis Cuyler. *Skiing in the Berkshire Hills*. Lee, Mass.: Berkshire House Publishers, 1990.

Stokes, Donald. *A Guide to Nature in Winter*. Boston: Little, Brown and Co., 1976.

Strauch, Joseph G. Jr. *Wildflowers of the Berkshire and Taconic Hills*. Lee, Mass.: Berkshire House Publishers, 1995.

Tyning, Thomas. *A Guide to Reptiles and Amphibians*. Boston: Little, Brown and Co., 1990.

Veit, Richard R. and Wayne R. Petersen. *Birds of Massachusetts*. Lincoln, Mass.: Massachusetts Audubon Society, 1993.

Weatherbee, Pamela. *Flora of Berkshire County, Massachusetts*. Pittsfield, Mass.: The Berkshire Museum, 1996.

A NOTE ON THE AUTHOR

René Laubach has been the director of the Massachusetts Audubon Society's Berkshire Sanctuaries since 1985. A resident of the Berkshire hilltown of Becket, he serves on its Conservation Commission. Since coming to the Berkshires, he has also been active in the Hoffmann Bird Club, serving as president in 1989 and 1990, and he is also on the executive committee of the Mount Greylock Protective Association. He has authored articles for the Society's *Sanctuary* Magazine and several scientific journals dealing with birds. With his wife, Christyna, and John B. Bowles, he wrote *A Guide to the Bats of Iowa*, published by the Iowa Department of Natural Resources. Both he and his wife are avid, licensed bird banders. Together they completed the Massachusetts portion of the Appalachian Trail in 1991. He is also author, with Michael Tougias, of *Nature Walks in Central Massachusetts*, published by Appalachian Mountain Club Books in 1996. Before coming to the Berkshires, René Laubach worked in science and natural history museums in Illinois, Texas, Iowa, and most recently Massachusetts. He served as a grant reviewer and panelist for the federal Institute of Museum Services from 1988 to 1993. Among his other duties at Berkshire Sanctuaries, he co-leads natural history tours to the American Southwest and Latin America.

BERKSHIRE COUNTY ROAD MAP